Divining Earth Spirit

– an exploration of global and Australasian geomancy

Alanna Moore

Python Press
Australia

Dedicated to Gaia, Mother Earth

And thanks also to contributors Steven Guth, Billy Arnold,
Junitta Vallak, Bill Jackson, Lee Barnes, Annie O'Grady, Frank Moody
Christine Rhone, Clyde Searle, Barbara Galloway and John Billingsley.

Alanna Moore, a professional dowser
and geomancer, is the author of
'Backyard Poultry – Naturally' 1998
and 'Stone Age Farming' 2001.
Both are published by Python Press.

She is also the editor of Geomantica magazine,
at **www.geomantica.com**

Python Press books are distributed by Geomantica.
Enquiries to: info@geomantica.com or snail mail:
Geomantica - PO Box 929
Castlemaine Vic 3450
Australia

'Divining Earth Spirit' was first published
by Alanna Moore in 1994.

This fully revised and updated 2nd edition published 2004.

Photographs by Alanna Moore and Billy Arnold.

Front cover: Eucalpytus tree,
Cooloola National Park, Queensland.

ISBN - 0 - 6462 - 1700 - 3.

Proudly produced in central Victoria:
pre-press by Midland Typesetters
printed at Centrestate Printing.

Contents:

Introduction

Geomancy is a huge subject and, while I have been working in this field for 20 years, I'm still only scratching the surface.

Despite my native Australia only having a relatively small population, it is nevertheless a huge country with awesome Aboriginal geomantic traditions. I can barely begin to speak of these. But I have met others who can.

Much of the geomancer's art is based on ancient traditions, but it is also about individuals' perceptions and responses to the landscape in the current era. Geomancy may be a very specialised subject and yet anyone can have these perceptions if they choose to be sensitive and receptive, especially at the special power places on the planet.

I use dowsing, also known as divining, as a super-sensory tool to help me to attune to environmental energies. Other people are blessed with clairvoyance and clairaudience. These abilities can be developed, to some extent, by anyone who chooses. I have explained the mechanisms of dowsing in my previous book 'Stone Age Farming'.

My 'Geomantica' magazine has been a medium for many individuals to air their ideas on all things geomantic since 1998. Before that, in the 1980's I produced other little newsletters – 'Dowsing News' and 'Earth Spirit Quarterly'. Many of the ideas, articles and interviews published there were compiled in the late '80's. Now it is time for them to reach a wider audience with this fully revised and updated book edition.

For there would be nothing better, as I see it, than to foster a healthy awareness of things geomantic, where there is often a climate of distrust between the Aboriginal and European mindsets of Australia. There is usually a huge gulf between the two. Yet we are all coming from a geomantic past, it's just that the white man lost theirs' hundreds of years previous to the Aboriginal people.

Landscapes are constantly under threat from insensitive and inappropriate developments. One way to help protect the sacred places is by helping to build bridges of understanding between the two seemingly different cultures.

In this book I want to take you on a journey through doors of perception which are both ancient and new to many. I want you to hear the voices of many in relation to Earth energy awareness and healing. And I'd like you to consider that we all have the potential to be able to divine Earth spirit, and that it is high time that its significance be acknowledged and nurtured.

Alanna Moore
Geomancer.

PART ONE
Gaian Geomancy

Geomantic Overview

Geomancy, the study of Earth's subtle energy and spirit, is an art derived from the intuitive observations and subtle energy perceptions of the ancients the world over. Geomancy analyses the esoteric interactions of Heaven and Earth, people and place, and seeks for harmony with mother nature. In China exponents of a sophisticated geomantic tradition known as 'feng shui' (pronounced foong shway, or foong soy) have long influenced landscaping and house design to ensure the wellbeing of their clients. Geomantic traditions are found around the globe.

Our sensitive ancestors observed the cyclic rhythms of Earth, Sun, moon and planets, with their benevolent or malevolent effects on life. Their observations were then applied to agriculture, astrology/psychology and ritual, as people celebrated and invoked the natural forces.

Earth's bio-magnetic field is estimated to have been 50% stronger in Neolithic times than now, and thus energies would have been more easily apparent. Ancient peoples called the Earth's energy many names: ch'i (China), pneuma (Greek), mana (Pacific islands), prana (Hindu) and baraka (North Africa).

Spirits of Nature

Earth energies, flowing in currents like the acupuncture meridians of our bodies, came to be personified as a sinuous dragon or serpent force. In the Chinese view the topography of mother Earth embodies dragons – watercourses being their blood vessels, mountain ridges their backbones and wells their eyes. Heavenly dragons control atmospheric events, while water dragons enspirit rivers and springs.

Earth dragons are disturbed and sometimes demonised, by such things as mining, the building of railroads, or fencing of commons. Disturbed dragon lines can spread tainted energies far and wide through the Earth energy network and whole areas can be rendered unpleasant to live in.

All around the world, animist cultures have perceived all nature to be imbued with spirit and consciousness. Not just the animal kingdoms, but plants and rocks as well. Unusual rock formations the world over have been recognised as the sacred abode of spirits.

In the Japanese Shinto religion these spirits were called kami, and in Indian tradition – the devas. To the Australian Aborigines the spirit world is loosely referred to as the Dreaming. The spirits honoured in oral traditions may still be perceived to reside in the land today.

Sacred sites

Geomancers have long sited homes so as not to disturb dragon lines or power centres and to live at a safe distance from them. For what might be a good energy in the land-scape can be over-stimulating and unhealthy to live around.

Places where Earth spirit is most concentrated – in springs, caves, rock fissures, stately trees, rocky outcrops and mountain tops – became the sacred sites. Here people interacted with the energies of place – of the Earth, sky, people and spiritual beings. When these sites were visited for short periods only, and approached properly with reverence or ritual, and perhaps during the correct astrological time, their special energies were found to be catalysts for revitalization, healing, vision, prophesy and personal transformation.

In some European cultures oracle trees, springs or wells were consulted on the highest matters of state. At the oracle centre at Dodona in Greece, a sacred spring that gushed out from under a gnarled old oak tree was the source of inspiration. Other sacred sites had a reputation for making barren animals or women fertile.

Australian Aboriginal sites were either associated with powerful nature spirits, or were places of initiation for either men or women into the mystery traditions, or increase sites, where plants and animals would be contacted telepathically and encour-aged to multiply.

Still today ancient temples, mounds, holy wells, stone circles, standing stones, Aboriginal sites and the like are often associated with powerful energy centres, detectable by dowsing as well as by scientific data gathering.

Geomancy in the historical era

Around the world spirituality was originally a most earthy occupation. Religions devel-oped around the theme of celebrating and encouraging the processes of nature to bring abundance to the crops and the hunt.

A classical example is that of the Eleusian Mystery traditions that were based on the agricultural cycle. The term Eleusis means a passage or gate, for these mysteries took one on a passage between the worlds. The holy sanctuary of Eleusis, dedicated to fertility goddess Demeter and her daughter Persephone, was built around a small hill in which there was a shallow cave. (It was totally destroyed in 396AD.)

The Mystai – those being initiated into the Mysteries, began their pilgrimage to Eleusis by walking in procession from Athens, and stopping at shrines along the way. One of these was the Plutonian, built into a cave for secret rites and considered to be the entrance to the Underworld. It was here in legend that Persephone was abducted by

Pluto into the Underworld, while Demeter desolated the earth in awaiting for her daughter's annual return.

Arriving at the sacred Eleusian precinct after dark, initiates were given a potion to drink, then proceeded through the temple complex for the final revelations – the epopteia.

Hippolytus wrote that the climax to the Mysteries is when an ear of wheat was cut and displayed in silence. Proclus recorded in the fifth century AD that Eleusian initiates uttered a sacred formula while gazing at the sky: 'Rain (O Sky), conceive (O Earth), be fruitful'.

The Delphi Oracle

Another classical example is the story of the evolution of the famous Greek oracle centre at Delphi, on the slopes of Mount Parnassus. Delphi (which means 'vagina') was a site sacred to the Earth goddess from the time of the Bronze Age.

Initially the Earth spirit that inspired oracular pronouncements was deemed to flow on just one day of the year from a fissure under the temple, and this spot was the haunt of the three Muses. On this day the resident sibyl-priestesses – the Pythia, would bathe in and drink deeply of the Castalian and Kassotis spring water (which was possibly radioactive). Thus under the influence of the Earth spirit, plus psychoactive substances (such as the smoke of burning laurel leaves) they would enter visionary trance states.

Plutarch explained it thus in the 1st century AD:

'Men are affected by streams of varying potency issuing from the Earth, Some of these drive people crazy, or cause disease or death: the effect of others is good, soothing and beneficial … The sun creates in the Earth the right temperament for it to be able to produce the exhalations that inspire prophesy.'

When, in the legend, the god Apollo came to do battle with Python (the Earth spirit) Delphi's age of innocence ended. The python was speared and ensconced beneath the sacred omphalos stone at the centre of the new Apollo temple. Delphi thus became the geomantic centre of the Greek world, with energies released from the Python made available on any day of the year.

Eventually, however, the power of the Delphi Oracle began to wane. Plutarch stated in his book 'The Decline of the Oracles' that the Earth currents had changed course, no longer coinciding with the temple. There was growing consternation in the priesthood, who frantically offered bloody sacrifices, to no avail. The spirit was gone.

Healing waters

The Earth was considered a source of healing as well as wisdom and water sources were particularly sought out. Greece had 300 odd Aesculapian healing centres at water sources where wells and reservoirs were used for ritual purposes.

The thousands of holy wells in Ireland were centres for pilgrimage for millenia and many were associated with healing certain ailments. To this day some people have 'miraculous' healings at holy wells.

Religious make-overs

In his book 'Republic', Plato extolled the strategy of re-using sacred sites when colonizing territories. Thus the Roman invaders reconsecrated holy hills, wells and caves etc to their own gods, erecting new temples over the old. Later, in Christian times, sites were re-dedicated again and standing stones had crosses carved into them.

Outwardly Christianity was savage in stamping out the pagan traditions it encountered. It's rapacious introduction was vehemently opposed by a peasantry who fought bravely to save the fabric of their culture and society. The only way the Church succeeded was through compromise – by incorporating pagan cultural practices, rewriting legends and revamping festivals and pilgrimages that celebrated the cycles of life with a thin veneer of Christianity enshrouding them. The winter solstice fire festival, for instance, became Christmas. Although a wealth of geomantic knowledge was lost (such as the oral Druidic traditions which took over 20 years to learn), many traditions have survived to this day.

Todays wishing wells were once sacred springs where a Water Goddess might be approached to receive her blessing; while foundation stone ceremonies seek the goodwill of the spirits of place. At the Beating of the Bounds, an annual perambulation around certain parish boundaries in England, residents still make pilgrimage to the local sacred sites and strike mark stones with twigs to ensure another year of agricultural fecundity. In the European countryside the removal of ancient megaliths (standing stones) has been cited as the cause of localised agricultural failure.

Even St Pauls Cathedral and the Vatican are located over ancient pagan sites!

Earth Spirit rediscovered in Europe

The knowledge and influence of the Earth spirit in the western world seemed doomed to fade out. But this changed around 1921 thanks to the insights of Alfred Watkins, who discovered 'ley lines' in English landscapes, while Xavier Guichard was making similar findings independently in France.

In Germany in the 1930's Nazis employed official state geomancers who abused esoteric knowledge and ancient geomantic systems to effectively convey their propaganda to the masses. This put geomancy into ill-repute and interest in it dwindled again during the era of post-war materialism.

Finally, in the 1960's, geomancy resurfaced with new generations of geomancers, particularly in Britain. And people nowadays are making practical applications of geomancy – in landscape design and nouveau pagan activities.

Many scientists are deeply interested and some study Earth mysteries with high-tech instruments and talk about geo-biology and bio-resonance (dowsing).

Modern perspectives

Modern understanding about sacred sites, based on scientific monitoring in the UK, confirm the presence of mind altering energies at such places. Often the megaliths used in stone circles and dolmens have been selected, it would seem, for their high paramagnetic energy level, which attracts magnetic fields to them. The effect of strong magnetic fields found at many sites can, according to Lenz's law, induce deep magnetic field turbulence in our brain, stimulating our visionary capacity.

Some sites are also high in background radioactivity and sacred sites above uranium deposit are visited for short periods only by people such as the Aboriginals of the Northern Territory in Australia. 'Some people have experienced transient visionary episodes while at places with relatively high background radioactivity and a condition we have nicknamed "radiation-psi" is hypothesized' says Deveraux.

One site in NT is called 'Sores Dreaming', as it is recognised that one will break out in skin sores if lingering over its uranium lode below. High levels of radioactivity can decrease our immunity to infections, it is now known.

It is warmly reassuring that we are rekindling that holistic sense of environment, long veiled and suppressed. Never totally lost, it has lain waiting quietly, like a great slumbering Goddess, a part of our psyche that merely needs awakening.

References:

John Michell, 'City of Revelation', Abacus, UK, 1973.
John Michell, 'The Earth Spirit', Thames & Hudson, UK , 1975.
Nigel Pennick, 'The Ancient Science of Geomancy', Thames & Hudson, UK , 1979.
Nigel Pennick, 'Earth Harmony', Century, UK, 1987.
Paul Deveraux, 'Places of Power', Blandford, 1999, UK.
Paul Deveraux, 'The Sacred Place', Cassell & Co., UK, 2000.
Charles E Hulley, 'The Rainbow Serpent', New Holland Publishers, 1999.
Dolores La Chapelle, 'Earth Wisdom', Fin Hill Arts, USA, 1978.
Rupert Sheldrake, 'The Rebirth of Nature' Random, UK, 1990.

The Earth's Energy Grids

Clues from the ancients

In Greek legend Socrates once told his pupil that if one were to view Earth from above it would appear like a ball sewn from twelve pieces of skin. Similarly, in Hindu philosophy, Earth is likened to a tortoise, whose shell pattern of interlocking geometric shapes develops and expands with time.

In the 1970's a report from Russia told of the discovery in Vietnam of 38 small gold objects of great antiquity, plus an identical bronze artifact in France. These they describe as tiny models of a dodecahedron crystal Earth, the geometry highlighted with lines of gold.

Could Earth be a crystal?

Substance to these ancient clues emerged with the research of Soviets, Nikolai Goncharov, an historian, Vyacheslav Morozov, construction engineer, plus electronics specialist Valery Makarov. In 1973 they announced their discovery of a crystalline grid, a pattern of energies that spanned the globe (Chemistry & Life Journal, Soviet Academy of Science). Cosmic energies, they said, ebbed and flowed rhythmically in a pattern of 20 equilateral triangles called an icosahedron. This connects into a series of 12 pentagons – a dodecahedron, to create an icosa – dodeca crystal lattice.

The evolution of this crystal form is apparent from an analysis of the magnetic stress patterns fixed in rocks during their formation through the ages of time. The original super continent Pangaea seems to have split up first into a tetrahedral form (of four equilateral triangles) which then evolved into an icosahedron. The current crystal pattern is an unstable one which looks to metamorphose into a pentadodecahedron form, by connecting the 12 pentagons point to point.

The three Russians found the components of the crystal grid to have certain peculiarities and associations.

Seismic centres

Seismic activity tends to mostly occur along the path of grid lines, where major geological fracture zones are found. These zones follow the boundaries between terrestrial plates that ride fluidly atop the softer inner material and periodically grate together. Some grid lines follow plate boundaries where major volcanic activity occurs. A fault line extending from Morocco to Pakistan, only discovered by satellite photography, has provided further confirmation to the Soviets' theory.

Animal Migration

All animals, it seems, are able to sense time and direction with the aid of magnetic sensors in their bodies. Using this vital sense they align themselves with Earth's magnetic field.

Animals often migrate along grid paths, where the greatest concentration of electromagnetism is found. Many spend their winters at grid nodal points (where grid lines cross). Whale stranding points are often found to be low in magnetism.

Anomalous regions

Ivan T Sanderson was the first to recognise that the Earth is ringed by ten centres of magnetic and climatic anomaly, 'vile vortices' such as the Bermuda Triangle and the Devil's Sea, near Japan. Five of these centres are equally spaced along the Tropic of Cancer and five along the Tropic of Capricorn. The Russians have since found two more at the North and South Poles. Each of these 12 vortices are found at the 12 nodes of the icosa grid.

Vortice areas feature concentrations of violent disturbances, combining wind, ocean and magnetic currents. Some nodal centres are the birthplace of cyclones, anti-cyclone and hurricanes, whose paths follow the grid. At three node points maximum solar radiation is experienced – a determining factor in air and ocean currents. Indeed many prevailing wind and water currents follow the grid pattern.

Grid lines corresponding to cloud and ocean streaking patterns were reported by American astronauts en route to the Moon as being one of Earth's most prominent features. The white waters of Bermuda, for example, are a series of thin parallel bright lines, sometimes echoed by vapour streaks in the air above. This could be the same phenomena as 'te lapa' in the Pacific, described by the Polynesians. The theory holds that the electrical field generated by the crystal grid could be the shaping force to determine patterns of water and air.

Ancient civilisations

Centres of ancient civilisation often correspond with grid nodal points, for example: Egypt, the Indus Valley, megalithic Scotland, Peru, northern Mongolia and Easter Island. According to Jalandris (Joe Jochmans) Australia's grid is also 'associated with megalithic structures – the lower node with Koonunda "Stonehenge" and Flinders Ranges, South Australia; the upper node with the Burunya megalithic region'.

Of these three places only Wilpena Pound Chambers Gorge in the Flinders Ranges are regularly accessed by researchers and new-age pilgrims. The Koonunda 'Stonehenge', actually a stone platform, is perhaps 800km off to the west, near Maralinga, an ex-nuclear-bomb-testing site. Harsh, arid country, it is off limits to all bar local Aboriginal owners. Captain Bruce Cathie has written about it and gives an exact location with map co-ordinates. It was originally found by Len Beadell, the South Australian government surveyor. I have no idea of the whereabouts of the Burunya site, but would assume it is on Cape York Peninsula in far north Queensland somewhere.

Not all monuments are found exactly on a grid line, some are up to 200 miles away. Some straddle or zigzag around lines as if to conduct the secondary energies that offshoot the grid along 'energy leys'. Clusters of structures are often situated at nodal points.

Paranormal features

Unique features often found at nodes include vitrified stone megaliths in Scotland and areas of weird disappearances, time distortion, UFO's, electrical and gyroscopic disturbance (which often occur in waves or 'flaps'). Another oddity, at two Russian nodes, is the lack of certain elements in the soil, causing freaks in animal and plant evolution. At one such node, Lake Baikal, three quarters of lifeforms are unique. At an African node it's been determined that a spontaneous atomic fission explosion of Uranium 235 occurred some 1700 million years ago.

UFOs and grids

In the 1960s Bruce Cathie, an ex New Zealand airline pilot, began to research the incidence of 'flying saucer' sightings which followed straight line and rectangular grid pathways. UFO researcher Aimee Michel had made the same discovery in France in the 1950s and American George Adamski in 1953.

Although Cathie's grid patterns are nothing like the Russian model there are points and lines in common between them. Cathie's books on the subject include 'Harmonic 33' (1968), 'Harmonic 695' (1971) and 'The Pulse of the Universe' (1977) and 'Bridge to Infinity'. His grids are based on spherical geometry proposed by Reimann in the 19th century and extended by Einstein in the 20th. Reimann said that there are no straight lines in the universe, only curved lines that eventually return to their beginning; a concept illustrated in eastern philosophy by the serpent swallowing its tail.

Cathie discovered that an American communications base at Kauri Point in Aukland harbour was positioned at an important grid node in both the Russian and Cathie grid model. He postulates that American military scientists probably know all about these energy grids and that the Americans have been developing the research of Nikolai Tesla (made at the end of last century) to harness universal free energy available at these grid nodes, just as the UFOs appear to him to be doing. He also says that nuclear explosions cannot occur unless carefully planned in time and location, they must match certain space-time geometrics of energy grid coordinates and the elevation of the sun. He extrapolated his theory by accurately predicting the times of the first atomic tests made by the French at Muroroa atoll in 1968.

Universal grid

A fourth century Chinese feng shui text refers to a multitude of horizontal and vertical energy veins on Earth, like a net with warp and weft weaving and communicating together. Similar such grid concepts may be found in Japanese, Indian, Roman, Etruscan and Freemasonry traditions. More recently Professor Calligaris has also discovered a straight line energy grid associated with the human body.

This fits with the concept of Dr. Neiman and many dowsers, who say that the major crystal grid can be subdivided into decreasingly smaller networks of energy lattice, down to the level of quartz crystals. Forty years ago Francois Peyre determined, by dowsing, the existence of a 4 m square planetary energy grid aligned to magnetic north. The positive nodes of this grid, he found, cause the human aura to expand, whilst the negative nodes contract the aura.

Elsewhere, Ernst Hartmann, founder of the German Society of Geobiological Research, announced his discovery of a grid of 2 metre squares, also oriented to north, its lines about 20cm wide. Prof. Zaboj Harvalik, scientific adviser to the American Society of Dowsers, and other dowsers find grid lines to have variable dimensions. Harvalik believes grid lines are created from the dip angle formed from the interaction of Earth's magnetic field and Schumann Resonance.

Dr's Wittman and Curry, in dowsing research conducted at the Medical and Bio-Climatic Institute in south Germany, discovered a second grid – juxtaposed at diagonals to the first. As grid nodes may be a factor in geopathic stress, a dowser's survey should always refer to these 'universal grids' for problem spots.

The dimensions of these universal grids vary according to your location on the planet.

They can also become warped, for instance by other energy flows, such as underground water streams.

Sacred geometry

Pythagoras spoke of five sacred solids in geometry – the first being tetrahedron, the fourth icosa and the fifth dodeca. Characteristics associated with the icosa (of 20 faces) are perpetual regeneration, water and the colour blue. The dodeca (of 12 faces) has qualities of unity and the shaping of the physical world, its element is ether and colour is white-yellow.

According to Plato – manifestation from the ether is through geometric forms, namely the five Platonic solids.

Matter in the making?

Australian Aboriginal legends tell of Dreaming Heroes travelling along pathways across an unformed landscape, at the onset of the Dreamtime. Landscape forms were created where these spirit beings rested, at lesser nodal points perhaps?

Dr. Vladmir Neiman, a Soviet geologist and mineralogist, suggests that Earth's crystal lattice provides a channel for cosmic pulses arriving from space. Nodal points in the grid, where lines and signals intersect and concentrate, are the likely place then for matter to be created and destroyed. If the web also extends throughout the universe, this might help explain the formation of planets and black holes, the crystal grid conveying the harmonic ebb and flow of the universe.

References:

Jalandris – 'Cosmos' Magazine May 1982 & March 1983
Prof. Harvalik, American Society of Dowsers Journal, May 1981,
'The Crystal Grid', compilation by Borderland Sciences, USA.
Bruce Cathie, 'Harmonic 33' Reed, NZ, 1968,

Chinese and Tibetan Geomancy

Tibetan animism
The ancient peoples of Tibet were animists, viewing the landscape as pulsating with conscious life forces. In their Tibetan Bon-po tradition, rocks, trees, rivers and soil were all recognised as being inhabited by spirits, while the heavens are filled with gods.

As in India, the naga rajas/serpent kings, ruled the spiritual domain and are connected with fertility, crops and water. They would have to be propitiated before a tree was cut, the ground ploughed or other disturbances created.

Likewise in Sri Lanka local cults venerated the nature spirits they call yakkha, which in Burma they call the nats. Gnas is the Tibetan name for a holy place, which is considered to be teeming with nature spirits and deities.

Sacred peak
Mount Kailash is Tibet's sacred peak, at 6,714 metres and of distinctive appearance, it lies in rugged, remote and desolate western Tibet. Kailash is regarded as the physical embodiment of mythical Mount Meru (aka Mt Sumeru in Buddhist cosmology), the axis mundi/centre of the universe in South Asian cosmology/geomancy. This is not surprising, as four of South Asia's mightiest rivers begin in the region of Kailash flow into India from there – the Tsangpo/Brahmaputra, the Indus, the Sutlej, and the Karnali.

A pilgrimage centre for over 2,500 years, Kailash is sacred to Hindus, Jains, Buddhists, and Bon-po followers. Limited numbers of pilgrims are allowed to visit Kailash each year, but this could change as the Chinese have proposed the building of a road around it.

Buddhism arrives in Tibet
When Buddhism arrived it displaced the Bonpo traditions somewhat, but also paid respect to some and incorporated aspects into a Tibetan Buddhist blend.

A Tantric master Padmasambhava who brought Buddhist teachings to Tibet was said to have faced the ancient gods of Tibet at Mount Hepori. This sacred hill overlooking Samye, which became a centre for pilgrimage, had been a seat of power for the Bon deities worshipped by the old aristocratic families of Tibet.

Giants in the land
When Buddhist Queen Bhrikuti came from Nepal in the 7th century to join the court of King Songtsen Gampo, she proclaimed that a gigantic demoness inhabited Tibet's landscapes. In order to subdue her (and thus the common folks' animist ways) she caused Buddhist temples to be built on the most prominent parts of her body.

At the heart of the demoness, her most vulnerable point – was a little lake in Lhasa, the capitol. This lake was filled in and the Jo Khang, Tibets holiest temple, was erected there. When the lake was filled in, the local snakes were rounded up and detained in a cave on the sacred mountain of Chakpori at Lhasa.

Other 'extremity subduing' temples were built on the hips and shoulders of the demoness. Thus Buddhism was seen to override the ancient belief systems, while placing it's own indelible stamp on the landscape.

However, inside Buddhist temples one finds the gon-khang. This separate chamber is reserved for the ancient gods who are still considered to be the custodians and protectors of the sacred places that once belonged to them, but from which they were expelled after the arrival of Buddhism.

Dakinis

An aspect of the divine feminine principle, the Tibetan Dakinis are mystical beings who can be either peaceful, playful, or wrathful. They appear in dreams and visions, can appear in human form or act upon one as subtle spiritual energy – activating the nerves, breath and essence.

With dakini contact the intuitive faculties are opened to transform the flatness of intellectual Tantric practises. Sometimes they tempt yogis away from rigid conditioning, such as by offering meat and blood to the vegetarians. Bringing a sense of freshness and magic they guide the development of profound, intuitive awareness, but should one become too attached or fixated they might pull the rug from beneath you!

The most ancient school of meditation – Dzog Chen – incorporates Bonpo traditions and exalts the Dakinis. These beings are said to have transmitted and concealed original teachings in a mystery cypher of highly condensed symbolism that is hidden in the Earth and discovered intuitively at the appropriate time. Only full linking with the Dakini energy can enable one to decipher these 'hidden treasures'. 'Mind treasures' are also received from birds, trees, light and space as divine revelation, in the Dakini's 'twilight language'.

Geomancy of China

In most ancient Chinese tradition Nu Wa was the mother of the world. She created the first human beings, from handfuls of wet mud. She appeared in many guises – as a beautiful goddess or child and other times as a human headed serpent being. Fu Xi, her brother or husband, accompanied her in later myths, and, as yin/yang serpent beings they coiled around each other, establishing universal harmony. Their images reminds one of the caduceus and DNA spiral. (Later Chinese myths attributed human creation to a male figure Pan Gu.)

Landscape dragons

Gigantic archetypal spirit beings were believed to inhabit the land – the formidable dragon of the rugged mountains, the tiger of the gentle foothills and lowlands, and the like. Great bioregional devas, spirits of place, were felt to protect local communities, warding off famine, sickness and bad luck.

Mountain dragons were said to have hatched from rocks – 'dragon's eggs', while other rocks are considered to be their bones, mountain ridges – their spine, the foothills – their arms and legs, watercourses – their arteries. The Great Wall of China curves around the contours of the landscape in order to avoid excavating and wounding the dragon, who might then unleash great wrath upon the land. One should never build on the dragon's backbone, head or tail, or under a cliff. Energy is very yang and dangerous there.

The potent image of the dragon's beneficent power was adopted by China's rulers very early on as an imperial symbol. The Chinese Dragon Emperor, arbitrator between Heaven and Earth, was centred at the hub of the empire. Imperial cities Chang-an (Sian) and Beijing were laid out in a chequer board pattern, having a north-south axis, its roads running east-west to channel energies towards the emperor. Beijing is said to be dragon shaped, the central gate being the dragon's mouth, the flanking gates it's eyes, and so on.

Water dragons

Dragons were also strongly associated with water and governed weather, tides and water levels. Originally rain deities living in lakes and rivers, they were regularly invoked in times of drought. The Dragon dance that's still performed at Chinese New Year festivities, was originally a ritual of rain making.

To bring rain water dragons fly to the clouds and, when harmonious, ensure the fertility of the fields and the prosperity of the people. Water is synonymous with money and success.

Although fearsome adversaries, dragons were generally regarded as auspicious beasts, protectors, who guarded treasures, waterways, clouds and winds, and even Heaven. During droughts their images were taken from the temples to show the dragon the damage done and to encourage precipitation.

But if the water dragon has been interfered with havoc can be unleashed. One should never build anything over a well (the dragon's eye), or spring (the dragon's ear). Storms are said to be battling dragons, droughts are sleeping dragons and floods are wrathful ones.

Flooding was often a great problem in ancient China and resident dragons could be called upon in times of flooding. An imperial edict of 1869 gave thanks for an impending flood that had been averted, stating that 'When the dykes of the Yellow River were in danger of collapse the repeated apparition of the Golden Dragon saved the day'.

The mightiest dragons were the sovereigns of the five oceans. Like the naga kings of India, they were said to live in crystal palaces beneath the sea.

Water dragons are said to live underwater for half of the year after which they rise into the sky at springtime, when the constellation of the Dragon is at its height.

A hierarchy of gods

The people had long worshipped a host of gods, some of the soil, of the elements, and of specific localities. Although they originally recognised no gods at all, in later times Daoist philosophers organized China's thousands of gods and goddesses into a heavenly hierarchy, ruled by the Jade Emperor, beneath which were posted an entire civil service of lesser deities, including a count of the winds and a lord of lightening. The celestial posts were often filled by deceased mortals.

Cheng Huang were the gods of the town wall and moat, in charge of cities and rural districts. Local deities administered individual streets, temples, bridges or villages. Every trade, craft and profession also had its own guardian deity, and up until the first half of the 20th century most Chinese guilds had a patron god, to whose image members would kowtow upon arrival at meetings.

The home was considered the domain of the Five Genii, who were responsible for front and back doors, the well, inner courtyard and the aisles around which the home was constructed. Pictures of fearsome looking guardian warriors were pasted up next to front doors each New Year. The kitchen god Zao Jun was the most intrusive deity in family life, as he dictated behaviour and the adherence to a great number of rules and regulations pertaining to everything from respect for elders to hygiene principles.

References:
Michael Willis, 'Tibet – Life, Myth and Art', Duncan & Baird, UK, 1999.
Tsultrim Allione, 'Women of Wisdom', Routledge & Keegan Paul, UK, 1984.
Douglas and Slinger, 'The Secret Dakini Oracle', Destiny Books.
'Land of the Dragon – Chinese Myth', Duncan & Baird, 1999.

Feng Shui

While ancient geomantic knowledge of landscape and Earth harmony was being greatly fragmented in Europe, Chinese geomancy, known as 'feng shui' (pronounced foong shway), remained relatively intact until modern times. While not sanctioned by the authorities in today's China, it is common in Hong Kong, Taiwan, Singapore and traditional Chinese communities around the world. Modern Chinese consortiums often refurbish huge office blocks in order to satisfy feng shui and thus enhance business prospects. And lately Asian-Australian real estate contracts are including sale clauses 'subject to good feng shui'.

Encapsulating ancient Taoist philosophy, yin/yang and ch'i theory, feng shui governs the relationship between people and place. The traditional Chinese home is designed to be a haven of peace and prosperity, harmonising with the Earth and Heavens above – a microcosm of the perfect environment. Ideal surroundings enjoy a healthy flow of Earth and atmospheric ch'i, as well as suitable astrological influences. Ancestor worship is also an important element.

In China two basic schools of feng shui practise developed over thousands of years. In the largely flat featureless Fukien and Chekiang provinces the Compass school developed an analytic approach. It stressed the importance of the directions, time, astrology, the I Ching etc, in proper relationship together. These various elements were charted on the feng shui compass, called Lo Pan, with up to 38 concentric circles containing nearly all Chinese symbols dealing with time and space. Few people employ the compass these days.

An older system – the Form School, takes the intuitive approach, feeling out the actual energies, rather than merely offering purely conceptual models. The Form School analyses the landscape forms and divines ch'i/Earth energy lines and dragon points. It developed in the southern mountainous regions of Kiangsi and Anhui provinces, and is now practised in Korea, Japan, Laos, Thailand, the Phillipines, Vietnam, Malaysia and Singapore.

In India a parallel geomantic system, called Vastu Shasta, also became a sophisticated tool for architecture and landscape design.

Environmental ch'i

According to Chinese thought life force, they call ch'i, has two forms. Yang ch'i is light and expansive, floating upwards; yin ch'i is heavy and sinks downwards, forming matter. Yin and yang ch'i, also, are not static, but constantly moving, changing, ascending, descending, expanding, contracting, inhaling and exhaling. Sometimes ch'i is mass (yin), sometimes vapour (yang).

Quality-wise, beneficial ch'i is known as shang ch'i and unhealthy ch'i is called sh'a. All types of ch'i interact and influence each other.

Personal ch'i is our breath, Earth ch'i is Dragon's breath, while Heaven ch'i is found in air, steam, gas and weather. Land with the most Earth ch'i is considered the most habitable because plants grow fastest there, animals are the fattest, and people are the happiest, most comfortable and prosperous.

Earth ch'i is said to spiral around and around inside the Earth, ever changing and pulsating; sometimes 'exhaling' towards the surface, sometimes 'inhaling' down to the depths. When rising to the surface it may create mountains, and, if extra charged – volcanoes. Should it recede too far from the crust then water will not flow and the landscape will be dry, flat, featureless, perhaps desert; while pollution, sickness and bad luck will fester. Our destiny is improved by the smooth flowing, balanced Earth ch'i that shapes our personal ch'i.

'Secret arrows' are a source of sh'a in both rural and urban landscapes. Straight alignments of structures or landscape features conduct sh'a, channelling it rapidly to pierce and reduce one's personal ch'i and convey dis-ease. Highways, railways and rows of office blocks create potential secret arrows, which threaten the most when pointed toward an entrance to one's home.

Water in the landscape is a yang element animated by ch'i. Water retains ch'i, whose quality defines the clarity, flow, course and depth of a watercourse. Rivers, ideally, flow neither too fast nor too slow. If a river meanders, all the better. If water drains away from a site too quickly ch'i will not accumulate there. A river with a straight artificial channel carries secret arrows that will injure people and reduce Earth ch'i. Sharp river bends also create sh'a.

Ch'i lines – 'lung mei' – flow sinuously through the living landscape, hugging the contour lines and conveying the cyclic pulse of the dragon force to the land. Ephemeral phenomena, like all things they are subject to decay.

Where yang dragon and yin tiger lines cross is said to be the 'dragon's lair'. Around it Heaven and Earth are in accord, and abundant shang ch'i will be evident. Where two tiger lines cross such a very yin site is deemed unfavourable.

Dragon nodes

Like acupuncture the goal of feng shui is to tap beneficial ch'i by focussing beneficial currents and deflecting or neutralising harmful sh'a. Best ch'i sites (for both living and dead) are carefully selected by sensitive observation. An auspicious site was described by a seventeenth century feng shui expert thus:

> *'There is a touch of magic light ... It can be understood intuitively, but not conveyed in words. The hills are fair, the waters fine, the sun handsome, the breeze mild; and the sky has a new light: another world. Amid confusion, peace; amid peace, a festive air. Upon coming into its presence, one's eyes are opened; if one sits or lies, one's heart is joyful. Here ch'i gathers, and the essence collects. Light shines in the middle, and magic goes out on all sides.'*

An ideal house site has slightly more yang than yin ch'i. Here energy may be transitional – rugged mountains might ease into foothills, or a hill rise from a flat plain. A screen of hills or trees protects the back of the site from prevailing winds and water is seen in the foreground. Dragon and tiger lines will be nearby. Ch'i will accumulate.

The best site is located halfway up the middle of an armchair shaped mountain range with a small hill in front – this is known as the 'mother embracing child' or 'dragon protecting pearl' site. This pattern can be created on a small scale with earthworks and strategically placed trees acting as windbreaks.

Vegetation & ch'i

Groves of feng shui trees were deemed sacred and protected in traditional geomantic landscapes. Ancient places where nature is revered, they often had equally important roles in staving off erosion and protecting sensitive topography.

An abundance of healthy, green vegetation denotes a good supply of Earth ch'i. The greener the foliage the better. Energy lines known as 'green ribbons' or 'dragon veins' may be traced, by dowsing, to connect all the greenest plants around. Buildings sited along such a vein tap into excellent Earth ch'i.

Tree planting stimulates Earth ch'i production and vine covered buildings enjoy enhanced ch'i as well. Trees are also useful to block afternoon sun, wind, pollution and noise, and to absorb sh'a from secret arrows. They are generally protective, but if planted too close to the house may cut off the flow of ch'i to it (via entrances, doors, windows, pathways), so keep them at a safe distance.

Urban feng shui

These days cities have taken on feng shui symbolism. Skyscrapers are the equivalent of mountains, roads are like rivers. The shapes, size, orientation and colour of buildings are analysed for ch'i quality. Secret arrows, such as from roads that point directly at houses, are very common in cities.

Often multistory buildings will be badly afflicted by secret arrows and, in trying to deflect them, the ba gua geomantic mirror is used, placed above entrances. This 'aspirin of feng shui' has sometimes unforeseen effects and 'mirror wars' may result from deflecting energies to neighbours' doors.

Modern feng shui site analysis (from a Form School perspective) considers the shapes of land, buildings and infrastructure; their position and orientation; the presence of ch'i lines; the vitality and harmony of plants, animals and neighbours; the history of the place and any bad omens which may occur during inspection.

References:

Sarah Rossbach, 'Feng Shui, the Chinese art of Placement' E P Dutton, USA, 1983.
Stephen Skinner, 'The Living Earth Manual of Feng Shui' Routledge & Kegan Paul, UK, 1982.
Evelyn Lipp, 'Chinese Geomancy' Times Books International, 1979.

Earth Mysteries in the British Isles

The Enigma of Stones Circles

When the Romans came to the British Isles and saw the great stone circles and barrows they were already vastly ancient, some several thousand years old. Herodotus marvelled of a 'singular circular temple', which may have referred to Stonehenge. There purpose was a mystery, as there are no accounts of Druid ceremonies to be had, and knowledge of them is long forgotten.

Many of the stone circles date to around 5000 years ago, to the Neolithic era. Building techniques such as those seen at Stonehenge indicate an even older tradition of wooden circles. In the later Bronze Age people were adding to and modifying the stone circle sites, and the process continued into the Iron Age, which ended some 2000 years ago.

The invading Romans were instructed not to destroy the existing temples, but to re-consecrate them to their own gods. Later, between 450 ad to 1066 ad, the Anglo Saxons renamed sacred sites in honour of their own Norse gods. In the eighth century Pope Gregory made the decree that pagan temples were to be Christianised. This saved many a sacred site from destruction, as many features, such as the holy wells, were embraced by the Christian religion.

The very first historical reference to a stone circle was when Stonehenge was described by Henry of Huntingdon in 1130. By these times there was not much respect given to the ancient megaliths, and the massive stones were being pilfered for building materials. Puritanical stone killer types often systematically set out to destroy the monuments in the name of the new god.

It was not until 1586 that, for the first time, William Cambden's book 'Britannia' spoke of other significant monumental sites of Britain. Antiquarians of the day were interested in the Roman and Saxon eras, but little else.

In seventeenth century England antiquarian interest finally turned to pre-history. John Aubrey (1626–1697) was the first person to associate stone circles with the Druids. He was also the first to document Avebury – the biggest stone circle in the world, as a vast monumental, ceremonial complex. Aubrey was the world's first landscape archeologist.

Aubrey must have been a great inspiration to William Stukely (1687–1765) who become the most well known antiquarian of his times, as well as the very first archeological fieldworker. Stukely was an excellent technical draughtsman who carefully reproduced what he saw. In those days sites were often being systematically destroyed with great fervour. He was able to document Avebury before much was lost.

Stukely published two celebrated and still highly collectible (and rare) books, for which he is most famous – 'Stonehenge – A Temple Restor'd to the British Druids' (1740) and 'Abury – A Temple of the British Druids, With Some Others Described' (1743).

Many of the interpretations and ideas about sites he observed may well be flawed, but nevertheless he must have stirred peoples' imaginations greatly. The stones of

Avebury, he asserted, were formed in the image of a great serpent, and to his mind it was a temple for serpent worship. This wasn't a very popular idea, but we don't really know much better nowadays. Stukely documented the existence of a second stone avenue, leading to Beckhamptom. Again his ideas were dismissed, yet some 256 years later the actual existance of this Avenue was finally confirmed by archeologists.

Stukely was a big inspiration for the modern revival of the Druids. The image of white robed Druids in ceremony was actually a fantasy dreamed up by self-styled Druid guru Edward Williams, who called himself Iolo Morganwg, in the late eighteenth century. His ideas certainly caught on in Wales, and new stone circles, erected for the purpose of Eisteddfods, are still in use.

But interest in understanding the ancient sites did not surface much until the dawn of the 20th century. Sir Norman Lockyer, the great astronomer and scientist, had surveyed alignments of astronomical significance amongst stones at Lands End, and, in 1909 he published 'Stonehenge and other British Stone Monuments Astronomically Considered'. Lockyer was the founder of astro-archeology/archeo-astronomy. Previously, back in 1770, Dr John Smith had already claimed in a book that Stonehenge had been a temple for the observation of the motions of the heavenly bodies.

In the 1920's Alfred Watkins, the respected photographer and inventor from Herefordshire, researched curious 'alinements' of ancient sites, including standing stones and stone circles, that he found spanning the landscape. Around the same time in France (and unbeknown to Watkins), Xavier Guichard was also tuning in to a similar geomantic system. And in Germany around this time, the regional planner J Heinsch independently announced his discovery of alignments in Germany, Britain and elsewhere. He spoke of 'holy lines', while Watkins called them of 'leys'.

Picnicking parties seeking 'ley lines' became a popular past time in the 1930's in England, until the World War broke out. The sites that lined up on maps were visited and inbetween them there would sometimes be discovered more 'mark stones' and structures hidden in vegetation, that all lined up straight.

In the 1930's in England mystic and author Dion Fortune, of Glastonbury, was perhaps the first modern person to suggest that there were special energies to be found at sacred sites.

Several dowsers in the early part of the 20th century independently discovered the presence of underground water streams and their intersections beneath the central or focal points of sacred sites in the UK – beneath the barrows, standing stones, stone circles and dolmens.

During the '30s in France dowsers Merle and Diot were finding prehistoric avenues to be aligned on water lines. Merle observed circular patterns of water around sacred sites and Diot also found circular water courses.

Then in 1939 Reginald Allender Smith, a well known and respected archeologist, and leading authority on the stone age, lectured on the subject to the British Society of Dowsers. He was the keeper of British and Egyptian antiquities at the British Museum, who, after retiring, had turned to dowsing. Smith had found that at the centre of every pre-historic temple there could be found a spot beneath which a number of underground streams formed a radiating pattern could be dowsed. He called this pattern a 'blind spring'. Barrows and tumuli, he found, were all located over blind springs. He also claimed to have found the locations of stones in the 'lost' Beckhampton Avenue of

Avebury, as well as an oval enclosure at its end, that had previously been described by William Stukely. It was not until 1999 that archeologists were able to confirm this to be true.

After World War II dowser Guy Underwood began to follow up on the earlier discoveries of other members of the British Society of Dowsers (which had been founded in 1933). In his retirement years he visited many ancient sacred sites, in Somerset, where he lived, and in Gloucestershire and Wiltshire. His articles, published in the Society Journals between 1947 and '51, were later compiled posthumously and published in book form as 'The Pattern of the Past'.

While his ideas have not all been well received and many seem outdated now, they nevertheless launched much food for thought. But many people think that his interpretations are flawed. Underwood felt that ancient peoples had deliberately sited their temples and structures over particular energy points. But what really came first? Did the energies come in afterwards as a result of the construction and use of the site? Was the chicken or the egg first? Both perhaps?

Another related theme emerged in the 1950's when UFO researcher Tony Wedd stated that UFO activity seemed to occur in straight lines and in association with physical site alignments. John Michell's first book – Flying Saucer Vision, was about this phenomenon. (And in New Zealand in the late '60's pilot Captain Bruce Cathie wrote about a planetary energy grid favoured by the UFOs.)

Other dowsers turned their attention to the historic era and found very similar energy patterns at more modern sacred sites. In 1965 W. H. Lamb told the BSD how he had found two or more underground streams crossing beneath the high altar of every church that he had dowsed. Independent of this research Muriel Langdon, another dowser, was finding 'water domes' (also known as 'blind springs') beneath altars, fonts, chancel steps and doors.

(In France dowsers have found no less than fourteen underground streams to be crossing beneath the altar of the medieval Chartres Cathedral.)

In 1967 Keith Critchlow discovered the sacred geometry inherent in structures such as the ruined Glastonbury Abbey, and foretold by the mystic Frederick Bligh Bond. This and the work of Professor Alexander Thom, who has 'entirely revised accepted opinion as regards megalithic peoples – with their amazing astronomical and mathematical knowledge as translated into monuments', led to the formation in 1969, of the group RILKO – Research into Lost Knowledge Organisation.

Thom, a Scottish professor of engineering, had published his first book in 1967 – 'Megalithic Sites in Britain' whereby he showed, by his accurate surveys, that 'the people who built them were guided by advanced scientific principles, particularly in the departments of astronomy and engineering'. At every stone circle he checked out Thom had found long sighting lines across the landscape for observing astronomical events. The circles recorded the lunar cycle of 18.6 years, he determined, and they were built using a unit of measurement, the 'megalithic yard' of 2.72 feet. (His surveys also showed that the circles are never true circles, but actually often ovoid in shape.)

In 1969 the scholarly research of John Michell, in his book 'View over Atlantis', helped a wider audience to understand stone circles and other 'Earth Mysteries' (which was a term coined by the Whole Earth Catalogue in the U.S. in 1974). Important books by such authors as Nigel Pennick, Paul Deveraux, Paul Screeton and Tom Graves and others followed.

What the dowsers found

Dowser John Taylor in 1975 studied a standing stone near Crickhowell in South Wales. He found a 'significant distortion' in the local geomagnetic field around the stone. It showed a doubling of the normal field strength of half a gauss – quite a variation. This field was found to wax and wane in a regular cycle. Taylor also found narrow bands of double strength geomagnetism running horizontally across the stone at various heights, which move up and down in their position somewhat over time on a cyclic basis.

Taylor, and later Tom Graves, found that standing stones generally had seven bands of this energy, although smaller ones of only 4-5 feet high might only have five bands. Two of the bands are dowsed to be below the ground. The bands were found to actually spiral up and down the stone.

'All seven bands, according to several researchers I've talked to, are tapping points into a spiral release of some kind of energy that moves up and down the stone following the lunar cycle … The spiral feeds energy from the ground to the sky during one half of the lunar cycle and feeds from the sky to the ground during the other half' Tom Graves wrote, in his highly acclaimed book 'Needles of Stone'.

Tom had found that he and other dowsers experienced a great energy release when, in a sensitive frame of mind, they touched the fifth and seventh energy band on the stone. Sometimes the thrust was strong enough to push one backwards or sideways away from the stone. Less sensitive people may feel their hands tingling at these points. A change of polarity was found to occur at the stones at the sixth day after new and full moon.

Tom noted that standing stones appear to act as giant acupuncture needles in the Earth, and that also the ancient practise of burning bonfires at 'beacon' hills at seasonal events could perhaps be considered a form of 'moxibustion' for balancing the Earth's energies.

Dave Sanguine of the British Society of Dowser's Earth Energies Group notes that 'Each stone of a circle can have controlling effects on detrimental Earth energies'.

Site energies

The locations of Britian's megalithic sites are often highly energized. 80% of the stone circles there are built within a mile of a geological fault line. Often individual stones are associated with magnetic anomalies. Many of the stones at circles are granite, which is slightly radioactive, or basalt, which is paramagnetic.

The Dragon Project in the 1970's measured various energetic anomalies at several circles, mainly at the Rollright Stones, over a number of years. They used gaussmeters, infrared cameras, ultrasonic detectors, dowsing and geiger counters.

Team member Don Robins suggests that the stones act as condensers, where an electric charge is stored until something happens, at which point the energy discharges. Stones can discharge when a person touches them and many people have reported mild shocks on contact.

The stones seem to also discharge when dawn light hits them. Audiosonic equipment at Rollright measured a high pitched sonic outburst from stones at dawn.

The central vortex

Carrowmore megalithic complex in County Sligo, western Ireland is the largest and most important megalithic centre outside Carnac in Brittany. (Interestingly, it has been found that there is a physical alignment between it and Tara in Ireland, Stonehenge and the Great Pyramid in Egypt.)

Irish dowser Michael Poynder has written about Carrowmore (and other) stone circles in his book 'Psi in the Sky', finding them to be located over several underground streams. 'Water spirals', he says, rise upwards at the circle centres, the crossing point of the underground streams.

Another Irish dowser Billy Gawn describes how he clairvoyantly sees a columnar vortex rising up vertically above dolmens and circles. The energy actually seems to go two way, he observes. 'Stone circles can have far reaching effects on the local area', he says. Earth energy lines that Billy can see seem to obey the laws of fluid dynamics (as do clouds).

When I visited Carrowmore's stone circles in 2003 I found the above described energy patterns by dowsing. I also dowsed Earth elemental beings that are stationed as guardians in the centre of the circles.

It is advised that when visiting stone circles you should dowse for the proper point to enter the circle, for if you walk against the energy flow you might start to feel sick, perhaps nauseous or spun out, as people have discovered when blundering in the wrong way.

Curiously, what ever energies you might find at a stone circle, dowsers told me at the International Dowsing Congress – you can also find at a crop circle.

Dancing circles

Stone circles are said to be the home of dancing fairies and once people would circle dance within the stone circles too.

'For untold generations, it has been believed, especially by the devotees of the old witch region' Tom Lethbridge wrote in the 1960's 'that by means of exciting people to execute wild circular dances, power could be generated and stored in stones and trees.'

'Perhaps the dancing is a memory of ancient initiation rites?' ponders Serena Roney-Dougal 'and perhaps the revival of this activity in 1980 in Britain and the circle dancing now done all over the country, is responsible for the concurrent appearance of the crop circles?' she muses.

Stone Circle Visions

Geoffrey Hodson was a highly respected clairvoyant of extraordinary ability who wrote and lectured tirelessly for the Theosophical Society in the early to mid 20th century. One day, in August 1922, while attempting to observe nature spirits in the area, he visited a stone circle near Keswick in the English Lake District. Sitting inside the inner circle of stones, he had a strong series of vivid visions of past events, which he wrote about in his charming little book 'Fairies at Work and Play'.

The visions were dominated by scenes in which a man of strong personality presided. This priest/teacher/healer cut a stately figure in white robes and long hair, as he stood inside the inner circle, behind a group of priests. Draped over some tall stones – a banner of white on which was displayed a golden serpent.

In one important ritual a large group of people watched from outside the outer circle, as the man, evidently a master magician, raised his hands to the heavens above and uttered a loud call. Hovering above him were a number of devas (angelic beings), some of whom, at his calling, formed a circle over his head some 80–100 feet in the air, their hands meeting in the centre bearing fire, each wearing a crown. Their fire descended down upon the altar stone in front of the priest and burnt brightly. The other priests went to the altar stone in two ranks chanting, while the other people made towards it too, and made obeisance to the fire, their heads bowed and arms stretched forward. Meanwhile the devas descended closely by them and a force like lightening played along the peoples' backs in the form of a huge cross above them. Many lesser nature spirits filled the air, some holding the force along the lines of the cross, others just as part of the congregation.

The priest prayed to some mighty spiritual entity and from whom a response apparently came. 'The effect of this prayer was remarkable' Hodson reported, as the heavens opened and a huge down thrust of force poured down into the central square, where everyone focussed their attention. This great pillar of living power glowed opalescent and slightly rosy coloured, reaching far into the ground and high into the heavens.

It caused the devas to become intensely active in trying to ensure the maximum force was reaching the people. Then a number of sick people were brought into the centre, for their great betterment. The priests distributed a yellow liquid for them to drink, while the high priest passed his hands over them for instant healing, while he channelled the tremendous power through him, his body glowing with a golden light. After giving the people a discourse, the high priest looked again up to heaven and spoke. The pillar of energy ceased to flow down and the people, chanting, returned to out of the circle by the three entrances they had come through. The high priest then turned towards the serpent banner and other priests and spoke and blessed them. Extending his arms towards them a stream of power flowed from him to them and the banner and the priests were lifted into a state of exultation. The banner was then rolled up and the priests moved off.

Hodson also saw ceremonies where just the priests saluted the rising sun, and on one night their attention was drawn to a particular star in the sky. In another vision people on the summits of Skiddaw and Blencathra were signalling with beacon fires.

'This temple appears to be in magnetic contact with a centre of the same religion lying to the south west and a great way off' Hodson senses. '... Much of the old magnetic influence remains and can be felt; so strongly impressed on the place are the ancient ceremonies that they rise up continually before the inner eye ... Other scenes far less holy and beautiful have been enacted here, other priests of dark and fierce aspect have stood within this ring ... (and) ugly as sin are the elemental shapes which hover around their ceremonials of blood ... (but) Down through the thousands of years which follow, it is the first, the nobler, the uplifting influence which lasts and which is the most strongly impressed upon the place, showing something of the grandeur of the religion of ancient days.'

Stone circle experience

There is a legend that a group of witches in Hampshire sent up a 'cone of power' to stop the imminent invasion of the Spanish Armada in Elizabethan times. A storm brewed up which wrecked the fleet in the nick of time. In modern times too, magic has been resorted to in warfare too.

During World War II it was discovered that Hitler was using geomancy, magic and astrology to help give him the edge for his plans of world domination. So adepts in magic and astrology were consulted by the British, in order to help understand the tactics the Nazis might employ, although this was kept very quiet.

Decades later professional clairvoyant Jill Bruce had life changing experiences which provided insights into this era, whilst camped inside a stone circle in Dartmoor. She has written a book about this and other aspects of her life's work, and told the Earth Energy interest group all about it during the International Dowsing Congress in England, 2003.

It all came to pass in the search for a lost dog, Jill told us. Three days after the 17-8-1998 eclipse of the full moon, after crossing Dartmoor, Jill camped in a little tent inside an important stone circle, where she had amazing visionary experiences. In her vision – the side of the tent melted away and revealed the presence of a ten foot high elf who was just outside of the circle, who told her that his name was 'Asulan'. He said that the elemental kingdom, of which he was a part, would help her, including looking for her lost dog.

She then had the frightening vision of an old Spitfire plane hurtling out of the sky and crashing down next to the stone circle, after which three beautiful siren-like women appeared. Asulan explained to her that during World War Two Churchill employed witches to help keep the Nazis at bay. Sirens were conjured up to lure the pilots to crash, and three psychics had died there.

Jill also saw that within the stone circle there was a huge city of the elves and later there she was able to discover fairy gateways and gates to important archetypes, which included Welsh Arthurian connections. And she received a gift from the devas in the form of an understanding about plant energies.

Sacred Site Abuse

With the revival in interest in things geomantic the sacred sites of Britain have attracted sometimes unwelcome attention in modern times. Not necessarily physically destructive, but nevertheless affecting the emotional and consciousness aspects of the sites.

The Dragon Project people, who have been studying the Rollright Stones in the U.K., sometimes came across evidence of black magic rituals having been performed there, including the remains of a dead puppy.

The Vale of the White Leaved Oak, a place in Herefordshire of great sanctity, has been found by local dowsers to have ten energy lines that radiate out from the area at 36 degree intervals out across the Midlands. Black magic rituals have been done there, and objects can be found dangling in the trees afterwards, while there is a very bad feeling there now. Let's hope that the bad energy does not radiate out further along the energy lines …

But even something as simple as leaving rubbish behind at a site, such as candle wax melted on rocks, can be enough to spoil a site to some extent.

Fascination with places like Stonehenge have led to their over use, degradation and isolation through the necessity of creating protection for them. Police have had pitched battles with pagans and wandering hippies denied access to their sacred sites. The tension has been somewhat resolved now in a more enlightened 21st century.

Stonehenge – Summer Solstice 1989

Police in helicopters, on horseback and on foot today stopped a ragtag army of hippies from illegally celebrating the summer solstice at England's best-known Bronze Age monument. 150 people were arrested, mainly for trying to breach a 6km 'no-go' area set-up to prevent a repetition of past midsummers day clashes. 800 police were involved and even the Druids were barred from holding their own sunrise ceremony.

Source: Northern Star 22/6/89

Stonehenge – Summer Solstice 2003

More than 30,000 people gathered at Stonehenge to mark the summer solstice on June 21st, 2003. English Heritage reopened the site to the public after the closures and clashes of previous years. Astrologer Roy Gillett, who was among the crowds there to watch the sunrise just before 0500 BST, said it was important to celebrate this the longest day of the year. He said Druids were joined at the 5,000 year-old World Heritage site by anyone who wanted to 'keep in touch with the flow of nature'.

Revellers were delighted that the good weather allowed the sunrise to be seen over the ancient stones. The sight of the sun breaking through trees on the horizon over the Heel Stone was met with a loud chorus of drums, whistles, whoops and shrieks and music from samba-style bands.

Because the solstice was at a weekend many more people were able to make the pilgrimage to Wiltshire from all over the country. The crowd was a mix of Druids, pagans, new age travellers, nature lovers and anyone else curious to take part in the experience. Police in the neighbouring county of Hampshire had warned they would not tolerate any illegal gatherings after the solstice. Officers were out in force in the area between Basingstoke, Andover and the Wiltshire border and thwarted any attempts to hold parties.

Source: BBC on-line, June 2003.

Chambered Mounds

These Neolithic structures are found in many parts of the world, with many in Europe and the British Isles. Inside the huge mounds, typically, are found huge stones arranged in passages and chambers. These are methodically covered with layers of sod, clay, gravel and sometimes quartz chips. According to energy researcher Wilhelm Reich the sand-wiching of alternating layers of such organic and inorganic materials can act as an orgone/energy accumulator.

The presence of clay layers, sometimes imported from out of the locality, can create a Faraday Cage effect and shield out electro- magnetic fields, thus creating ideal conditions for enhanced psychic communications and experiences. This would have been ideal for their ritualistic use.

When I visited Newgrange, the famous 'passage grave' in Ireland's Boyne Valley, it was fascinating to dowse inside this massive Neolithic chambered mound, which is faced with lumps of white quartz. There I found a huge and regal Earth spirit that inhabited the massive mound on the hill top.

My guess is that it is the spirit of the hill, who gained in status when this important ritual centre was in use. In legend the site is associated with the great god/king Dagda the Good, it's builder, who passed it on to his son Aengus.

Visiting the Carrowmore megalithic region in 2003, it was sad to observe the earthworks being done to re-build one of the 'passage graves' there, probably as a result of archeological studies opening it up. This work was being done with metal cages/ gabions of stone being constructed as an inner core. These metal structures may well disturb the energetic nature of the site. 'Metal interrupts energy' as TC Lethbridge would put it.

Dew Ponds

Man made shallow ponds that collect moisture are another enigma of British tradition. Like the chambered mounds, they are built of alternating layers of clay then straw, usually over chalk. Could they be acting as an orgone acumulator, one wonders?

Olivers Dewpond, near Devizes, is diamond shaped, but unfortunately is not working now, Shaun Ogbourne told us at the International Dowsing Congress, 2003.

Dowsing this dewpond people have found the important dragon line, known as the St Michaels Line, to pass through it and three underground streams to cross near its centre. This sort of pattern is seen in many other dewponds. This leads Shaun to believe that dewpond locations were dowsed for.

But this is not necessarily the case. Perhaps the dewpond attracted the underground water?

References:

Guy Underwood, 'The Pattern of the Past', Abacus, UK, 1969.
Neil Mortimer, 'Stukeley Illustrated', Green Magic, 2003.
Paul Deveraux, 'Earth Mysteries', Piatkus, UK, 1999.
'Earth Mysteries – A Study in Patterns', various authors, R.I.L.K.O., UK, 1977.
Geoffrey Hodson,'Fairies at Work and Play', Theosophical Publishing House, 1982.
Sig Lonegren, 'Spiritual Dowsing', Gothic Image, UK, 1986.
Michael Poynder, 'Pi in the Sky', The Collins Press, Ireland.
Tom Graves, 'Needles of Stone', Turnstone Press, UK, 1978.
Serena Roney-Dougal, 'The Faery Faith', Green Magic, UK, 2003.
Tom Graves editor, 'The Essential Lethbridge', British Society of Dowsers, 1980.

A sacred stone in Ireland from the Iron Age, the Turoe Stone (sadly not in its original position).

North American Earth mysteries

Landscape alignments
While in Britain the idea of ancient sacred site alignments was not to emerge until the 20th century, William Pidgeon, an American ahead of his time, was the first westerner to discover and record site alignments in America from around 1853. His informant, an old native American De-Coo-Dah, the last medicine man of the Elk Nation, showed Pidgeon the massive earthworks and effigy mounds which ran in alignments and spanned hundreds of miles, in 'lineal ranges' as he called them. Pidgeon was led to believe that they were division lines marking territories. (Likewise in England ley lines often mark parish boundaries.)

Dowsers' findings
Dowser Sig Lonegren writes that the structures found along the alignments in Ohio had ceremonial rather than defensive purposes. 'There is primary water under each of the markers' he finds.

Sig, together with the American Society of Dowsers Earth Mysteries Group, have also studied energy patterns in over 30 ancient underground chambers in Vermont. They conclude that 'primary water' found at any sacred space 'has a pattern to it that links it directly to the structure itself'.

Effigy mounds
In the USA there are an estimated 10,000 effigy mounds of which some 5,000 remain, almost all in the state of Wisconsin. At the Lizard Mound Park there can be seen 27 well preserved mounds. Mound shapes there are commonly conical, or cigar or so-called 'panther' shaped, with all but the panther mounds having water dome and ley energies associated with them, writes dowser Neal Sagar.

Most impressive of them all is the unique Lizard mound, about 120 feet long and from 4 to 40 feet high. Sagar reports powerful dowsing reactions over the Lizard Mound, with water domes and leys present. The dowsing survey left him feeling greatly energised. Burials have been excavated from some of the higher linear mounds, and these had the least detectable energies. Archeologists date the earthworks to about 800AD or so.

The serpent to many native American peoples is a symbol of life energy and the gigantic Serpent Mound, near Locust Grove in Ohio, is the most well known effigy mound. It's enormity (over 500m long) and shape can only be viewed properly from the air. The massive earthwork, that winds across the top of a bluff near the Ohio River, depicts a serpent grasping an egg in its mouth, with a tail that ends in a spiral.

Geologists tell us that it is located over a 'crypto-volcanic' feature unique in America, plus a dense cluster of fault lines.

Ceremonial mounds
'The earthworks and ceremonial mounds of Native Americans seem to differ in many respects from the earthworks typical of the British Isles and Europe. Only in the New England region are found ancient stone chambers, dolmens, standing stones, and cairns

similar to those found in the Old World' writes dowser Lee Barnes.

'Most of the ceremonial mounds in the south-east are earthen structures, layered upon previously built mounds, often with evidence of ashes from burned council houses between successive layers, each built with the addition of thousands of basket-fuls of earth. These mounds are mostly limited in the Appalachian Mountains to the broader floodplains south of Asheville – researchers suggest that there were not large-enough populations in the smaller valleys to the north to support the labour to build large ceremonial mounds' Lee exlains.

'Near the southern edge of the Appalachian Mountains is the famous Nikwasi Mound at Franklin, North Carolina, considered one of the more important ceremonial mounds along the Little Tennessee River. The mound was presumed to have been constructed with numerous earth layers over a much older, primitive Earth Lodge cere-monial chamber, representing different mound-building periods long before the Cherokees superseded earlier cultures in the late ninth century.

'Early explorers, including the colourful botanist William Bartram, describe the mound and it's townhouse and surrounding village. The British Army, under pressure from colonists inching into Cherokee lands, marched on the valley in 1770 and destroyed dozens of village sites, occupying the mound's Town House as a field hospital, before finally burning it down, along with 1500 acres of corn fields.

'Today the Nikwase mound is located between two busy streets which meet at a bridge and near the "old ford" of the Little Tennessee River, at the base of the county seat, Franklin. This mound was also heavily damaged by cultivation before it was preserved as a public park. My dowsing was limited to a quick once-over, since the site is elevated and clearly visible to passerbys in this conservative Baptist community. I found background Hartmann Grid lines around the mound and stronger, dowseable energy lines going out in the Four Directions, (North-to-South, East-to-West) from the central top of the mound.

'These dowseable lines seem to have been ceremonially-created, rather than pre-existing earth energies – an energetic manifestation of prayers offered to the Four Directions. There are numerous local fault lines in the crystalline geology, but none are obviously connected with local mounds.

'I have continued to find this pattern of dowseable energy lines in the Four Direc-tions at over a dozen additional sites in the southeast and midwest. Larger mounds in the nearby region include Etowah, near Atlanta, Georgia, as well as Ocmulgee Mounds in southern Georgia, and the Kolomoki Mounds in southwest Georgia.

'I have only noted two mounds in my travels that are associated with major springs – this includes Kolomoki, a large mound complex in southwestern Georgia and a large unnamed mound on the private commercial attraction, Biltmore Estate, near the confluence of the French Broad River and Swannanoa River.

'Kolomoki was a large ceremonial center near the Chattahoochee River with two prominent burial mounds directly west of the major mound. This site was built about 800 A.D. and apparently abandoned after 1300 A.D.

'Besides finding background Hartmann Lines in the plaza between the mounds, I found an extremely powerful line between the burial mounds and the largest mound. At the time, I had programmed my L-rods to cross when detecting DELs, but in this case my rods literally flew widely apart, suggesting a vastly different energy line from those which I was familiar.

'This "burial line" was about a foot wide and, curiously, was located just a couple of feet adjacent from a well-worn visitors' foot trail between the mounds. I followed the "burial line" by deviceless dowsing, noting an intense contractive pressure in my chest. It was clear that other visitors avoided this line by a few feet when walking the shortest line between the mounds.'

Mystery Hill

'I only know of two sites east of the Mississippi River which are clearly archaeoastronomical. The well-publicized Mystery Hill- Americas Stonehenge, in southern MA and our own "Woodhenge" at Cahokia, near present day St. Louis. Mystery Hill is a partially restored "tourist-trap", catering strongly to the New Agers who want clear views of the sun on solstices and equinoxes, as well as, and lunar maximum and minimums. The site has been initially carbon-dated to about 2000 BC.

'I found extremely narrow, 1-2 cm wide DELs marking significant solar and lunar points upon the horizon. My sense was that these DELs were thought-forms created by people staring from a central viewing point. The only other significant observation here was of a strong DEL from a low, linear tear-dropped shaped wall with a powerful DEL extending off to the northeast. This orientation was similar to that found at several larger rock piles seen the previous day in southern Vermont during a field trip to a private site.'

Rock Eagle

'At Rock Eagle, a stone effigy ceremonial site built in the Middle Woodland Phase, east of Atlanta, GA., I searched for DELs associated with the site.

'The Rock Eagle, is constructed with bread-loaf sized, pure white quartz rocks piled 8 ft. deep in the center and shaped in the form of an eagle with arching wings, measuring about 102 ft. from tail to head, and 120 ft. from wing tip to wing tip. Of particular interest is that these quartz rocks are only known from a quarry site more than forty miles distant. I found numerous DELs apparently flowing into the base of the tail.

'There is a three-story viewing tower along the base of the tail, and I was able to dowse the same parallel DELs from each of the levels, showing me that these DELs had considerable vertical height. I was also amazed when dowsing around the arching wings, to find a series of DELs radiating in diverging directions – this was the first time I found anything other than parallel lines associated with ceremonial sites' writes Barnes.

References:

Neal Sagar, 'The American Dowser', fall 1989.
Sig Lonegren, 'Spiritual Dowsing', Gothic Image, UK, 1986.
John Michell, 'The Earth Spirit', Thames and Hudson, UK. 1975.
Lee Barnes, 'Meanderings among Native American Mounds' in Geomantica no. 13 (included in Lee's article are very useful lists of books and websites on these subjects.)
Paul Deveraux, 'Secrets of Ancient and Sacred Places', Blandford, UK, 1992.

Modern trends in northern hemisphere geomancy

The Fascination with Earth Mysteries.

There are many traditions of geomancy, but I tend to look to those of my genetic heritage, of England and Ireland, as something of a bench mark. Here the modern tradition is labelled 'Earth mysteries' and this field can encompass many aspects, from the mythic to the pagan, from UFO and crop circle research to dowsing and scientific studies with instruments.

I interviewed John Billingsley, the editor of 'Northern Earth' magazine, in West Yorkshire in 2000, to find out more about the current state of play of the British Earth Mysteries movement.

JB: There's a popularisation of interest in the Earth Mystery field. For the 30 years I've been involved I've seen it grow from being part of an interest in all things alternative, like natural healing and lifestyles, folklore, u.f.o.s, etc. It's narrowed a lot since then and Earth Mysteries is now more archeology, the sense of place and sacred landscape. So it's become more focussed in its own area, with u.f.o.s pushed off into the background. There's a bit of a dichotomy between the intuitive and what you might call the empirical approach, which is very solid research based; but there's a lot of interest in the intuitive. It's the only field which combines both approaches and it's trying not to say that one is better than the other.

This is very much a British based tradition. There's something like it in France and a bit in Germany, but within Europe it's fairly unique. It could be because of the relationship we British have with our monuments. There's a lot of megalithic monuments that are highly accessible here. You just can't ignore places like Stonehenge or Long Meg. In Sweden there are also lots of monuments, but they are generally in the very inaccessible regions.

Antiquarianism has held a role in British literary tradition since the 17th century. It's been very strong since then and Earth Mysteries has been the heir to that, to the antiquarianism of people like William Stukely. It's almost as though there's been a traditional fascination with the ancient monuments, tying them together with the folklore, which has found its way into novels. Folklore in the 19th century was very popular in Britain, but it's almost nowhere now. This constant fascination with heritage, the past, the mysterious has been a constant in British culture, more with English culture. The Welsh and Scottish approach is more folkloric. The English approach is characterised by this synthesis of the intuitive and empirical approaches.

So the state today is that we have two wings in Earth Mysteries, with each side tending to see from its own belief system. One wing is represented by the highly empirical set of researchers, who have more in common with academic fields; and the opposite wing is coming from the new age/pagan perspective. The latter wing tends to object quite vocally to any attempt to objectify these monuments, any attempt to date or understand what rituals happened at them. It's really only the approach taking the middle ground which has got anywhere.

Writers like Paul Deveraux's strongest works are, for me, where he has used his own intuition and also worked with some very solid research to find out about whole landscapes and how they've fitted in and are seen together as a living landscape of ritual and meaning. This is one of the great things about Earth Mysteries – it's never seen sites just as sites but as places that are connected to everything you see around them. They're seeing archeology as whole landscapes and this is something that archeology has only recently caught up with in the last couple of decades. The whole idea of the phenomenological approach to land has come into archeology from geography and was really pioneered by earth mysteries. (If only we'd had more funds in the 1970s we would have made much more progress!) It's been the amateur researchers that have been pushing together and chivvying the academics with little ideas that seemed a bit off the wall at that time, but over the years it's come to be seen to make more sense.

Alignments, for instance, such as were suggested by Alfred Watkins in the 1920's, were laughed out of court by the archeologists and although ley lines are not accepted, the idea of alignments in prehistory are now accepted as a standard archeological fact. Astroarcheology, the alignment of ancient monuments to astronomical features, once again, was laughed at when it was proposed in the 19th century, and now this too is accepted. Not to the accuracy to what some people would like to think, but it is accepted that prehistoric people in the Stone and Bronze ages had an interest in the celestial bodies and their movements. Although it's a very small or minor field I feel that the ideas have chipped away at academia, which is now a much more open minded academia and this is why earth mysteries has moved more toward it. But nonetheless it has widened the gap between the more belief centred earth mysteries people, who prefer sites to just be mysterious. So that is the state of play of the British Earth Mysteries field.

Rollright Stones

AM: What's the situation now at Rollright Stones?

JB: A few years ago the owner of Rollright Stones, Pauline Flick, who's always been a tremendous guardian of the site and maintained access for the archeological and other organisations, decided she had to sell the stones and there were a number of people who wanted to buy them. Some developers wanted to buy the stone circle site and they were seen off early on, she didn't want to know about them; and there was some archeological interest. But the successful tenders were a group that was started by a couple of pagans in nearby Banbury. They got the message out to a number of people, and in the end the stones were sold to a couple of young stockbrokers who then got onto the board that involved members of the Rollright Appeal, run by John Atwood of the neo-pagan Rollright Fund.

So what we have now is a board running the Rollright stones that is very sympathetic to pagans, with active pagans high up in the decision making process. We've got people manning the site as much as possible and they allow it for use for various groups for rituals, with the strict condition that no damage is done to the site. They've built their own fire pans, so that ritual fires could be lit, because pagan groups tend to light fires everywhere. Pagan groups have been responsible for lighting fires at places like Boscawen stone circles and the Nine Ladies in Derbyshire, and damaging the stones. At the moment pagan groups have as good a record for causing damage as weekend tourists have, so it's been distressing for all of us really. But in the case of Rollright Stones they're now being managed for as wide a use as possible, for instance they're also being used for

Shakespeare plays. So the long term future of Rollright stones is as an active sacred site, not just as an archeological/ heritage site, and whilst not detracting from the condition of it.

I feel it's a wonderful step forward. If it can have the affect of pushing some responsibility into the neo-pagan movement in Britain, which is a largely urban movement, this can help the situation. We have the problem that the popularity of paganism and the background it's coming from seems to be causing certain negative affects, which is giving earth mysteries a problem as we now find ourselves thinking whether we should be publicising sites. This is an issue coming up for discussion increasingly from time to time over the last few years. Are people loving these sites too much?

AM: It's something like the situation with Aboriginal sacred sites in Australia. They usually keep quiet about their dreaming places and only when development threatens do they suddenly start to talk about them. Then the white population often think it's all made up and demand proof, when it may actually be an offence in Aboriginal law to divulge these secret stories and locations.

'Seahenge'

JB: Yes indeed. Its traditional that communities tend not to tell outsiders about their own traditions and beliefs. This has a downside to it as well, for while it keeps those traditions you do get the possibility that outside interests will come in and take the object of those traditions away. This has been the case with the so called Seahenge structure, on the foreshore at Norfolk. Seahenge, an ancient Bronze Age complex is a good example of how outside interests clash with local interests. It's basically a circle of oak wood posts found in a peat bed on the seashore. There's an upturned oak stump in the centre and it looks like an excarnation platform, where dead bodies could have been placed and stripped of flesh by birds, the weather and natural decomposition processes. Excarnation sites are known elsewhere but its the first time a timber circle, although perhaps four thousand years old, has survived. So its one of the most exciting archeological finds of the century, certainly in the last decade.

With the site covered by the tides twice a day, great anxiety arose for the archeologists, as the tides were wearing away at the site. But as soon as the problem arose of what to do with the circle, then another set of problems came up. The archeologists wanted to remove it to rescue the timbers, which possibly meant taking it away from the site, where it had been standing for some 4000 years, then relocating it, or reconstructing it somewhere. At this point they made a decision about what to do with it with the very barest of negotiations with the local bodies, only discussing it with local archeological groups. The ASLAN (Ancient Sacred Landscapes Network) people, which is a group that focuses on the protection of ancient sites, got in touch. But the first thing the local community heard about it was when they announced that they were going to take it away, and the local community was livid! They said they'd known about the site for 50 years, but they just hadn't told the archeologists. Somebody did, then suddenly they were faced with losing it.

Now Norfok is not rich in ancient sites, there's no stone there, so this incredibly unique site, that the locals weren't blabbing abut but nonetheless they valued, was suddenly removed as soon as outside interests came in. So this is a parallel to the situation in Australia with many Aboriginal sites. The sites are treated as if secondary to other narratives. In this case the archeologists took a look at Seahenge and thought 'We are archeologists, this is an archeological site, therefore our narrative has priority. This is our site, we can do what we like.' The pagans were still on the outside with a different narrative and this was also different from the local narrative. So we were watching, in the case of Seahenge, these competing narratives, with the politicisation between the archeologists, the pagans and the locals, and this turned into a face off which developed into a sit-in of this ancient monument with the archeologists trying to remove it.

And out of all the narratives the one that was pushed to the bottom of the pile was the one held by the local people. And this is the same scenario with tribal people where, if they don't express their knowledge of the land, the outsiders barge in and make it their own. So Seahenge doesn't now exist as it was. It's been taken away and the place has not been preserved and the local community are very upset. This is perhaps an area we all need to look at, where a place becomes a focus for different narratives. An ancient site built for a purpose by a particular culture and we can never really know what went on there, only guess at its purpose. What we have today is all these people who love these sites are all bringing their different ideas to the site, maybe earth mysteries, maybe new age, maybe pagan, maybe Christian.

Now I feel that sites are probably big enough to tolerate all these different interpretations that have come and gone over thousands of years, but the trouble is that these interpretations may be competing. We might have one lot of people saying 'This is our site!', like we see in the Middle East, where Christian and Islamic groups are fighting over the same sites. We see it in some sites here, where goddess movements and other pagan groups are squabbling over the correct interpretations. And we also see the difficulty for local groups in fighting off the demands of other narratives where archeologists or folklorists come along and give well reasoned, well backed up arguments about something- then its a good narrative, and if you've only got the local folklore which actually integrates it into the community but doesn't explain the site, then its easily displaced. This is the problem. We have to see places as harbouring changing narratives. There's a sacredness that's always adaptive and we have to make sure that our views do not exclude other people's. As this is what we're seeing more and more of, such as pagans going into stone circles or barrows leaving offerings, candle wax or whatever, and they're saying 'This is our site' and they're excluding the interaction of other people with a different, but very sincere, approach. And we have archeologists going in and saying 'We have to put a fence around this site' and they don't care that people want to use these sites.

'Rollright Stones seems to balance these issues together. I think its a model for the future, not perfect by any means, but a step in the right direction – accommodating archeological and ritual use in a balanced way. Seahenge is an object lesson in what not to do.'

Leyhunters of Today

Christine Rhone, a keen student of geomancy, travelled from Australia to attend a Leyhunters Moot in London in July 1986, and wrote about it for 'Dowsing News' on her return. Speakers included Sig Lonegren, Jamie George and John Michell.

'This was the first moot I had ever been to so I can't compare it with others. From my point of view, living in a rather small city in Australia, the mere fact of being in the same room with so many people interested in Earth mysteries, with a large selection of books for sale in the lobby was enough to make me feel like singing an old chant.

'I thought of my friends who channel for peace in the natural temples of New South Wales, my friends in the Blue Mountains interested in leylines and the healing properties of places. I was grateful that circumstances had allowed me to come and hear about some of the new research, directly from the researchers themselves.'

London geomancy

'I must say that during the whole moot I was suffering from a severe case of jetlag and felt like a robotised zombie, merely going through the motions of being there. I was disoriented from the transition from bush atmosphere to city and really had no idea where I was. It was a big city called London and there were ornate buildings called pubs on every corner with strange paintings hanging in front of them. Through this daze, I managed to hear some of the material, and will try to give parts of what struck me most …

'Just when I thought I couldn't possibly take any more information, Nigel Pennick came on like a whirlwind, churning a sea of words, to take us through a talk on London geomancy at a frantic pace, with bits of humour thrown out every now and then to keep us from going into a catatonic state.'

Rhone remembers Pennick explaining how the symbol for the London underground is one of the alchemical symbols for the Earth, and that Queen Bodesire is buried under platform ten at the Kings Cross tube station, at a spot once called Battles Bridge … But there was more London geomancy in store.

'The next day Andy Collins took us on a tour that began at the Tower of London and explained that because of the braincells he had lost overnight he couldn't remember much to tell us. His mind seemed to revive after we left the Tower area, not surprisingly, since the gigantic shadow of an axe has been seen there most recently by psychics.

'The London Stone, one of the city's two omphaloi, could be one of the saddest looking ones left on Earth. But maybe we should be happy that anyone has bothered to preserve it all. The stone is behind a grill, in a cage, in the side of a bank building, surrounded by chewing gum wrappers and ashes. Directly opposite is a huge monolith of a building, black, with gargantuan criss-cross studded girders on the outside. A reminder that in modern society we must "kept it together", no matter what.

'We went to the Temple of Mithra, St Pauls, a couple of other places, and then St Brides, which made a great impression on me. Several people reported physical reactions in the lowest levels of the church, one person feeling a sense of heat, another – headache, and a third – tearfulness. We ended up at the Temple Church, another very powerful site in quite a different way, on Watkin's St Paul's Cathedral Ley Line.

'On the whole, being used to situations in certain parts of the world where workshops and events are beyond the means of many of the people who are most involved, I was happy to see that the Moot, at least, was one area of vital interest left in 1986 that has not succumbed to the pressures of being slick and pricey.'

Source: Dowsing News, Nov 1986.

Crop circles

Without doubt the enigma of the crop circle is the greatest Earth mystery of the modern era. Although a global phenomena, with over 10,000 crop circles reported up to October 2002, the occurrence of crop circles is mostly concentrated in the chalk downs of the English county of Wiltshire.

What often began as simple circles in ripening crops, usually located near important ancient sacred sites, such as Stonehenge and Avebury, patterns have evolved in complexity over time. Nowadays there are a myriad of geometric forms appearing in the crops. Sometimes ice circles are found too, in Scandinavia, Canada and Finland. They feature a free floating circle of ice which doesn't wobble but rotates around its axis completely over 24 hours.

Scientistic study of Crop Circles

Research into the subject got serious in England when a Centre for Crop Circle Studies was set up in 1990, an article in the Weekend Australian told us. But until recently few scientific studies had been made. In the USA the BLT Research Team Inc. is an organisation that has been formed to investigate physical changes in plants and soil at crop circles. Geologist Diane Conrad analysed surface soil samples from a crop circle that appeared near her home in Utah. She found that they had a characteristic generally only found in sedimentary rock that is subjected to pressure and heat over long periods.

Another researcher, Dr Sampath Iyengar, a Californian mineralogist, discovered that clay minerals in samples also showed a very orderly pattern, that is – increased crystallinity. No-one had ever seen anything like it in soil. This phenomena is usually observed in geologic sediments exposed to low temperatures and pressures over millions of years.

In a laboratory, soil would have to have been exposed to temperatures of 500 to 800 degrees celsius to achieve such a crystal growth effect. Iyengar could offer no explanation but stated that 'It's some kind of energy, an unknown force that's causing this.'

Others have checked this and found the same effects. An intrigued Dr Robert C Reynolds Jnr, a renowned mineralogist of Dartmouth College, stated that 'I believe that our present knowledge provides no explanation.' This is the first time that a scientist of his standing has taken an interest in crop circles.

W C Levengood, a Michigan biophysicist, began investigating plants from crop circles in 1990. He studied the pin head sized holes appearing in plant nodes subsequent to crop circle formation, calling them 'explosion cavities'. His explanation for these phenomena is that moisture in the plants stem has been heated rapidly, turning to steam and then either stretching the plant fibre or blowing a hole in the stem.

'It seems to be a powerful microwave energy that is causing this, it heats from the inside out. The interesting thing is that these holes occur in microseconds.' Such effects have never been seen in control plants taken from outside crop circles.

Levengood also noticed changes to seeds and germination capacity of plants in crop circles. Seeds germinated up to five times faster than controls if the crop circle occurred when seeds were fully formed. The seedlings are able to tolerate lack of water and light for a considerable time without apparent harm. In 1998 Levengood patented a method to emulate the effects, with a process he calls 'molecular impulse response'.

What is the meaning of it all?

For many people there is deep meaning to contemplate in some of the complex geometrics and glyphs presented in the patterns. Some think it is the Earth trying desperately to communicate, and that it is a cry for help!

Marko Pogacnik states that crop circles 'bear witness to the awakening of Gaia and represent her way of opening to universal space and her attempt to talk, through the language of cosmograms, to all people and all beings populating the planet's surface.'

They tend to occur in high energy times and places. They appear in clusters around the equinoxes, which are times of high geomagnetic energy in the Earth. And they are frequently seen in the areas where there are concentrations of ancient megalithic sites, and also close to radio and microwave transmitters, Cowan and Silk tell us.

Dancing Lights

Adding to the exquisite beauty and mystery of the circles, are observations of floating balls of light that are seen, usually at night time, bobbing around in the vicinity before a circle appears. Sometimes they have been accompanied by high pitched trilling sounds.

Balls of light have historically been seen around sacred sites since long ago and also in seismically active and geologically unstable areas. Traditionally these have been referred to as 'fairy lights' in times past, and, in more recent times, as 'Earth lights'. Inexplicable malfunctioning of electrical equipment at crop circles has also been a common occurrence.

Intelligence at work

There is a sense that the energies involved are highly intelligent and are somehow consciously interacting with the minds of interested people. Sometimes crop circles have appeared in shapes that had only just been thought of by researchers in the field the day before. It is as if there is an ability to dip into the researchers' minds and borrow some appropriate thoughtforms.

This type of intelligent ability has also been noted in relation to UFOs and nature spirits, who are apparently capable of taking images from our mind to 'clothe' themselves in forms familiar to us.

Nature spirits and devas are known to enjoy creating geometric shapes for themselves to inhabit. These are sometimes called 'angel houses'.

Dowsable energies

As for dowsable energies – people have been consistently finding that the sorts of energies found at sacred sites are also found around crop circles. Underground water is always present beneath crop circles, which are usually found to be over a 'blind spring', notes dowser Jim Lyons.

'Many people find deep underground streams and there were a number of water veins close to the surface that ran from blind springs and downshafts. These often followed the outline of key shapes. It is these shallow veins of water that appear to have been moved when the circle was formed.' Tony Hathway.

Not only do dowsers find crossings of underground water lines and earth energy lines, but also energy vortices with radial lines emanating from them.

Shaun Ogbourne of Wiltshire told me of his experiences of dowsing, with other researchers, the two and three dimensional energies present within the crop circles. The dowsers were interested to find out whether the energy patterns directly corresponded with the perceived patterns in the crops. They often did, but many also had similar patterns that were only loosely aligned.

Four crop circles had high radioactive counts. Shaun compares the feelings elicited at radioactive sites, such as a Holy Well in Cornwall where he feels warm, relaxed or sleepy. (The normally beautiful feeling, was too strong at the Holy Well, where he felt sick.) At radioactive crop circles, Shaun finds, one also feels sleepy.

What to expect at a crop circle

Sitting inside a crop circle a sensitive person can feel the cyclic movement of energy over several minutes. The energies can also change according to the people who are in them.

Dowsers describe swirling layers of energy that are detectable by dowsing. The direction of energy flow in the circle relates to the direction of energy flow of its main Earth energy lines and the 'whole thing seems to obey the same laws that govern the direction of rotation of electric motors!' says, researcher Jim Lyons.

'The precision and complexity of these patterns of movement of ionised air (plasma) can only be understood in terms of recent research in plasma physics. The plasma state is naturally unstable and short-lived; thus the whole process is complete well within a minute, as has been attested to by a number of eye-witness reports' he adds.

There's a right way in

The safest approach to investigate a crop circle is to find the appropriate entrance point. For a good experience enter at the right spot and join the energy flow.

If you walk against the energy flow you might start to feel nauseous or spun out, as people have discovered when blundering in the wrong way.

Hormonal effects

Hormonal changes in people exposed to crop circles have been studied by Lucy Pringle and others. They find that our pituitary and pineal glands are very responsive to the energy fields of crop circles. After five years of research they have found that peoples' hormone levels (oestrogen and progesterone) experience a 30% change within 5 minutes of being in a crop circle. Some post menopausal women have experienced a return of their menstrual cycle after visiting crop circles. So this helps to explain the tradition of fertilizing effects from some sacred sites.

After visiting crop circles some people have experienced time warps – as they do at stone circles, as well as spontaneous healings of chronic health problems.

References:

'Mystery of the Crop Circles', Weekend Australian magazine, Oct 19–20, 2002.
Marko Pogacnik, 'The Daughter of Gaia', Findhorn Press, UK, 2001.
Tony Hathway, 'Who Makes The Crop Circles?' March 2001, BSD EEG.
Jim Lyons, 'The Crop Circle Phenomenon', Caduceus magazine no. 46, 2000.
Lucy Pringle, 'Crop Circles, The Greatest Mystery of Modern Times', Thorsons, UK, 1999.

Neo-Megalithics

Were the crop circles attracted to energetic locations, or were the energies attracted to the site as a result of the crop circle formation? Perhaps a bit of both I suspect. In many instances dowsers are finding that modern geomantic structures have attracted energies to them that were not there initially.

Energies of medicine wheels

Canadian dowser Henry Dorst gives us an insight here. 'After inspecting one medicine wheel in Alberta and finding two (energy) ley lines converging on its centre I assumed that the Native builders of such monuments chose them because they had, somehow dowsed these energies. I was disavowed of this notion after building a brand-new wheel, and again, after helping construct two labyrinths. In all of these cases brand-new, dowseable "water domes" and "ley lines" appeared after people began to use these constructions meditatively. In other words, my assumption that aboriginal North Americans necessarily dowsed – in the way that we understand dowsing – for these energy phenomena before setting up a site for sacred practices, was erroneous.'

Walking the Labyrinth. Mornington Peninsula, Victoria

Energies of labyrinths

'The labyrinth pattern itself can draw in energy and water to around its location' Shaun Ogbourne explained, at the International Dowsers Congress in 2003. 'But this happens more so with the actual regular use of that labyrinth. The more energetic it gets, the nicer the atmosphere feels around a labyrinth.'

Jim Lyons told the Congress how a Chartres Cathedral styled labyrinth was made on an energetically neutral site. It has now attracted several underground streams of water to beneath it, and there are also magnetic and gravitational anomalies now to be found there. These effects occur whether it's made from basalt rocks or just sawdust. Cats love the energy of labyrinths, Jim reports.

'In parkland, near Moulton in Northamptonshire, the local council had constructed a labyrinth by placing gravel to form the pathway' dowser Billy Gawn writes. 'I first observed this about two years ago, shortly after it was constructed, and there was a blind spring several yards away to one side. When I was there again, a year later, the blind spring was close to the centre of the labyrinth. I could continue to give many more examples where a structure and not human intent or activity had caused underground water to be diverted so that it is now underneath it.'

'Marty Cain, a dowser and labyrinth builder in New England (USA) has been finding this for several years now.' Billy Gawn says. 'I am also hearing talk about this on the Internet. Labyrinths call in water? Apparently'.

Modern stone circles

Jim Lyons told the International Dowsing Congress of 2003 about a stone circle made by dowsers at Arigna, Co. Roscommon, Ireland in June 2000. The 60ft diameter circle was located intuitively and the big rocks were placed on 'messy' water line crossings, while the small rocks went on small 'perfect' crossings. 'It cleared the area of detrimental energy for some three miles' he said.

Shaun Ogbourne continued. 'It was made with the intention of clearing the detrimental energies from a wide an area as possible. The bigger the stones the bigger the effects, so we used stones up to two tons in weight! (You can also use a larger number of more smaller stones.) Afterwards it was noted that the difference in the local community was dramatic. A lot of peoples' squabbling had quietened down.'

After making the circle in record time, there was one more structure to be made, continues Tony Hathaway. 'This was the building of a dolmen using three uprights and a large triangular slab of stone. The dolmen was built over an ascending spiral of beneficial energy, using an angled capstone to reflect the energy back into a sphere within the chamber. It had the effect of acting like a transformer, which boosted the local supply of earth energies. Everyone who sat within the dolmen found it a very relaxing and peaceful experience.'

However Dave Sanguine warns of putting up a standing stone, stone circle or labyrinth that may attract unwanted energy lines. This could mean that underground streams may be attracted to pass beneath your home, if the structure is near it. You might end up with geopathic stress in the house, as shallow underground water flows may be diverted from a nearby underground stream, or a blind spring might even appear.

'I have inspected several places where stone circles were recently constructed and the builders did not take into account the underground water present on the site.' Billy Gawn has written. 'I found, at these, that under most of the stones small flows were present and that a blind spring or springs could also be dowsed within the area of the circle. The thing that was absent in most cases was the presence of major flows, and where some did exist, there was a lack of the relationship between the stones and the intersections of the edge lines. This would indicate that major flows of underground water are not influenced by these structures but minor flows are. Similarly so with human activity and intent as most of these circles were constructed and used for ceremony and such like things.'

Although you can build a stone circle on energetically neutral ground, Shaun Ogbourne finds that the best energetic effects occur when an already energetic site is used and there is regular ceremonial use of the site. Energy affects have been noted a mere three months time after construction.

Making Labyrinths

Alex Champion has been making labyrinths since the 1990's in the USA at West Coast Dowsers' gatherings. He considers labyrinths to be good focussing devices for Earth energy. He encourages users to feel the energies and experiment with them. Some people feel dizzy, tired, warm, tingly and other body sensations when walking the labyrinth. Spiritual healing can be facilitated within them and challenging feelings can arise during a walk, as we contemplate a 'barrier we need to get through'.

To locate the centre point of a new labyrinth Champion dowses for permission, or asks the local spirits where it should be. He finds three dimensional paths are more powerful than two dimensional (flat) ones. Their effects, he finds, are transforming and he has found greater inner peace with them.

Looking through the hype – not all labyrinths turn out well. I asked a friend near Melbourne how her labyrinth was going and was surprised to hear that it didn't exist any more. She explained that they didn't like the energy of the person who had made it nor the energy of the labyrinth itself. So they had it removed.

Making stone circles

Ken Ring is a maverick long range weather forecaster in New Zealand. He believes that weather is controlled by the moon and is fascinated by the ability of stone circles in Europe to mark time in the moon cycle and predict eclipses. Every year he travels to the UK to study ancient stone circles. During eclipses, he says, which are always either at the full or new moon, there can be earthquakes, volcanic eruptions and dangerously high tides. Perhaps this is the reason for the ancient fascination with the lunar cycle?

'A stone circle can be made from big stones or tiny pebbles' he says. He gives all the instructions required to make a stone circle that can be used as a cosmic observatory in his book 'How to Make a Stone Circle (Southern Hemisphere)'.

References:

David Cowan and Anne Silk, 'Ancient Energies of the Earth', Thorsons, UK, 1999.
Henry Dorst, 'Some Experiences of Dowsing among the Indigenous People of Canada, March 2001 BSD EEG.
Billy Gawn, 'Black Chicken, White Egg' BSD/EEG, 2001.
Billy Gawn, BSD/EEG 2002
Tony Hathway, 'Building a New Stone Circle', BSD EEG 2002.
Virginia Westbury, 'Labyrinths – Ancient Paths of Wisdom and Peace', Lansdowne, UK, 2001.
Ken Ring, 'How to Make a Stone Circle – Southern Hemisphere', Milton Press (PO Box 60197, Titirangi, Auckland), NZ, 2001.

(Note: many fascinating articles from the BSD EEG -British Society of Dowsers Earth Energy Group – are available for all to see at their website: www.britishdowsers.Org/EEG.html)

PART TWO
Geomancy in Australasia

Australian geomancy

Aboriginal people keep the oldest continuous geomantic traditions in the world. Vast networks of Earth energy pathways in Australia were maintained in sections by tribal clans, who followed seasonal migrations along the rainbow serpent lines and kept up the spiritual obligations of the sacred site network along the way.

Dance, ritual and the chanting of these 'song lines' thus delineate territory and define and integrate the cultures of the many tribes. Individuals and families who own sections of songlines that pass though their territories have the authority to only relate their particular portion of an unfolding Dreaming story and song. Only people initiated to a high degree are allowed to know the deepest meanings of sites and stories, for knowledge entails great responsibility.

With such Earth centred spirituality Aboriginal people have stewarded the integrity of Australia's landscapes, maintaining one of the last, vast natural areas left on the planet – by minimising their impact, controlling population and living simply, without greed. (Although admittedly Aboriginal fire regimes were often largely responsible for changes in vegetation types.) There is so much to be learned from these gentle and visionary people.

In my work as a geomancer I assess the invisible hazards in the environment that can influence our wellbeing for better or worse. Looking at the overall 'feng shui' of a home or building site can involve checking a lot more considerations than the Chinese geomancers of old could have dreamed of. And being in Australia means addressing the haunted aspects of our landscape, so that people can avoid building on Aboriginal sites. It can be a bit of a let down to clients when they are told 'you can't build just there'! But, in understanding the risks involved they are usually very grateful!

Many of Australia's sacred sites have been lost, as the old rules where invaders protected them were long forgotten. This has cast many shadows of sadness across the land.

Sites were sometimes marked by carved stones and trees, artifacts and paintings, stone arrangements or bora grounds (in the middle of which I always find a powerful energy vortex). Many are sites of significant landscape features – rock formations, special trees, caves and waterholes. Other sites might be non-descript and not obvious.

Important sites were used for initiation ceremonies (with exclusive male or female use), plant or animal increase, dance grounds or burials. Many sites have been completely razed or forgotten. But their energies remain. One may be plagued by feelings of anxiety, irritation or anger at disturbed sites.

The location of sacred sites is usually kept secret by the Aborigines, who know the consequences of speaking out. The sites can become targets for vandalism or worse. Film maker Sandra Holmes, who has told me of her life in the Northern Territory, was shocked to find one day, at what had been a magnificent site of rock art, that all the art work had been totally removed. One presumes that this was the work of mining companies not wanting any trouble in obtaining mining rights over the area.

Site dowsing may indicate the location of a desecrated sacred site. Homes unlucky enough to be close to or over such sites may suffer from continual bad luck, illness, accidents, psychic disturbances, hauntings and a high turnover of occupants. Geomancers can offer help to harmonise the energies, but consultation with local Aboriginal elders may be the best starting point for healing work.

Massacre sites

Sites of massacres are probably the most hideous legacy the Australian landscape bears. They are particularly disturbing to those unfortunate enough to live in the vicinity. In north coast New South Wales, where I lived for several years, massacre sites are many.

For instance – Ballina pioneer James Ainsworth wrote in his 1922 reminiscences a detailed account of an unprovoked massacre of 40 tribespeople in the early 1850's at East Ballina. Troopers had opened fire on a campsite, where 2–300 unsuspecting people slept, at 3am in the morning … 'Men, women and children were slaughtered without mercy … and many who got away were badly wounded. Their graves may still be found on the fatal ridges' he wrote. All concerned know the whereabouts of this mindless slaughter.

The trouble now is that the site has been swallowed up by yet another housing estate, built in the early 1990's, despite the protests of Aboriginal people and other environmentalists. It has been reported to me by residents that there is much sickness amongst the unfortunate inhabitants, my informants' health going downhill rapidly after moving in.

What to do? Finding a solution for those who have invested in the Australian Dream and found themselves stranded in a nightmare isn't easy. Suing local councils who allow such developments may well help prevent a repetition. (In this case planning laws in relation to Aboriginal sites were flouted.) But preventative measures are always going to be a whole lot better than fighting bitter battles later on.

The rape of the land from mining, inappropriate agriculture, and development is an ongoing onslaught and still inflicts suffering. The Earth is crying out and there is much healing required. Hopefully one day all land management in Australia will involve geomantic, indigenous perspectives, just as the European ancestors of white Australians would have done.

Reference:

Rory Metcalf, 'Rivers of Blood', Northern Star, NSW, Australia, 1989.

The Rainbow Serpent

by Junitta Vallak

In May/June 2000 I travelled from Broome to Perth with Judy O'Donnell, Geoff Linnell and Robyn Adams, with whom I have been on spiritual trips before. Our aim was to link up with the 'Journey of Infinity'* and to connect with the Rainbow Serpent energy.

According to Robert Coon in his book 'The Rainbow Serpent and the Holy Grail, Uluru and the Planetary Chakras' – the Rainbow Serpent enters Australia at Beagle Bay, north of Broome. I must admit that I had not delved into Robert's book in depth and it wasn't until I returned home and checked out what I saw clairvoyantly with what he has said, so I had no preconceived ideas.

I have always understood that the Aboriginal people say that Creation came into Australia through the Kimberley – the areas are not too far apart and when I 'saw' the Serpent, I was amazed how big it was.

The Sacred Heart Church at Beagle Bay is full of mother of pearl shell, which is the most sacred object representing the Serpent from Bali to Uluru. I was astounded at the magnificence of the Altar in the Church, with intricate designs made of pearl shell glittering all over it.

The actual bay is almost inaccessible, so we continued to Cape Leveque to do our Wesak Full Moon meditation. The tide was out so we were able to access a small rocky cove which gave us some privacy.

I slipped easily into a meditative state and 'saw' the Rainbow Serpent rise out of the Arafura Sea, curve around and enter Australia. It was so huge that it covered all of the Kimberley. It was magnificent, vibrant and glittering, with rainbow lights that were in no fixed pattern, but shifting and flowing within it.

It travelled through Uluru, the Flinders Ranges, then exited at Wilsons Promontory, went down through Tasmania, Macquarie Island and skirted the Antarctic. When it approached the Antarctic its colour changed to white, with rainbows shimmering through it, like opals from Coober Pedy.

It then approached South America and went up the coastline, where its colour changed to golden brown. When it came to Lake Titicaca it huge jaws opened and I thought it was going to swallow the lake, but it dived into it instead. It's hard to describe how I felt watching all of this, but I think I was just astounded at the beauty of its form. Gobsmacked in fact!

That was all I 'saw' at that time, but when we meditated at Monkey Mia – the new moon was in Gemini – much to my amazement I 'saw' it emerge out of Lake Titicaca and travel across the Pacific through Easter Island and on to the North Island of New Zealand. As soon as it touched there it changed to the full rainbow spectrum again, the golden brown colours seem to have been 'fixed', whereas the rainbow ones swirled and moved within it.

From New Zealand it forged across to Mount Warning on the east coast of Australia – the first place to receive the sun. It then headed for Uluru and, as its nose touched itself at Uluru, there was an enormous explosion of rainbow light – up into the strato-sphere, down into the Earth and out in all directions. It created a huge energy field – a stunning sight.

It continued on to Monkey Mia/Shark Bay and headed out across the Indian Ocean, skimming under India, through the Maldives then down past Madagascar. It went past South Africa and then elegantly curved upwards and entered the Cape at Table Mountain. Curiously, it didn't have any colour when it left Australia. I don't really understand what I saw or its significance and I haven't seen anything since, but I guess there must be still more to be revealed – in more ways than one, going by the following quotes!

In Charles Mountford's book 'Brown Men and Red Sand', he says that 'Nothing shows more clearly than the legend of the Rainbow Serpent that the Aboriginal people were never entirely disassociated from world thought ... The Rainbow Serpent is essen-tially the water element in nature and is related to everything that the Aborigines associate with water – rainbows, pearl shell, rivers, permanent springs and rock holes.'

In 'Voices of the First Day' Robert Lawlor says 'The Rainbow Serpent is the first cosmological model for the spectral order of the universal energy ... Only a small portion of these energies is visible in the seven colour spectrum of natural daylight ... The electromagnetic spectrum, like the Rainbow Serpent, is a profound metaphor for the unity that exists between the tangible and the invisible worlds'.

*The 'Journey of Infinity' – Energy Build-Up for the Olympic Games. Junitta wrote about it in the August 2000 Casurina Bulletin:

'There is a huge build-up of energy prior to the Olympic Games in September. We have many groups travelling around Australia with the focus on completing their Journeys to co-incide with the Olympic Opening Ceremony. The "Journey of Infinity" began in March and they have been joined by many people doing segments.

We also have a group walking for peace from Lake Eyre – which is full again for the third time in a century – to Sydney; two groups of horse people are travelling in opposite directions through Australia to meet also in Sydney in September. There is also the Sacred Run and we can't forget the torch which is going around the country!

So we have an enormous focus of thought form energy which we can utilise to help raise the consciousness of everyone on the planet.

On Sunday September 8th the Journey of Infinity group will ground the energies collected during their trip, and the crystals and earth they gathered will be buried on Peace Hill in Canberra.

Brynn Matthews has finished his part and is back in Cairns. He tells me that the energies that went through people during the trip were incredibly powerful as they connected into them. Their trip from Kalgoolie across the Great Victoria Desert, the Gibson Desert, onto the Gunbarrel Highway to Katajuta (aka The Olgas) was extraordinary. They drove on dirt for 4 days and Brynn remarked on the clarity of the air, the landscape, the wild camels, wildflowers and the fact that they were on Aborigi-nal land. Approaching Katajuta from the west was an amazing sight.

The Mystery of the Coiled Palms

I first read about Queensland's mysterious coiled palms in an Australian Plants Society study group newsletter and was hoping for several years to get to see the phenomena for myself, and dowse over the site.

Ever since seeing the remarkable cover photo of a corkscrew-twisted palm on Harold Tietze's book on earth rays I have suspected that palms may be particularly susceptible to electro-magnetic radiation. Tietze said that three radiation lines crossed around that palm, causing it to spiral upwards, trying to escape the irritation.

Finally I got the chance for an expedition in August 1999, when a friend and I headed towards the palms at the coast, east of Yeppoon. On the south side of the bridge at Causeway we found the entrance to the Cool Waters Caravan Park, on the shores of the Causeway Lake. We parked in the visitor's car park down the back and wondered how we would find the walking tracks behind the cabins that led to the palms.

I'd just got out my pendulum when a man appeared who asked if we needed help, then gave us the directions we needed. We dived into the lakeside rainforest and followed a sign pointing to the 'Coiled Palms'. Passing the outdoor chapel (some benches) we were soon gasping in astonishment at the sight of this botanical mystery.

There was a pair of palm trees that lay coiling on the ground, looking like a tangle of pythons, more animal than vegetable. Nearby tall, straight palms grew perfectly normally. Nobody, until then, had been able to give any explanation for this phenomena.

Dowsing soon gave me some answers. It revealed a powerful yang energy vortex at the centre of the two palm's double coils, from whence a dragon (Earth energy) line emerged. It certainly felt like a site of power, of perhaps Aboriginal Dreaming significance. The palms were responding to the powerful energy.

We felt uplifted by the energies there and could have spent many happy hours, but for the ferocious mosquitoes that made meditation difficult. Later, walking down the Cathedral Walk, we found tidal inlets with many more Livistona palms growing all bent and floppy looking, but only one other one had a perfect coil. They were existing side by side with naturally straight members of their species.

Dowsing revealed that every bent palm was affected by a line of underground water flowing beneath it. None of the naturally straight Livistonas were located over energy lines of any type.

The amazing coiled palms of Queensland

Inside Our Lady of Yankalilla Church, the apparition corner of the back wall is top right.

An Earth Mystery in South Australia

The discovery that churches are found, by dowsing, to be located over Earth energy flows and 'hotspots' might be the case in Europe. In Australia no such association exists between churches and strong energies. Well, not usually, anyhow.

But a church at a little town in South Australia has proved an exception to this rule. It is the (Anglican) Christ Church, in the town of Yankalilla. I was travelled through the region in late 2001 and, having been told it was a 'must visit' for a dowser, made a beeline to see it.

The church had seen a range of phenomena ('miracles') manifesting in recent years and had become a centre for pilgrims from all over Australia and the world. They flocked to see images of Mary and baby Jesus that had been appearing on the plaster of one of the walls. And the diocesan Bishop had declared the church a Marion shrine.

This story of the history of the miraculous at Yankalilla is best told by the parish priest Father Andrew Notere, in leaflets provided at the church.

'Yankalilla is a small community just an hours drive south of Adelaide, where Mother Mary MacKillop established one of her early schools. That was in the year 1867. Now Yankalilla is the centre of a growing resort and retirement community, and Mary MacKillop is on her way to becoming Australia's first saint.' Notere writes.

'Lourdes, Fatima. Medjugorje, Guadalupe, and now Yankalilla. Is Yankalilla the Guadalupe of Australia? Our Lady in Guadalupe chose to appear to a peasant Indian in a land that had just been colonised by conquistadors from the Christian culture of Europe …'

An Aboriginal site

'In Yankalilla, the land on which the church stands was once thought to be a corroboree site. According to legend there was a terrible massacre of Aboriginal babies on this site, sometime in the last century before the church was built (1857). The Apparition of Our Lady of Yankalilla may well be calling us to the need for reconciliation between the original peoples of this country and today's European descendants' says Notere.'

The apparition in the plaster on the wall has reportedly shown Mary with dark skin and, at one time, an Aboriginal man's face, looking over her shoulder.

Notere continues 'The Apparition itself may be seen upon entering the church from the west door. Its clarity surprises many of our visitors who come here with low expectations of seeing the holy image. The clearest part of the Apparition is the face of Mary. Her features, her eyes, nose and mouth are uncannily clear and lead to the conclusion that this is indeed an icon not made with human hands.'

'The Mother and Child are now enclosed within a metal frame high up on the east wall behind the altar. Mary is crouched in adoration, her head bent in that familiar Marian way. So suggestive of maternity and compassion. That Our Lady has chosen to appear at this exact position in the church is not without significance, for immediately below her is the tabernacle containing the consecrated bread which is the very body of her son.'

When I visited with Billy Arnold we could see no such image. The church was empty and felt perhaps a little sad for it. The photo that I took showed the metal frame on the wall, inside of which was just a mouldy area, while the rest of the walls had been freshly painted. It would appear that the image of Mary and Jesus had been growing in the mould. Perhaps the new paint fumes proved toxic to the mould within the frame and killed off the medium of the miraculous?

History of the miracles

'The image of Our Lady was first noticed on August 24, 1994, by one of our parishioners' Notere goes on. 'At that time it was possible to see the Apparition only from the first two or three pews on the right side of the nave. The diocesan Bishop was invited to view the image on the wall. He is the patron of a number of Anglican Marian societies, and thus is well placed to guide us in our present work here in Yankalilla.'

'The Bishops visit to Christ Church confirmed our own feelings that the image of Our Lady on the wall in front of us could well be an authentic sign from God. But was the image merely a fluke, a result of salt damp or poor plastering? If so, would it continue to evolve into a meaningless jumble of bumps and glips high up on the wall, leaving us below with a lot of explaining to do?'

'Since that time the Apparition has been continuing to evolve, becoming clearer and more defined as if an artist were in the process of completing a sketch in a small country church Photographs taken of the Apparition over the past year reveal an evolving image, surpassing now the limits originally prescribed by the metal frame. The best evidence of this is to be found at the bottom of the image, laying at Mary's feet. It is not difficult for even the most sceptical visitor to see there the representation of a rose, complete with curled petals, a leaf, and a stem coming from the direction of the frame. This rose, Mary's signature, was first noticed after the church began hosting pilgrims in July 1996.'

'Other photographs taken by pilgrims have unexpectedly revealed the face of Jesus, as on the Shroud of Turin, and winged angels large and small on the Apparition wall. Perhaps the most important photograph to date is the one taken in October 1996. The developed prints revealed an unusual white surface on an otherwise darkened window at the front of the church. On closer examination, the white colouring revealed a startling and inexplicable image of Jesus bearing a small baby on his shoulder. The brightest part of this image is the radiance of light coming from his Sacred Heart. The diamond shaped leadwork in the window has been completely obliterated by the image and the shadow cast over the left side of the glass has been erased by the baby's body.'

Other photos have shown ghostly figures sitting in the pews and yes, there was the sense of a somewhat mystical atmosphere inside this church. It was silent and peaceful when we were there, no sense of a massacre …

Notere continues 'In the summer of 1996 I had been asked by the Bishop to write an article for the diocesan paper. The time had at last come to share the story with a wider church. To our surprise the Adelaide Observer picked up the story and ran a feature on July 2nd 1996 (the day of the feast of the Visitation of the Blessed Virgin Mary). Within 24 hours all the major networks, newspapers and radio stations were covering the Yankalilla story. The church was warming with its first pilgrims. They were coming from metropolitan Adelaide, from tiny rural communities that make up South Australia, from interstate and overseas.'

A legend foretold

'One of our senior parishioners recalled a talk a former Rector had given to the Ladies Guild in 1980. He had mystified the group when he stated that one day their church would be filled with pilgrims from all over Australia and beyond. Fr Rod Opie is remembered as a deeply spiritual priest, a prophet and one who suffered deeply for his faith. It has even been suggested he received the stigmata during his care of the parish. Fr Opie died shortly after resigning the parish in 1980.'

'The pilgrims have been coming here every day since July 1996. Many have told us of seeing this church in their dreams over a period of many years. One lady from Adelaide claimed to have been healed of a life threatening disease in 1957, through a vision she had of a "beautiful lady" whose presence filled a small church. Little did she know that she would at last see that church when she came with others on a bus tour in November 1996.'

'Others have told us of healings large and small. Three persons close to death have been restored to health through the intercession of Our Lady of Yankalilla. Many others have been granted healings, small graces, relief from extreme pain. Others have prayed for restoration of broken relationships and many have made their way back into the Church after wandering in the wilderness for too many years.'

'A number of people have moved to Yankalilla area to be near the shrine. One of these persons has been receiving interior messages from Our Lady which are being regularly recorded in a journal and shared with the Parish priest. She will be one of the founding members of our "Oasis of Peace" community, whose work it will be to give ourselves radically to prayer and to respond to the many urgent needs of pilgrims to this place.'

The sceptics might laugh off the whole thing and put it down to an effective bit of publicity mongering. They may not see the same features in the images that others claim to. Perception is in the eye of the perceiver after all. And they may well be amused by the fact that the Father has changed his name subtly from Andrew Nutter.

Holy energies – a dowsers survey

We wandered around the entrance area looking at the literature and souvenirs on offer there. There were tiny bottles of 'holy water' on sale, collected from the bore at the back of the church. Billy clairvoyantly perceived the presence of water spirits, but none very special. A bit of dowsing was called for.

But before I got a chance to do a dowsing survey of the church I happily discovered, with some amazement, that it had already been done. A plan copy had already been posted on the back of the entrance door!

And so I discovered that 16 streams had been dowsed to be flowing beneath the church! The largest underground stream corresponded with the line of the back wall, where the apparitions have been. No wonder the wall had gotten so mouldy!

One of the underground streams was marked in as 'holy water'. This was the stream from which the water on sale was taken from.

It all felt to me to be very consistent with the European experience of sacred space. Sacred sites have tended to be high energy places in traditional societies, where magic and miracle is more likely to happen. Places with powerful magnetic fields have been triggering places for visionary experiences. Spending time around water energies may well alter our state of consciousness and potentially encourage spiritual experience.

Reviving the spirits of place

Ancient pagan/animist beliefs link the presence of powerful water energies with visions of 'beautiful ladies', the guardian spirits/deities of the holy wells and water ways both above and below the ground. These have traditionally been personified as a goddess of place, and later as a saintly manifestation in Christian times. For example – there are many Bridget Wells in Ireland deemed holy and sacred, first to the ancient local goddess, then Celtic goddess Brigid (a solar deity originally) and later to her Christianised self, Saint Bridget.

People have long pilgrimaged to the holy wells to give their offerings and to ask for favours and healing. The healing waters have been attributed to many curings, thus ensuring the continuity of this practise. You don't have to even drink or bathe in healing waters, just sitting beside them is enough to absorb their energies.

The research of Masuro Emoto in Japan shows that we can imprint energy and emotion into water, giving the old traditions some scientific credulity too. He has demonstrated how water can be imprinted by our prayerful thoughts, giving it a sacred quality.

Sacred sites sometimes find us before we find them. Like the woman who received miraculous healing through the dream of the beautiful woman whose presence filled a small church, which turned out to be the church at Yankalilla.

But the church at Yankalilla is over a desecrated sacred site. Like Notere, I feel that the spirits of place have been calling out for a healing to take place, a clearing of the psychic wound of the massacre of the original inhabitants, of the killing of babies. The influx of pilgrims and their prayers must have had a wonderfully harmonising effect, as Billy and I had no sense of the trauma that one might expect to feel at a desecrated site.

As for the images on the plaster, these might be attributed to the work of the devic kingdoms, who love to manifest the thought forms of the prevailing ethos as tools of communication. Nature spirits are the designers of the shapes and evolution of the life forms. Directing the growth directions of mould/fungi would no doubt be an easy task for a water spirit, which may well be a guiding force present here.

Perhaps in Yankalilla we are seeing sacred space as an incubator of religious longing. As a connection point to the spirits of the Earth and her underground waters, which on the one hand would seem to present an entirely pagan situation and yet again, could be viewed as an experience over time which personifies the very essence of the evolution of Christianity.

References:

Fr Andrew Notere, 'The Events at Yankalilla' from 'The Medjugorje Sentinal' – June 1997.
Marko Pogacnik, 'Nature Spirits and Elemental Beings', Findhorn Press, UK, 1997.
Dr Emoto's website: www.hado.net

Tower Hill

by Junitta Vallak

Just as the area around Glastonbury is a vast Landscape Temple formed by human endeavour,(the 'Glastonbury Zodiac') so Tower Hill, near Warrnambool in southwest Victoria is also a Landscape Temple, but formed by the dynamic forces of nature.

Tower Hill is a volcano which last erupted six or seven thousand years ago. It is one in a line of over 30 volcanoes which stretch from Colac in Victoria to Mt Gambier in South Australia.

Tower Hill formed over 25,000 years ago when hot rising basaltic magma came into contact with the subterranean water table. The violent explosion that followed created the funnel-shaped crater which was later filled by the lake, creating the present day islands.

A wide crater was formed by the eruption. Volcanic scoria and ash was deposited along with the fragments of the underlying limestone and calcareous clay, the latter sometimes being ground down to a white dust. All these materials formed regular layers around the crater rim, creating the volcanic landform known as a 'tuff ring'. The nature of the eruption changed and this led to the growth of numerous small cones within the main crater.

When I saw these cones, I was reminded of Haleakala Crater on Maui which also has cones within the volcano's rim. Haleakala is much bigger, but a similar energy prevails in both places. Like Haleakala, the cones at Tower Hill are miniature volcanoes as some have their own small craters.

I was struck by the similarity to Glastonbury Tor, as I climbed the cone which has a crater called Yatt Mirng or White Eye. The local Koroitgundidj Aboriginal people named it Yatt Mirng probably because the light coloured reed bed surrounding the darker water looked like an eye in the almond-shaped crater floor. Nowadays a nearby tree looks like a pupil and surrounding vegetation looks like eye lashes.

The highest point of the Cone has a very feminine feel and looks like a breast. It even had a large rock protruding from it on the top just like a nipple. As I walked around the rim I felt a very powerful magnetic pull and almost toppled over the edge of the rim of this miniature crater. Immediately I had begun to 'tune in' and was alerted to the fact that this was no ordinary place.

I suddenly realized I was looking at a Mandorla, the almond shaped inner space of the vesica pisces symbol. Mandorla means almond in Italian. Two mandalas form a Mandorla so when I consulted a map of the whole area, I was pleasantly surprised to see the Landscape Temple emerge within the vesica piscis.

The effect of white settlement on Tower Hill was disatrous. Deforestation, the introduction of rabbits and hard hoofed animals stripped bare the heavily timbered volcanic cones within twenty years. Today the whole area is preserved and a restoration program is helping to bring the area gradually back to its original appearance, as the French explorers in the ship the Geographe saw it in 1802.

Knowledge of the spiritual practices of the Koroitgundidj have been lost to our present consciousness, but from the relics found in the volcanic ash layers we know that the Tribe were living in the area at the time of the eruption. Only their spirits remain and for those who can tap into this dimension, much knowledge is waiting to be retrieved. Using psychometry as a method is also another way to tap into the interesting past of the area.

Tuning in

To be conscious of Landscape Temples requires an awareness of the totality of the landscape and the ability to be able to tune your eye and body to the patterns and invisible energies which surround us.

Knowledge of sacred geometry, dowsing ability and awareness of ley lines are definite advantages. It also helps if you can refer to maps of special areas and when you are flying, keep your eyes peeled. Conscious astral travelling and lucid dreaming are two other methods of locating these hidden Natural Temples.

When I first saw the wonderful Natural History Centre, it was obvious that the architect, Robin Boyd, was very conscious of the landscape. He has echoed the shape of the cones and the flow of the landscape in the building. I don't believe that it is an accident that this stunning structure is almost right in the centre of the large Mandorla. Feng shui principles were obviously applied within the building and its location. I suspect that many natural Landscape Temples lie undiscovered in this and other volcanic areas. Secrets of the past are waiting to be revealed in these powerful places and I believe that their natural healing energies can be used for personal and planetary healing work.

When the amazing photos of the face, pyramids, Tholus and crater on Mars were published, some fascinating correlations were revealed. It seems that there are similar geographic similarities with Avebury, Silbury Hill and one of the crop circle glyphs. Landscape Temples, natural and artificial, are probably not restricted only to our own Planet. The Solar System and worlds beyond are waiting for us to reconnect. Is this the way back?

Dowsing Aboriginal Sites

Water Divining at Aboriginal sites

Professional water diviner Paul Davis is highly experienced at dowsing underground water stream and domes. At a talk he gave to the Dowsers Society of NSW he also spoke of Earth energy vortices with '8 magnetic lines' surrounding them (the number can vary).

'Certain Aboriginal sites are located over water domes. A strong reaction may be felt by many dowsers at these sites. They receive a positive reaction from their rods or pendulum, particularly when dowsing over a carving on a rock surface that is located at the centre of an (underground) dome. This energy was obviously of importance to the Aboriginals, who could probably detect it through their hands or feet.'

Paul himself can stand at the edge of a dome and feel the energy located within its diameter and the lack of it outside. He also states that it is noticeable that the energy from a dome has a harmful effect on trees within its influence.

Source: Dowsing News Feb. 1988

Aboriginal Site Dowsing

Clyde Searle wrote of his experiences of dowsing Aboriginal sites in the Sydney region for Dowsing News in the 1980's. Clyde had been particularly fascinated with Aboriginal sites of occupation, relics and artifacts. For 25 years dowsing such sites was his main spare time interest – locating, examining and photographing occupation sites, stone arrangements, rock engravings, middens and the like. Much of the time he spent in the Royal National Park and Glenbrook National Park. He laments that over the years many Aboriginal sites and relics have been destroyed or vandalised.

Clyde dowsed for, found and followed ancient trackways through wilderness areas that the Aboriginals used for tens of thousands of years. Down across the Emu Plains at the bottom of the Blue Mountains and Glenbrook NP many of the ancient tracks were the basis for the first European roads. It seems that the first European settlements were located over Aboriginal occupation sites too.

Clyde has walked extensively around the Lapstone Hill area and discovered many signs of Aboriginal occupation, including stone arrangements and ceremonial sites. One such site has been dated to 7000 years ago. While many of the sites have been already recorded he has found map dowsing of great assistance in locating previously unknown sites and relics in this area.

To pinpoint the exact spot he has to still do the foot work, dowsing as he goes to find the right direction. 'Sometimes the pendulum will lead to a site where the object sought can no longer be found, but its remanence remains' he says.

Finding faint engravings

He has made a number of intriguing finds of small, fine engravings on sandstone rocks, that are located either in a creek bed, or on its bank and on hillsides above creeks. They are highly worn, often sporting small pits or holes. They have no particular pattern and often appear in groups of 5 to 6 rocks in close vicinity.

One exception to this was an engraving he found which may well have depicted a map of the region and its rivers. Engravings are often associated with stone arrangements, rather than occupation sites. The lines are very fine and are obviously made with a sharp pointed tool, Clyde found. He doubts if many could be found without the use of dowsing, as most are covered with accumulated debris.

Ritual objects

'Certain artifacts found in the area have had some form of energy imparted into them which can be detected by dowsing' Clyde explained. 'These artifacts are those which were used in unknown ritual ceremonies. Among them are pieces of quartz with crystals embedded in them, and stone mounds in stone arrangements. It is interesting to note that similar energy can be detected in the mysterious stones, found on the western plains of New South Wales, which are called cyclons and which are believed to have had ritual significance' he says.

Site Alignments

'Another interesting fact which has come to light as a result of map dowsing in this region' he adds 'is that all the important ceremonial sites in the Glenbrook National Park, Lapstone Hill and Castlereagh regions are connected by straight lines of energy from a central point. This point is a well known site called "The Circles", where, on a rocky outcrop, there is an engraving of a spiral or circular design. Some of the ceremonial sites linked by these energy lines are also interconnected by similar straight lines.'

Aboriginal stone arrangements are found all over Australia, but are not common. Not usually being very large, the stones are easily removed or damaged. The top photo shows an unique small stone circle that was used as a men's initiation site, near Sydney.

Below are two spiral stone arrangements in a Heritage Park in Mullumbimby, northern New South Wales. They were found elsewhere (in the path of a new road being made) and were re-located to the park and cemented into position. Their purpose can only be guessed or intuited.

Kumarangk – The Sad Saga of Hindmarsh Island

A 'troubled bridge over the waters' that now links Goolwa, on mainland South Australia, to Hindmarsh Island/Kumarangk has been called the most litigated structure in Australian history. Opened in March 2001, it's construction destroyed sites sacred to the Ngarrindjeri nation, particularly to women traditional land owners. Before then a battle was fought in many courts, which mainly served to bring into disrepute the very culture of the traditional land owners, the profession of anthropology and the credibility of just about everyone who stood up to oppose it.

Opponents were silenced and freedom of speech compromised by ongoing defamation cases. The term 'secret women's business' became part of the Australian language, as it was dragged through the mud ...

The bridge divided the community, both black and white, and has become an ugly symbol of the greed of developers triumphing over indigenous concerns. When their land is harmed in this way, Aboriginal people suffer terribly and some would call it an act of genocide.

Let's take a look at the story, from its most ancient origins, to today ...

Stories from the Ancient Time
Ngurunderi is the supreme mythic deity of the Ngarrindjeri nation, a tribal Aboriginal group living around the region of the mouth of the Murray River in South Australia. In a well known story from the Dreamtime, describing the formation of the landscape features of the region, Ngurunderi 's two wives ran away one day , so he followed them in hot pursuit, paddling his canoe down the Murray River. The river was only small in those times but as Ngurunderi travelled he followed a huge Murray Cod whose great tail kept hitting the banks and widening the river, while the splashing water formed swamplands. Trying to spear the fish unsuccessfully, each time the spear was thrown it formed river islands.

Finally Ngurunderi's brother in law speared the fish and the cod was cut into many pieces which were thrown into the river, each becoming new fish species. Making camp, Ngurunderi's footsteps on the beach were changed into rocks. On another day he saw some people who were afraid and hid from him, so he turned them into the birds that live there today.

One day, smelling fish cooking- which was taboo for Ngarrindjeri women- he knew his wives must be near, so he rushed off in further pursuit. The huts he left behind were turned into hills and his canoe shot up into the heavens to become the Milky Way. His wives made a raft to escape and dashed across Lake Albert, where their raft was turned into reeds and trees. Still in hot pursuit, at Kingston Ngurunderi met a sorceror, and a great battle between them took place. Defeating and killing his enemy, the burnt body came to be marked by granite boulders. Ngurunderi then travelled along the Coorong. At each camp site he dug into the sand to find fresh water and fished.

He continued past the Murray Mouth and Victor Harbour, still searching for his wives. More granite islands were formed at Victor Harbour where he threw his spear and at King's Beach a bluff was formed where he threw his club. His wives heard all the noise and fled across the (then) land bridge to Kangaroo Island. He saw them fleeing and called up the waters to drown them. And so they were swept into the sea and turned into the Pages Islands. At this point Ngurunderi knew that his time to join the spirits was coming soon. He dived into the sea to cleanse his spirit and went up into the sky. He can still be seen today as a very bright star.

(From the story told to Ronald Berndt and seen on the video film 'Ngurunderi', SA Film Corporation.)

Kumarangk Dreaming

What you can't read about or discover easily are the dreaming tales pertaining to Hindmarsh Island, in Ngarrindjeri country at the point of the Murray Mouth.

Kumarangk is the ancient name for Hindmarsh Island and in the Ngarrindjeri language this means 'the points'. There are many celestial associations on the island – places linked to Venus, Jupiter, the Southern Cross, possibly Mars and most importantly to the Seven Sisters/Pleiades Dreaming.

At the closest point to the port town of Goolwa on the mainland there is a very important point – the Nonpoonga, the 'ancient place of the golden sun on the water', where time is measured. At the spring equinox the sun and the moon shine down at this point and it is also the meeting place of the salt and fresh waters at that time of year. The location of the meeting of the waters changes throughout the year, or it used to. Goolwa means 'mixed water'.

At either side of what used to be the vehicle ferry between Goolwa and Kumarangk there were caves, now either hidden, lost or destroyed. These are, or were, an important part of the Dreaming, because this is where the great spirit Ngurunderi camped whilst giving out the Law to the people of the area. It's a site central to the formation of the Ngarrindjeri Nation.

Now that the bridge, which the Ngarrindjeri people resisted for some ten years, is completed still much heartache and bitterness prevails in the Ngarrundjeri community. With the destruction of the Nonpoonga, the sun shadow will not be seen again and the continuity of the tradition of that ancient time will be no more.

Part of the island's Dreaming importance involves 'secret women's business', the revealing of which could attract a tribal death sentence. Traditionally the dissemination of Ngarrundjeri (and other tribal) knowledge is restricted on the basis of age, gender, family affiliation, aptitude and connection with place. So it has been the subject of much dispute and ridicule. The island women have had years of bullying, and the divisive tactics employed on them have caused some rifts.

Yet the general significance of the island to the women, that a Dreaming story involving the presence of the Seven Sisters at Kumarangk in Ngarringjeri land and legend, has been documented from the mid-nineteenth century onwards.

Dreaming tracks

The straight track 'ancient way', proscribed by the great spirit Ngurrundjeri's wanderings, crosses the island of Kumarangk. Several other dreaming tracks converge there too, including one which comes down from the north and over the mouth of the Murray.

The Island has traditionally been used like a kind of 'conference centre,' where different clan groups would gather together to share knowledge at regular times.

Beyond Kumarangk and further along the path of the Ngurunderi Dreaming track a curious phenomena has come about. The Anglican Yankalilla shrine of Our Lady is written about elsewhere in this book.

A World of Richness

When the white explorer Charles Sturt saw the region around the Murray Mouth he described it as perhaps the richest river delta in the world. This area, which includes the Coorong National Park, is under an international Ramsar Agreement to protect the migratory birds and animal breeding grounds there, and is recognised as a wetland of international importance. The Ngarrindjeris call it the Picaninny Waters.

Once one of the most densely populated regions in Aboriginal Australia – the environment was so rich, that Ngarrindjeri had no need for a nomadic lifestyle. The people lived in their 'wylies' – solid wattle and daub structures, on the southern shore of Kumarangk in the summer, and on the more sheltered northern shore of the island during winter. Their food sources were endless, until the white man came and cleared much of the island for wheat and grazing.

Environmental concerns

Yet no management plan has been created to look at the impact of the bridge and the resulting large scale housing development on Kumarangk's sensitive environment. This was highlighted back in 1993 when University of Adelaide academics addressed a public meeting in Adelaide. (Campus News, 16/8/93)

Associate Professor Dr John Noye explained that the State Government plan to build the $6.4 million bridge would cause serious environmental damage. Noye is an expert on computing coastal tides and currents and their effects on beach erosion, fish larvae movement and the like. He spoke of the fragility of the coastal, estuarine and riverine environments, and the fact that many bird species are on the decline. Already, in '93, the numbers of visitors were contributing to environmental degradation.

The barrages that were put in place between 1939–40 have caused steady siltation, restricting water movement between the sea and the estuary. The Murray Mouth had became completely blocked by the mid 1980's. The area is also faced with ever deteriorating water quality due to increasing salinity plus chemicals and fertilisers finding their way into the river upstream and accumulating in the Murray Mouth lakes, causing toxic blooms and making water undrinkable even for cattle. The area urgently needs a management plan, said Noye. 'Putting a large housing development in and attracting hordes of day trippers … makes little sense.'

In December 2002 the Government announced a $375 million package to help the Snowy and Murray Rivers. Some of this has been spent on dredging and removing barrages at the Murray Mouth to help restore the river's original flow pattern.

What the Women say

'The significance for Ngarrindjeri is the island's sacredness, the land is sacred to us … Our ancestors suffered at the hands of the white settlers. When they saw what the white settlers were doing to their country, they would cry and feel the pain of seeing everything that was of value to them being destroyed … After 200 years we, the indigenous people of our country, are still feeling the pain of the white man's developments. The destruction of sacred land is another form of genocide.' Ngarrindjeri elder and Kumarangk traditional owner Dr Doreen Kartinyeri has stated.

'Hindmarsh Island is, and always was, a place of spiritual, cultural and heritage importance to Ngarrindjeri people and in particular women. It is part of the Seven Sisters and therefore is a place of importance for all Aboriginal women. I have seen and continue to see the pain, suffering and struggle of the Ngarrindjeri women in the fight to protect Kumarangk and it breaks my heart. But no matter what they throw at them (Court cases, Royal Commission, Lies, Discrediting etc) the spirit and belief of the people are strong and remain strong.' Says Sandra Saunders, a traditional owner.

Bridge history

A previous council signed a deed with developers and the government of the day to cut up part of the island into house blocks to pay for the bridge infrastructure – without any sustainable management plan.

The Ngarrindjeri women began their battle. As custodians they were simply fulfilling their responsibility to protect their sacred traditions and places.

An Inquiry into the Hindmarsh Island Bridge Project was tabled in 1993 by the Environment, Resources and Development Committee of the South Australian Parliament, having involved the local community and all major political parties. The committee found unanimously against the bridge, but the State Labor Government ignored the recommendations to protect the island and oppose the bridge.

During the next state election campaign the Liberal Party opposed the bridge. Samuel Jacobs QC was appointed to investigate the bridge's legal and contractual issues only. His report was never released. The new State Liberal Government decided that likely litigation and compensation costs would be too great if they reneged on the bridge deal, so they quickly changed their stand.

In 1994 the Lower Murray Aboriginal Heritage Committee applied for protection of the site from federal authorities, because the State Minister for Aboriginal Affairs, while agreeing that there were significant heritage sites at risk, used special powers under the State Aboriginal Heritage Act to authorise damage to them and allow the bridge's construction. The Federal Government subsequently accepted Professor Cheryl Saunder's findings on the matter and, on 10/7/94 banned the bridge for 25 years. This decision was then overturned on legal technical grounds.

In 1995 a Royal Commission was established by the State Liberal Government to investigate whether the secret women's business was fabricated. This was the first time in Australian history that a Royal Commission was used to investigate Aboriginal beliefs. The women refused to participate. The Government was forced by the Supreme Court to go back and consult the Ngarrindjeri people in an appropriate manner and found that 85% of Ngarrandjeri people were opposed to the Royal Commission and to being forced to divulge sensitive cultural information. Public opposition also came from many other quarters.

The Royal Commission ending up by deciding that the whole of the women's business was a fabrication. Despite the State Liberal Government's keen acceptance of the report its legitimacy has been questioned, for its terms of reference were inappropriate and denied basic human rights of religious freedom.

The subsequent Mathew's Inquiry showed that a number of the Royal Commission's findings were wrong. An attempt to have the Commission made subject to a Judicial review foundered because a State Government Act disallowed any review process at all.

Another attempt was made to apply for protection under the Federal Heritage Act in 1996. Justice Jane Mathews was appointed to investigate, but a change in government brought in a new Federal Minister for Aboriginal Affairs and thence Senator Herron refused to appoint a female Minister to read the report. On those grounds the Ngarrindjeri women refused to include evidence that they felt was sensitive, for women only. Mathew's report verified that the Seven Sisters Dreaming Story was connected to the Ngarrindjeri lands, with documentation from long back, refuting the Royal Commission's finding on this matter. But when her report was finished she was deemed, as a judge, to be ineligible to have carried out the inquiry and her report was ruled ineffective.

In 1996 Justice Elizabeth Evatt was appointed by the then Federal Labor Government's Minister for Aboriginal and Torres Strait Islander Affairs, Robert Tickner, to report on the effectiveness of heritage legislation. Of the Federal Heritage Act she reported that 'The Act should recognise and respect Aboriginal customary law restrictions on information about significant areas. The (present) Act does not protect confidential information or respect Aboriginal spirituality or beliefs which require that confidentiality be maintained. Aboriginal people want the Act to be maintained and strengthened.'

Once again a change of government came about before Evatt's report was completed, and so, despite her findings, little has changed with the Act to protect confidential beliefs. Having twice attempted to gain protection from the Federal Heritage Act, the Ngarrindjeri again requested that the Minister conduct an investigation, as required by the Heritage Act. Instead they got the Hindmarsh Island Bridge Bill which Senator Herron introduced to parliament. This was passed in early 1997 and had the effect of preventing the Minister from making any orders under the Heritage Protection Act relating to the bridge.

The Ngarrindjeri then challenged the constitutionality of this new Act in the High Court. The court case was given a high public profile because of the possibility that it might have a bearing on future legal challenges to John Howard's Wik 10 point plan (in relation to Aboriginals' gaining of title to their sovereign lands). The Ngarrindjeri plaintiffs lost their case. The High Court ruled that the Bridge Act was an amendment to an already existing Act and that if Parliament had the power to make a law, it must follow that Parliament had the power to unmake it.

2000 saw the marina developers Tom and Wendy Chapman suing for $25 million damages that they claimed they suffered when construction of the bridge was halted. The case went on for over 6 months. The judge heard evidence about the secret women's business before an all women court room, demanding the secret details recorded on camera.

Eminent American anthropologist Prof Diane Bell, director of women's studies at George Washington University in Washington, DC, gave evidence. 'I have come to conclusions that the Hindmarsh Island, Murray Mouth area has significance to women and that there are Ngarrindjeri women and men who believe a bridge threatens the health of women, the social order and the land' she stated. Bell is the author of the book 'Ngarrindjeri Wurruwarrin – a world that is, was and will be'. (The Advertiser 16/8/00)

Tom and Wendy Chapman eventually withdrew their appeal over the 2001 Federal

Court decision to deny their claim for $25M compensation, in which Justice Von Doussa rejected the assertion of the SA Hindmarsh Island Bridge Royal Commission that the Ngarrindjeri fabricated their cultural and spiritual beliefs. They were forced to withdraw their appeal because there was no evidence to show the Ngarrindjeri women fabricated their opposition to the Hindmarsh Island Bridge.

'Last year (January 2002), the Conservation Council of South Australia lost a defamation action brought against the Council and some of its individual members. Now the action was brought by Tom and Wendy Chapman, the developers of the Hindmarsh Island Marina and the associated controversial bridge. Judge Williams, in the Supreme Court found that the defendants had indeed defamed Mr and Mrs Chapman in various publications and in his judgement he made much of the fact that Mr and Mrs Chapman are upstanding and esteemed citizens of Adelaide, while the defendants were malicious in their crusade against the Chapmans and the building of the marina and of course of the bridge. The Judge awarded the Chapmans $130,000 in damages and ruled that they had been defamed in three different publications. Well last week, again in the Supreme Court of South Australia, three judges overturned two of the judgments of Judge Williams and they were split 2–1 on the third matter. So the damages, payable to the Chapmans were reduced to $50,000 …

'Now that the marina has been developed, how much money has been pointlessly spent on legal actions?' asked Terry Lane on ABC Radio in December 2003.

Bruce Donald (a senior Sydney lawyer and many years ago the ABC's chief lawyer): 'Oh, you couldn't count it and this is the chilling effect of defamation proceedings in public interest matters and why really the Australian legal system has a lot to answer for, developing it into such an arcane and rocket science. Millions of dollars will have been spent, bearing in mind the Royal Commissions before Jacobs and then before Justice Matthews, that was truncated, cases up to the High Court. I mean there were in relation to these cases some 11 defamation actions, not just this one we're talking about here, but 10 other cases, some involving the ABC, involving 45 publications. Now the courts and legislatures have really got to wrestle with this problem. It's a really serious issue of free speech in a democratic society when the great beneficiaries of debate are the beach houses of the lawyers. Not mine, sadly.'

'Defamation actions against a large number of defendants including conservation groups, academics, politicians, media operators, printers and individuals who have spoken out against the controversial Hindmarsh Island Bridge have earned the developers some $850,000 with at least one action still outstanding,' wrote Mike Parnell, a solicitor with the Environmental Defenders Office (SA) Inc., when the Adelaide Advertiser of 11th February 2002 reported the partial lifting of suppression orders relating to 10 defamation actions in which the Chapmans were successful or had obtained settlements.

'It's time that there was an unconditional apology made to the Ngarrindjeri people by the Australian and South Australian Governments on behalf of the Australian people and the Crown over the treatment given to the Ngarrindjeri people by the 1995 Royal Commission (for its concoction of the defamation that the Ngarrindjeri people fabricated their spiritual beliefs and culture to assist "Greenies" with their opposition to the building of the Hindmarsh Island bridge), and the subsequent use of this unsound and false Royal Commission finding by the Commonwealth Parliament to the injury of the Ngarrindjeri,' states the Roma Mitchell Community Legal Centre communique.

Meanwhile the building of the bridge blew well out of budget and since it's opening

Aboriginal people refuse to use it. The Marina development has been greatly facilitated, of course.

Visiting Kumarangk

In 2000 I arrived at the Hindmarsh Island ferry, the bridge looming above it half built, and had a strong impression of the tainted energy of the island, the sense of desperation, fuelled by the desecration, bitterness and frustration there. There was a lead weight feeling of crushing oppression that was hard to handle, that I have never encountered before.

Just beforehand there had been a Ngarrindjeri youth suicide and two young Ngarrindjeris were killed in a car chase, under suspicious circumstances. Not long before that an important symbol of Ngarrindjeri culture, a canoe tree (where a canoe shaped section of bark was removed long ago, leaving the tree alive) had been ringbarked, causing great distress. Then, in early September 2000 an historic big river boat, lovingly restored for use as a tourist venture by the Ngarrindjeri, and not long delivered and moored close by the half built bridge, was totally destroyed by a fire. Just beforehand someone in the night was seen swimming away from it …

Geomantically, I found, the power of place was strong. I dowsed a very powerful ley line passing over the Murray Mouth and this, I was told, is one of the important dreaming tracks. As well, the island is affected by a magnetic anomaly, as various old measurements of the island have been 1000 yards out, and the shoreline hasn't changed that dramatically to explain this discrepancy.

When I took Billy Arnold there in 2001 he was stunned to clairvoyantly tune in to a congregation of highly unusual nature spirits near the Murray Mouth. They were so different and seemingly so ancient that he could not compare them to any others. It was like stumbling across a lost civilisation …

The massive Marina development that we saw later in 2003 was a gigantic and ugly scar on the landscape, filling up quickly with luxury holiday homes and gigantic marinas.

Discovering Ngarrindjeri Culture

The Ngarrindjeri nation has fought to uphold their law on every level to no avail. It's a sorry state of affairs. Tom Treverrow, a softly spoken Ngarrindjeri elder, feels that the cause is probably lost. The whole affair has greatly embittered the Ngarrindjeri community.

Tom is a director of Camp Coorong, across Lake Alexandria on the Coorong shore. It's a 'Centre for Race Relations, Cultural Education and Recreation', that is run by the Ngarrindjeri Land and Progress Association. They specialise in school camps, excursions and conferences and have cabins and dormitories for stay-overs. There's a museum and conference room and you can learn all about Ngarrindjeri culture there, from bush foods to history to traditional basket weaving. This centre is playing a valuable role in not only keeping Ngarrindjeri culture alive, but in bridging the cultures of black and white.

In the words of the Kumarangk Coalition, in a statement prepared for their Long Walk peaceful protest –

> *'This is a journey for peace where as a family we strengthen our bonds of love and trust. A journey of knowledge handed down from generation to generation. A journey of creation, of spirituality, customs, culture and languages.*

'So it is in this spirit of true reconciliation that we pledge to protect our heritage, the legacy for our children and the children of generations to come.

'To continue our commitments to shared beliefs, our sense of each other and our intimacy with the land, our mother. We in all conscience, STAND AGAIN, in another non-violent protest, to honour the spirits of our ancestors, our Elders of time immemorial, those for whom we continue the struggle for justice.'

References:

Pam O'Connor, 'The Aboriginal People of the South East', South East Book Promotions, Australia, 1994.

'Unfinished Business – Kumarangk' produced by the Kumarangk Coalition c/o PO Box 3168, Rundle Mall, Adelaide SA 5000.

Proceedings of the Royal Society of South Australia, vol 25, page 324-325.

ABC Radio National's, 'In the Public Interest', 14/12/03.

Personal communications from island residents.

Communiques from Roma Mitchell Community Legal Centre – rmclc@ozemail.com.au

Camp Coorong – PO Box 126 Meningie SA 5264, ph 08 8575 1557, fax 08 8575 1448.

Nimbin Rocks

Nimbin Rocks, those iconic volcanic plugs, great fingers of rhyolite at the entrance to the Nimbin Valley in northern New South Wales, have great Aboriginal significance and were used as male initiation ground. Their potent yang power is not suitable for constant habitation in the vicinity, especially so for women, Aboriginal poet Kath Walker told my friend when we went to live there in the 1970's. But it's a good place to spend a few days charging one's batteries, and that is enough, she explained.

One time Aboriginal custodians of Nimbin Rocks and well known identities, Millie Boyd and her niece Lorraine Mafi Williams (now both deceased) tried to warn people to take these energies seriously. The local Nimbinji spirit can be cheeky to downright malicious, Lorraine told us at a workshop she ran in the Blue Mountains in the mid 1980's.

Katrina Smythe was living up close to the Rocks for a while and wrote to Dowsing News to say that 'I can notice the change in my energy after leaving the vicinity. It certainly has a way of sucking you down and spacing you out.

'Not long before we left my sons (both aged 7) and I all saw a small yellowish glowing light to the south of the rocks, against the background of cliffs. It hovered for a few minuted there and then rose, dimming as it went, to finally fade against the rather light, nearly full moon sky. That night and the next there were barely perceptive flashes of pale light streaking in all directions in the north west section of the sky. There were faint colours with them, mainly blue, yellow and some red … On the whole I'm glad to have lived there, somehow it made my astral travelling easier.'

I had my own experiences of unusual phenomena in the region. I've seen 'spirit lights' bouncing along the tops of the Nightcap Range, on the route taken since the Dreamtime by deceased Aboriginal spirits, via Byron Bay's headland … But I have never gone up close to those men-only Nimbin Rocks, following Aboriginal law. I went back to live in the Nimbin Valley in 1989 and stayed in the area for 11 years. I was told that I would not be able to write there. This was true, I would have to go elsewhere for that.

So I know from experience that the energies are indeed intense there. The Nimbin Valley has many sacred initiation areas, including some for women on the more feminine north side, where the Blue Knob basalts lie. Just as we were first warned – I never saw women thrive in that valley and I can't say that I did either. Peoples' relationships, new businesses – so many seemed to be floundering, or on the rocks. Poverty is a major problem there, with a great many welfare dependants. But on the positive side – I learnt a lot, about nature, the fabulous rainforests and natural farming and gardening.

Sadly these days, despite there being no jobs available, the lure of cheap land in a spectacular environment beckons. The whole valley seems to be filled with land subdivisions. The atmosphere in Nimbin town itself, so close to the Nimbin Rocks, once full of the starry eyed idealists of the '70's, has degenerated badly. The spectre of junkies dealing and alcohol fuelled aggression on the main street is a bit hard to handle. The Nimbinji spirit at work, perhaps.

Don't let me put you off though! It's a magic region for a holiday or a training course. But if you are a female – don't go and explore those Nimbin Rocks, or that Nimbinji spirit there might come out and spook you!

Reference:
J. G. Steele 'Aboriginal Pathways in Southeast Queensland and the Richmond River' University Of Queensland Press, Australia, 1984.

At the Nimbin Fair

Sacred Alice Springs

Alice Springs, in the red heart of central Australia, is a fascinating and unique place where Aboriginal culture is strong. Sacred sites can be seen everywhere , marked by signs, surrounded by modern development and protected by law.

Here even the most ordinary landscape feature can have spiritual significance. Some sites, like the dingo puppy sites, are just a tumble of dog sized rocks. There are many sacred trees growing around town, one of which grows in front of one of a bank, and developers face heavy fines if they destroy them.

A sacred rock in Alice Springs

On the weekend of September 8–9th 2001 Alice Springs hosted the biggest corroborree ever held and it was also Australia's most significant centenary of federation event of the year, according to Geoffrey Blainey, the Chairman of the National Council for the Centenary of Federation. A major reconciliation event, with a crowd of some 30,000 people watching (– more than the population of Alice!), the festival was also a celebration of the most important Dreamings (geomantic traditions) of the town – the Caterpillar/ Yeperenye Dreaming. Technical infrastructure came courtesy of the Sydney Olympics and was state-of-the-art with a 30 foot high TV screen so all could see.

A showcase of indigenous talent, of the many Aboriginal musicians and artists, the entertainment was tempered by moving ceremonies, such as the honouring of the members of the 'stolen generation' (Aborigines who had been removed from their families by government policies and forced to live in institutions). Some of these people came onstage and were greeted and hugged by local Arrente women elders. Ex-prime ministers Gough Whitlam and Malcolm Fraser took part in the event and were honoured for their contribution towards Aboriginal land rights.

'Some 1200 children carrying lanterns danced and giggled among six golden 12 metre tall caterpillars around 5 separate circular stages, representing traditional song lines,' the local Centralian newspaper reported. The Yeperenye Spectacle portrayed the convergence of the caterpillars along the dreaming tracks at Alice Springs. Then came the fierce battle between the ntyarike caterpillar and the iriperenye (stink beetle), the creation of the surrounding MacDonnell Ranges (a spectacular sight as the ranges behind were lit up by powerful spotlights), the caterpillars' transformation into cocoons and, in the final scene, their re-emergence as hawk moths.

John Williamson sang an emotional couple of songs with his Hermannsberg Aboriginal mate Warren Williams including 'Thousand Feet', which is about the many generations of Aboriginals who have walked around Uluru, reported the Centralian. To quote – 'Williams said – It is the spiritual centre of the nation – I felt maybe it was pretentious of me to write about a place of such spiritual significance. We sang Thousand Feet while the caterpillars representing the five mobs met together for the first time in decades, and tears were streaming down Warren's face. It is the kind of emotion that inspires young Aborigines to hold their traditions close to their hearts.'

I can verify that there were many very emotional moments over that momentous weekend and an important and major act of the recognition of Aboriginal suffering and healing had occurred. It felt as if a great deal of tension had been released, and, as if to assist the purging process, the brooding skies opened up after it was all over and Alice copped some lovely rain showers.

The weekend's events, rather than send ripples or waves of healing energy across the country via positive media reports was totally eclipsed by other contrasting events that happened the next day in the USA. Consequently the average Australian would not know that this wonderful event of national significance had even occurred.

The Story of the Yeperenye

'Alice Springs, called Mpwarntwe (pronounced ahm-barn-twa) is built on the traditional lands of the Arrernte (Arr-un-da) people. Arrernte people understand that their Dreaming, known as Altyerre (al-chair-ra), was established during the creation period and remains within the landscape around them today.

'The Yeperenye, Utnerrengatye and Ntyarlke caterpillars were the major creative forces for the Alice Springs area and are among the most sacred and important of all Arrernte totems. They formed the ranges that surround the Festival grounds. The Caterpillar ancestors came from many different places. They travelled from the north at Apmerrknge (Central Mount Stuart), from Urlatherrke (Mt Zeil) in the west, Atula to the east and Apwetele to the south. The Caterpillars converged at Mpwarntwe, the epicentre of Caterpillar culture, where they held pitched battles with the Irlperenye (stink bug men). The area is rich in battle grounds, "cocoon" sites, dance grounds and campsites used by the Caterpillar ancestors.'

References:
Centralian Advocate, Sept 11th 2001.
Yeperenye Festival leaflets.

Flinders Ranges Dreaming

The spectacular Flinders Ranges run for 480 km, starting north of Adelaide and heading to the north east of arid inland South Australia. Some say they lie on the path of the main Rainbow Serpent line that crosses Australia diagonally, starting at the Kimberleys in the north west. Many consider them to be the location of 'Grid Point 44' on the Earth's crystal grid, and Chambers Gorge seems to be the most likely candidate for this.

The local Aboriginal tribe, the Adnyamathanha, are rich with the deep cultural meaning of ancient Dreamings of the area. Ashes at foot of the Arkaroo Rock have been dated to 15000 yrs, the oldest in the area. Very rich geologically, an important ochre deposit at Bookartoo was traded in 30kg slabs on peoples' heads up to distant Cape York, and ceremonial shells were brought back in exchange. The last fully initiated tribal man, who lived in Leigh Creek, died in 1996.

The jewel of the region – a great circle of ranges forms Wilpena Pound, marking the Dreaming tracks of two immense maned snake spirits, central to Flinders Ranges dreaming. The nose-to-tail bodies of these Akurra are the walls of Wilpena pound.

The Adnyamathanha say that in the Dreamtime the two Akurra encircled an important corroborree that was being held in Wilpena Pound. They gorged themselves on the participants.

Turlu the kingfisher man was one of the few survivors of this attack . An important participant, he signalled that he was on his way to the ceremony by lighting a big fire. His fire produced a great bed of ash that white man later called brown coal. (There's an open-cut coal mine at nearby Leigh Creek.)

Pauline Coulthard and cousin Joe Mckenzie, of Adnatma Yarta cultural tours, explain that St Marys Peak (the highest point in Wilpena Pound, at 1188m) is the head of the female Akurra. Her name means (approximately) 'trying to find your mind' and the Adnyamathantha (meaning people of the rock) believe that walkers get lost in the pound because she disorientates them.

According to another Adnyamathantha legend a great Akurra in the northern ranges drank Lake Frome dry. It then dragged its distended body through the adjacent hills, carving a big gorge to Mainwater Pound, in the Gammon Ranges. Its passage was marked by Arkaroola Creek, its string of important waterholes being places where the Akurra camped each night.

'Akurra often leaves Yaki Awi, a waterhole where he resides today, since the end of his Dreamtime journey, to sunbake on its banks. From a long way off you can hear his tummy rumbling in the sun. Some say the noises are just rock falls,' Coulthard says.

Adnyamathantha say that the Pleiadies cluster are considered to be a group of women eaten by an Akurra, who later died in a flood. When the belly of the then rotten snake burst open, the women were blown into the sky.

Rock art in the mysterious Chambers Gorge is as much a mystery to Adnyamathantha as it is to white people, with very ancient origins.

References:

Melanie Ball, 'Serpent Dreaming', The Sunday Age, Aug 3rd 1997.
'Glovebox Guide – The Flinders Ranges', Australian Geographic, 2000.
Adnatmatna Yarta Cultural Tours, PO Box 187, Hawker SA 5434.

The Battle for Timbarra

Timbarra plateau near Tenterfield in northern NSW has been a battleground for environmentalists and Aboriginal people since plans by Ross Mining for a gold mine have threatened to destroy a sacred wilderness and water catchment area.

A lease was granted to Ross Mining in April 1996 for a 400 hectare gold mine to be located within the Poverty Point and Tin Can Swamp areas on the Plateau. The gold would be extracted using the heap leach pad method. Arsenic released from the cyanide processing would be a by-product. The mining process would release less than one gram of gold per tonne of granite processed.

Ross Mining planned to use 700 tonnes of cyanide each year to extract gold from the mine. One gram of cyanide is the lethal dose for humans. The mine would also use 75 tonnes of caustic soda and 60 tonnes of hydrochloric acid to extract 50,000 ounces of gold, worth $20 million a year. These chemicals represent a significant environmental threat to the region because the mine is on a highlands, which feed into the Clarence River.

There is opposition to the mine from five government departments, including the New South Wales National Parks and Wildlife Service. The NPWS considers the Timbarra plateau to be of 'outstanding and unique conservation value'. A great many endangered and vulnerable plant and animal species live there.

Ross Mining and the government have ignored the wishes of local Aboriginal people, who have taken out a number of native title claims on the area. The Timbarra Plateau is one of the most sacred sites to several local tribes of the Bundjalung/Malera people.

'Revered by Aboriginal people as their place of creation, law giving, initiation, healing and communion with god; and spared from hunting – Timbarra is a sacred site,' says John Wilson member of the Timbarra Protection Coalition.

Initiation cycles lasting two years climaxed on this plateau. The sites contain many rare and sacred artefacts such as scarred trees, engravings and stone marked sites. Bold Top Mountain, an arrangement of granite tors, is a spectacular natural wonder and a sacred Aboriginal place. This area is yet to be gazetted as a mythological site by the NPWS.

What do traditional landowners say?

'Malera country is Gold Dreaming and we of the Malera people are the children of the Gold Dreaming,' said Kathy Malera Bandjalan. With the voice of her family, Malera-Bundjalan has vowed to stop the mining of her ancestral land on the Timbarra (that they call Malera).

'The proposed mine is an attack on the Malera people, their land and identity,' argues Malera-Bandjalan. 'Malera is sacred to us as a people. To attack our land is to attack our people. To mine Malera is to totally kill our spirit. It is to kill everything we believe in. It is to cease our existence as a people. We have lost enough without losing any more, especially our Dreaming and sacred sites. Especially those that are of particular strength to women.'

There has also been two other land claims by other tribes of the Bundjalung people who claim this mountain to be of extremely high cultural significance to their people. Yet the right to ancestral beliefs is one of the basic human rights.

'Previous studies have demonstrated that the Timbarra plateau has important Aboriginal archaeological and heritage values. The NPWS considers that, given the Aboriginal heritage significance of the area, there is the potential for the proposal to impact on Aboriginal archaeological and heritage values as a result of pipeline construction and associated clearing and ground disturbances, and upgrading of relevant access roads to the pump site.

'Of particular concern are relic-based Aboriginal sites ... and ceremonial sites which must be identified in conjunction with the Aboriginal community. The NPWS notes that no assessment of the Aboriginal heritage values of the Nelsons Creek area, impacts of the proposed activity on those values or measures to mitigate impacts on identified values has been provided in the REF reviewed.' Gary Davey (Director of Environmental services, NPWS).

After much protesting and after much damage was already done, in September 1999 Ross Mining closed the gold mine. The reasons were purely economical. The price of gold had dipped low enough to make the venture too costly. But the infrastructure is there, ready for the ugly spectre of rising gold prices to get it back into gear ...

References:
Internet articles
Personal communications.

Timbarra Lament

Sacred forest
Of my heart
You own me
And I need you

And we should not be
Torn apart
Lose true nature
Wild parts

But some would shave
Your tangled locks
Dam fresh waters
Slay your elders
And waste
Your body bare

But without the shade
Of your green glades
We're all diminished

For it's a fools gold
That they seek
And they're blinded
By its glare.

Alanna Moore

Geomancy in New Zealand and Polynesia

Who are the Polynesians?

The ancestors of the Polynesian people emerged out of South China and Taiwan some 5-6000 years ago. This has been established by the many similarities between the fourteen indigenous languages of Taiwan and the proto-Polynesian tongue, plus other clues. They migrated their way down via the Phillipines and Melanesia, and spread out to populate the southern reaches of the vast Pacific ocean.

Not only great sea-farers, they were farmers, hunters, gatherers and fishers, who were adepts at reading the oceans, the waters and the stars.

Their ability to navigate incredibly vast distances is renowned. It is possible, if not probable, that they visited South America, where they acquired the staple crops of potato and kumara/sweet potato, not naturally found in Oceania, as well as some religious practices associated with it. (The Maori name for potato is 'peru-peru'.)

New Zealand was difficult to find and thus it was the last large island on Earth to be settled by man (not counting Antarctica). Waves of migrations of Polynesian people started to arrive there from around 2000 years ago, as evidenced by 2000 year old remains of kiore/ domestic rat; as well as the oral history and whakapapas/geneologies of the earliest tribes, such as the Waitaha nation. Waitaha people say that their ancestors sailed there from Rapanui/Easter Island, some 4,200 nautical miles due west from Cape Reinga. While it is an incredible distance – prevailing winds would have taken them directly there.

Cultural similarities, such as the top knot of hair on the head, tend to reinforce the stories of a migration from Rapanui. In the nearby Rekohu/Chatham Islands (to the east) the style of fish hooks made by the indigenous Moriori people (seen in Te Papa, the national museum in Wellington) is the same as that at Rapanui, as it is with those found from Pitcairn, an island inbetween. Moriori wood carvings are also reminiscent of Rapanui style too. The Moriori may have arrived there directly from Rapanui and never made it further on to New Zealand, although there is evidence that some of them, at least, came via New Zealand's South Island.

Later migrations to New Zealand – the so-called Fleet Maori, arrived only around 800 years ago. Often they were fleeing unrest on the overpopulated islands of central Polynesia, to the north-east, with many wakas coming from the Cook and Society islands. A Maori saying states 'I am a seed sown from Ra'iatea' which is one of the Society Islands, 200km west of Tahiti.

Surprisingly, the human genome project has traced the forebears of the Maori back to a mere 70 odd individual women of Asian origin. This has largely silenced the arguments for the so-called Polynesian-Aryan theory – giving a Celtic or white ancestry for the Maori. Some tribes are darker or fairer than others and this could perhaps be explained by the amount of mixing with Melanesian people en route to New Zealand.

The new tribes were followers of the god of war and aggressively dealt with the existing tribes they encountered in the new land. They wrested sovereignty from them, according to their law, by depleting them of their mana/spiritual power. They did this by desecrated the sacred sites they found and eating and enslaving the people. Sometimes they ate their victims at their sacred sites. As an act of revenge some areas had curses put on them.

In the 1830's the peace loving Moriori in the Chathams were almost wiped out by a displaced Taranaki tribe (from the south west of New Zealand's north island), and the pitiful few left are now trying to re-assert their land rights. Their cruel fate has been finally documented, in a book on the subject by author Michael King (who was killed in 2004 in a car smash).

Star lore

Polynesian peoples developed an intimate knowledge of many of the vast canopy of stars above the Pacific Ocean. The heavens were often consulted, not only in relation to navigation, but also for knowing when to plant and harvest food crops.

The Pleiades were a favourite. They were considered a woman and her six daughters, the Matariki/'little eyes', who were guardians of the skies. Their advent heralded the important time when preparations began for the planting of the next crop, and also when the foods of the forest and sea begin to multiply. There is an old Maori saying that the Pleiades are the food bringers.

In some districts the time of Pleiades' rising (in June) was considered the new year and to celebrate this there was much singing, chanting and dancing. When the Pleiades appeared on the horizon in the morning, this sacred/tapu time was especially reserved for festivities and rejoicing, the women singing and posture-dancing as they gazed at Matariki.

The Pleiadian new year was also recognised in the Cook Islands homelands, while in other districts of New Zealand it was Rigel's rise that heralded the new year.

When the crop was well sprouting, sacred food would be held out towards the Pleiades, while karakia was recited, at dawn, then the food hung up on a pole as an offering. The first fruits of the harvest were always offered to the Pleiades.

An Indonesian tradition says that the ancestors learned agriculture from someone who learnt it in the Pleiades. The Dyaks of Borneo/Kalimantan believe that rice, their staple food, has a soul which originates from the Pleiades.

Although they are not farmers, Aboriginal traditions all over Australia also give great significance to the Pleiades too. Like the Greeks, they considered them to be seven sacred sisters. A painting by one of Australia's best known Aboriginal artists Clifford Possum makes a telling comment, at an important retrospective of his work seen at Sydney's Art Gallery in 2004. Possum juxtaposed the seven stars of the Pleiadies on the one side of the work with the cross of Jesus on the other, to show the two ends of the religious spectrum in his world.

Star gods

Many of the pantheon of gods in Maori and Polynesian lore are linked to the stars. In one legend agriculture god Rongo-maui, younger brother of Whanui, the star Vega, acquired the seed of kumara from Vega. When Vega rose in the sky, around March, it heralded a time to prepare storage pits for the kumara harvest. Around that time a lookout watched for the rising star. When it first appeared the cry went out 'Here is Whanui!'.

Rongo himself was associated with the moon, while the forest god Tane was linked to the sun. Sirius was known as Rehua, the Man Eater.

The goddess Hina (called Sina in some parts of the Pacific) was a female personification of the moon and sister or mother to the great ancestor Maui. In Tahiti she was held responsible for the tides and generally connected with fertility and childbirth all over Polynesia.

Geomancing the Land

In voyages of discovery around the south Pacific the great pioneering ancestor/god Maui is said to have 'fished up' the islands of Tonga, Cook, Hawaii and New Zealand.

New Zealand's north island is likened to a great sting ray (Whai Repo or Te Ika Mango-roa) and is otherwise known as Maui's Fish; while the south island is referred to as a great waka (Aotea Roa). Whenua means the land and also a placenta.

The early Maori personified the landscape as an extension of themselves and their voyaging history. Landscapes features were sometimes honoured as ancestors. The peak of Te Whara at the eastern end of Bream Head, near Whangarei, is thus revered by the Ngata-Wai iwi /tribe, who consider the whole mountain, including its tracks, as wahi tapu/sacred space. The area was used as burial ground for the chiefs of several tribes. The volcanic range is 19-21 million years old and features spectacular jagged rocks and some of the finest coastal forest remnants left in Northland.

Mountains were said to be either male or female. This had useful spin-offs. Following the resolution of an inter-tribal conflict, the daughter of one tribe's chief was married off to the chief of the other tribe. In addition two local hills, from the territory of each tribe, were also ceremonially married together. The result was enduring peace.

Some stories of the mountains of the central north island speak of their sexual jealousies and much in-fighting amongst each other. Some mountains moved location to avoid conflict. (This would have helped make sense of the volatile nature of the volcanic regions.) Matronly mountains were referred to as 'mother'.

At Moeraki Beach, near the mouth of the Waitaki River in the South Island, well known stones of mythic import are found. Curious, large spheroid and ovoid boulders, these are said to be the petrified eel pots, gourds and kumara of ancestral waka, the Arai-te-uru. The entire crew on arrival from the homeland were transformed into local mountains, hills and pillars of stone in legend. The waka itself had overturned at Matakaea Point, near Oamaru, where she was turned to stone and can be still seen there. Her companion waka, Takitimu, landed at Southland and was transformed to the lofty blue range of Takitimu, a 'fairy haunt' which does indeed look like an upturned canoe.

The Navigator

On the northern coast of New Zealand's South Island stands a large upright stone of great mythic value – 'The Navigator'. Emerging from the beach sands near Anapai Bay, in what is now the Abel Tasman National Park, this craggy stone could possibly represent Rakaihautu, an ancestral navigator of the Waitaha peoples. Brailsford says that the Navigator is where Uruao came ashore from Rapanui/Easter Island some 67 generations ago.

Some say that this limestone karst was carved, for it looks somewhat head shaped, with a top knot of both Rapanui and New Zealand style, and a big beard. It is also said to be the site where legendary trail blazing ancestor Maui observed the nearby coast of the North Island, where he checked the currents by floating a fine line on the tide and watching the drift patterns, before setting off to 'fish up'/'discover' the north island.

'The Navigator', South Island, New Zealand.

Easter Island statue, Christchurch Museum, New Zealand.

Dowsing the Navigator I detected three powerful energy leys above it converging and sending a pillar of energy down into the stone. Nearby a huge Earth spirit/deva guardian resides in the adjacent limestone bluff, no doubt soaking up the energy, which is probably partly derived at least from the focus of human thought and action. Hamish Miller had earlier (in 2003) detected some 80 lines of energy radiating out from this stone.

Omen Mountains

Each Maori iwi had its own special omen mountain, where lightening flashing in a peculiar manner, particularly on a calm day is seen as an omen of death or misfortune. Such a 'rua-kanapa' is Matauhaura Mountain, at the eastern end above Lake Rotoiti.

Tarawera is another tapu mountain where the bones of the dead are kept. There was a belief that whenever deaths were about to happen a supernatural waka would be seen travelling towards the mountain. Just before the massive eruption of June 1886 two boat loads of tourists, led by well known Maori guide Sophia, saw such a phantom waka with thirteen paddlers. The great eruption occurred that night.

Sacred ceremony

In ancient Maori lore culture came down to the people from above, in the form of three baskets of knowledge. One was the basket with the knowledge of the creation stories, one was the knowledge of the ritual procedures for good magic and the third contained the knowledge of black magic. Also inside them came the sacred atua – stone statues, which acted as focii for ceremony and mana.

Generally, ceremonies would pertain to birth, sickness or death. Rituals performed would gain special mana/spiritual power imparted from the site and its resident atua /god or gods. There was much prestige in having the various rituals performed over one at the special sites. Rites were often performed at sunrise facing the sun.

Another important sacred site for ceremonial ritual was the wai tapu of a hamlet – a stream or pond. Such sites were set aside and not trespassed on. Ceremonies of lustration and immersion were an important feature in Maori ritual.

Shrines of stone and earth

The sacred shrines of the Maori were called tuahu. (In a similar lilt, the South American Incas called their sacred places huacas.) Eminent anthropologist Elsdon Best wrote in 1924 that unlike in other parts of Polynesia, where there are massive stone structures for temples, no temple like structures are known to have been erected in New Zealand. In the Society Island homeland Ra'iatea ancient ceremonial stone platforms, known as marae, are found. In Maoridom today a marae is just a plaza for community gatherings, with associated wooden buildings.

Larger stone monuments are found elsewhere in the Pacific. For example, in Tonga is the famed Ha'amonga-a-Maui ('Burden of Maui'), a trilithion of coral rock some 16'/5m high, with slabs weighing 30–40 tons each. But it is relatively modern, constructed around 1200AD as a monument to a ruler.

The Maori's tuahu were usually not marked in any way, only sometimes a rough unworked stone or several , or worked blocks of stone were set upright, but otherwise the place was left natural. These places were used for ceremony, some for black magic. Occasionally a stick platform (tiepa) was made to put offerings on, or small mounds (ahu, puke) were used.

Making and sanctifying a tuahu was the first serious task undertaken by the first peoples as they moved across the country. An early job for the invading tribes' tohungas/priests was the tamoe rite, whose purpose was to weaken the powers of any earlier or local gods.

Tuahu in the south island were generally fenced off enclosures some 12'/3.6m by 6'/1.8m in area, with a wooden image in the centre. Only the tohunga was allowed inside. In the Chatham Islands the Moriori tribe had their tuahu sites, which were marked by a stone upon which offerings to the atua were made.

The Maori also had special sacred stones that were buried under the ground as talismans and a source of mana. These were put under peoples' homes and behind places of learning, to help impart knowledge and power.

Stone markers also clearly delineated areas for hunting and gathering and were associated with prominent features, such as distant mountains and headlands. Sometimes boundaries were even tied to the stars above.

In Waitaha legend six sacred tuahu were placed around both islands, as points of connection to communicate with the stars, Brailsford writes.

Other special stones were placed as talismans for fisheries (known as mauri-kohatu) and for rivers and forests. But by the early 1800's many had been removed. 'Neglect of the stones is said to be the reason for increased mortality of the Maori' Jenkin writes.

Some Maori tuahu were ahu – a mound of earth either specially made, or a natural feature. Sometimes wooden pillars were used. Sometimes in an emergency a tuahu could be improvised to contact the atua. For example a tohunga might just cup his hand and use that as a shrine. But it was best to use long established ahu which had the most mana. A tuaha was occasionally moved, in which case some of the earth from the original spot was taken with it.

A special and legendary shrine was established on the summit of Puketutu Island in Manukau Harbour, by the tohunga/priest Raka-taura. It was used by the people of Tainui. It was from here that the tohunga of the Manukau people karakaied a chant that led the taniwha Ureia to its death. Another famous such shrine was on the hilltop at Te Ahurei, at Maketu in Kawhia harbour.

The tohunga was a highly tapu person, a seer, spirit medium, healer as well as war general. The position was hereditary, passing from father to son, taught at night or under trees away from disturbance. They learned ritual chants (karakia), sacred history and knowledge, and they were said to be able to receive knowledge directly at the sacred places.

Forest lore

Special stones carefully placed in wilderness areas became shrines for the wild gods of the forest. The stones were selected for the job for their unusual shapes. The stone might be placed at the foot of a famed bird catching tree. There the tohunga would liberate a lizard (a tree lizard or gecko) to act as a guardian of the mauri/life principle of the forest. The stone represented the mana of the forest and acted as a medium between the spirit worlds. It stood there as a talisman of protection and it was a place for ceremonies to increase the forests' fruitfulness.

When abundance was low a tohunga would be called in to arouse the mauri with karakia and sometimes feathers would be placed on the stone to encourage more birds. The first bird caught each season would be given as an offering there. Sometimes a hollow stone was used, inside of which a tapu object, such as a lock of hair, would be concealed.

Trees were only cut down with great respect and ceremony, and seedlings were then planted to replace them. Trees were cut with sacred adzes made from pounamu/greenstone, found in the South Island of New Zealand

Greenstone

Pounamu itself is a highly sacred semi-precious stone – nephrite jade – much esteemed by the Maori. It is said to absorb the mana and prestige of its owner. Many New Zealanders wear greenstone pendants around their necks, carved with a spiral, a popular design. The spiral – 'koru' is symbolic of new beginnings, of growth and harmony. Brailsford tell us of a Maori elder, who, attuning to the pain of a place where a massacre had occurred, placed pieces of pounamu in a stream, as a healing gesture.

Sacred Stones in Hawaaii

In Hawaii the Pohaku-a-Kane (Stones of Kane, known as Tane in New Zealand) were sacred stones between 1'–8'/ 30cm–2.5m high that were erected upright as altars for placing offerings, such as pieces of coral, on a daily basis. They were discovered in visions and dreams with Kane's help, and were ritually sprinkled with water or anointed with coconut oil, their upper part covered with black tapa (cloth made from bark). Similar traditions exist in Fiji.

Other upright sacred stones, or small stone platforms, are found scattered around Hawaii. These were where offerings of leaves, stones etc were placed to placate the local deities and spirits of place when travelling through their territory, to help prevent getting lost or injured on the way. Fishing shrines had fish shaped stones.

Also at one time every island around Hawaii had a fertility shrine, consisting of a single upright stone, where infertile women made offerings and slept overnight.

While only men prayed at the household shrines, women had their own special temples such as the 'House of Papa' the Earth Mother, a small house like structure with stone walls.

Gardening magic

The Maoris were great farmers and gardeners. In their gardens they created focal points of stone and wood for the atua and mauri, or resting place of the life principle, of the garden. Here, at crop planting time, the tohunga recited ritual incantations, and again at harvest. And if rain was needed, a wooden bullroarer would be ritually employed to bring rain to the crops.

In legend, Rongo, the god of cultivated crops as well as of peace, would mate with goddess Te Pani, the Earth Mother, and from the success of that union Kumara, the peace child, would be born. In the peaceful tradition of the Waitaha nation, sadness or anger had no place in the garden and growing the sacred crop was a joyful occupation.

Stone carvings of Rongo were used as a representative of the god. When placed in the gardens they were to ensure fertility of the crop and success of the harvest. Statues of Rongo's wife Te Pani were also placed there, so she could watch over crops, her wide eyes to search for poor seed, her big head for her wisdom and large body to encourage ample tuber growth. Both had offerings made to them.

The garden godstones were around 12"–18"/30–45cm high, were quite round, and have only three fingers depicted. This is a tradition from all around the Pacific, including several statues that were recorded from remote Pitcairn Island.

Stones carved with male and female sex organs have also been found in New Zealand's Taranaki district. Basaltic stone phalluses are known from the Austral Islands, and from the Society Islands there are stone phalluses in the form of a human body with a glans head.

Godstones were kept at the tuaha, or concealed elsewhere. Here they stayed until taken to the garden, when planting had begun, and placed at the head of the field. When it was time to plant the kumara, and to ensure a good crop, the tohunga would call upon Rongo to take up residence in the statue. During planting an appeal would be made to Te Pani – 'Oh Pani – pour out thy basket on this field'.

A favourite planting time was 'Orongonui', the 28th day of the moon cycle, named after the god Rongo. 'I don't need to tell Maori people about growing crops using the

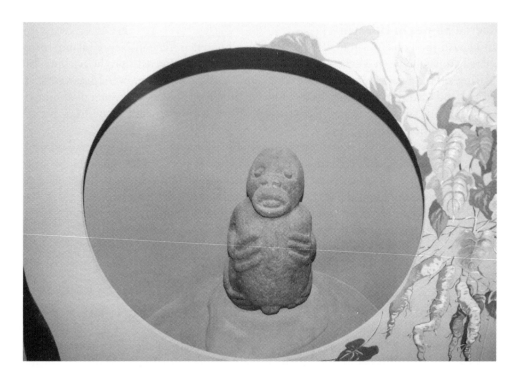

moon. They have been doing that for hundreds of years' permaculture farmer Joe Polaisher wrote in a Community Employment Group newsletter, in February 2001.

When a field was to be planted and prior to the special karakia necessary for that, four special wooden 'godsticks' provided by a tohunga (called toko, also whakakok atua and taumata atua) would also be stuck in the ground, one at each corner of the field.

Godsticks were used in many rites. In other parts of the Pacific, such as Tahiti and Rarotonga, god sticks represented a hybrid god Rongo-ma-Tane, combining the god of cultivated plants with Tane, the god of wild forests.

(Elsewhere in Polynesia (such as the Cook Islands) Rongo was often the chief god, either called Rongo, Ro'o, Longo, and, in Hawaii, where his home is said to be the waters, Lono Ono. A secondary appellation in New Zealand – Rongo-marae-roa – means Rongo of the far-spread expanse i.e. the ocean.)

The bones of the ancestors/elders were sometimes brought out and suspended from the godsticks, or placed around their base. Sometimes dried heads were brought out and displayed, to encourage fertility. The tradition of placing human remains to encourage crop fertility has also been seen in parts of India and Egypt.

Trobriand islands garden magic

The Trobriand islanders had similar traditions of garden magic. In one magical spell the magician sits in a sacred grove with two mythical personalities, blessing and anointing with coconut cream, invoking the small yams to grow quick and straight. 'The belly of my garden lifts' one magical affirmation implored. They used a magical wooden wand, symbolic of the magicians office, to strike the garden, to impart fertilising energy.

Miniature 'houses of spirits', and 'stakes of the spirits' or miniature fences associated with ancestral spirits were placed in gardens. Other small sticks acted as signs, warning that a taboo of not gardening was in force, such as when sacred ceremony was scheduled.

Binabina is a generic name for stones of volcanic origin imported from the D'Entrecasteaux archipelago to the Trobriands. These are placed on the yam house floor for magical ceremony, where they are called the 'pressers of the yam house floor'. On special hearthstones the magician deposits the oblation to the ancestral spirits and rites of magic are performed.

Over in South America farmers have traditionally placed large stones in their fields to honour Pachamama, the Earth Goddess.

Stones of significance in New Zealand

Travellers treated a special atua landmark – a tree, log, rock or pond- with great respect in order to avoid disasters. At such places people would perform ritual, make offerings and recite karakia, acknowledging the mana of the spirit within the place.

Cowan cites this typical karakia: 'Arrived at Point-of-Earth,
> arrived at Point-of-Sky,
> arrived in this land, as land.
> The stranger's heart is food for you.'

Sometimes the tipua stone would become a focal point for the spirit of a deceased important person. A man in the sixteenth century, Uenuku-tuwhatu, upon dying was said to have become a tipua stone near the mouth of the Awaroa Stream in the Kawhia Harbour. In this form his mana was so great that it was believed that the stone had the power to make childless couples conceive.

South east of Orakau in King Country, near Wharepuhunga Mountain, is the 'Walking Rock' an 80'/25m high rhyolite monolith that was considered to once be human. If one wished to avoid heavy rain or inconvenience on journeys one pulled a handful of fern or manuka and laid it at its base, saying
> 'Behold thy food,
> feed thou on the heart of the stranger'.

Mokoia island in Lake Rotorua was considered a very enchanted place. This 'Olympus' of the Arawa tribe was an abiding place of ancient gods and a hiding place of stone images. There is a little hillock there below which was kept the sacred stone image of Matua-tonga. Despite its very fertile kumara growing ground, few people lived there- it was so tapu. One who did live there was the greatest of tohungas – Unuaho.

When Bishop Selwyn paddled over for a visit in the late 1840's he was hoping to make a convert. But Unuaho challenged him and his god to perform an amazing feat. He demonstrated to the Bishop how he could make a cabbage tree wither and die with a deadly charm, then send another karakia and bring it back to life again. The Bishop gave up and went home.

Hatupatu was a legendary ancestor who once found sanctuary in the hollow of a peculiar rhyolite rock, that was somewhat armchair shaped. It was located at the foot of Ngatuka Hill, on the left of the old road from Rotorua to Taupo, just before the Waikato River Bridge at Atiamuri. Here, in the 1920's, travellers were still making offerings of manuka twigs or fern fronds placed into the cavity to avert bad weather, wrote Cowan.

A similar tradition was connected to sacred boiling mud pool Whanga-pipiro, on the ancient track from Rotorua up the Waipa Valley. When passing this pool travellers would drop a branch of manuka or fern frond into it, and if this was not done it was expected that a big rain storm would soon come. As well, they would recite –

>'O spirit of the Earth,
>feed thou on the heart of the stranger'.

UFOs

New Zealand pilot Bruce Cathie's discoveries of energy grids began when, as a pilot, he observed Unidentified Flying Objects following particular aerial pathways. In his books, such as 'Harmonic 33', he has identified some hot spots for UFO activity. These include the island volcano Rangitoto (near Auckland), Nelson, Wellington and Blenheim.

In Northland, at South Head, north of Helensville, there has been much UFO activity observed, I was told by Julie, a friend who used to live there. The biggest lake at the northern tip (Lake Ototoa) has a light shining up out of it at night and Julie once saw a UFO coming down from above and going into the lake. The locals know all about the light, she told me, and sometimes international visitors come to look for UFOs there too.

Another big centre for UFO activity in New Zealand is north east of Warkworth at the Dome Valley, Northland, she told me.

My Trip to Maunganui Bluff

Earth mystery researcher and author Martin Doutre is of the belief that the pre-fleet Maori were erecting standing stones, stone circles and astronomical marker points back in antiquity, although his conclusions aren't all shared by his contemporaries. His theory that Celtic peoples with great astronomical knowledge came here long ago has been thought by many to be quite ridiculous.

In his book 'Ancient Celtic New Zealand', which has the image of a stone circle computer simulated onto a landscape on the cover, Doutre describes discoveries at Maunganui Bluff coloured with a wild imagination. Trying to re-create stone circles from rock piles, he has taken measurements from rock to rock and recorded them with exactitude. But then he superimposes ancient sacred geometric forms (the Temple of Jerusalem and the like) over drawings of the scattered rocks – with very little correlation between them. 'Sites were destroyed and rocks moved' he gives as defence. Nevertheless any correlation is purely speculative.

I went to Northland to check it out for myself in November 2002. The Bluff is an outstanding headland, that plunges its vertical rock face down to the beach on the west coast, next to the little holiday village of Maunganui. The volcanic feature (the only one around for a long way, in hilly country) is an obvious siting point for other nearby land-scape features as well as those a great distance away.

At Aranga I headed south down the Aranga Coast Rd to Maunganui Bluff Beach until I reached the cluster of beach huts (called batches here) and was able to admire the great cliff close up. A signpost said I could walk up to the summit in an hour and a half, but I didn't attempt to.

Above me, by dowsing, I could detect four ley lines going in various directions from the top of the Bluff's summit. They seemed to possibly correspond with the four major alignments postulated by Doutre and said to be based on ancient Maori knowledge.

Not knowing where to look, I decided to give up on sighting anything like astronomical markers. So I drove back onto the main road, but fortunately instinct told me to stop at a high section of road and get out to check if anything could be seen from a distance. Staring out over the Bluff, marvelling at its massive jagged shape and dowsing a big landscape deva present on its summit provided some interesting past time.

It was then that I saw a pyramidical shape on the mountain side, all cloaked in grass. The Bluff's natural shapes were rounded, but this had acute angles and gave me the immediate impression that it was man made. Casting my eyes over the Bluff again I saw other sharp angled shapes, all distinctly different from the natural rounded lines of the Bluff. I had surely found what Doutre was on about. And indeed, flicking through the book, there was a photo of the distant Bluff, probably taken from a similar viewing point, with these same features marked out. Bingo!

Astronomical markers are one thing. But as yet I have seen no evidence or references to an ancient megalithic culture having existed in New Zealand. And I've heard that it was the British Israelite Association that funded the no doubt expensive publication of Doutre's large book. It does seem odd that Jewish people might be pushing a Polynesian-Aryan theory ... But mysteries within the Earth Mysteries field never cease!

References:
Nigel Prickett & David Bateman, 'Maori Origins – From Asia to Aotearoa', Auckland War Memorial Museum, 2001, NZ.
Barry Brailsford, 'Song of Waitaha', Wharariki Publishing, C/o McBrearty Associates, PO Box 35-036, Shirley, Christchurch, NZ.
Barry Brailsford, 'The Tattooed Land', 1981 (updated edition) Stoneprint Press, NZ.
Barry Brailsford, 'The Song of the Stone', 1995, Stoneprint Press, NZ.
Michael King, 'The Moriori – a people rediscovered', Viking, NZ, 1989.
James Cowan, 'Maori Folk Tales of the Port Hills', 1923, Whitcombe & Tombs, NZ.
James Cowan, 'The Maoris Yesterday & Today', Whitcombe and Tombs, NZ, 1930
Elsdon Best, 'The Maori' Vol 1, Whitcombe and Tombs, 1923, NZ.
Elsdon Best, 'Maori Culture', Dominion Museum Bulletin, 1925.
Elsdon Best, 'Forest Lore of the Maori', Whitcombe and Tombs, 1942
Bruce Cathie, 'Harmonic 33', Reed, NZ, 1968.
T Barron, 'Art and Life in Polynesia', Pall Mall Press, UK, 1972.
Longman Brown, 'Traditions and Superstitions of New Zealand', Brown, Green, Longmans and Roberts, London, 1856.
Bronislaw Malinowski ,'The Language of Magic and Gardening', Allen & Unwin, UK, 1935.
Brian Leigh Molyneux & Piers Vitebsky, 'Sacred Earth, Sacred Stones' Duncan Baird Publishers, 2000, UK.
Robyn Jenkin, 'New Zealand Mysteries', Reed, NZ, 1970.
Scott Cunningham, 'Hawaiian Religion and Magic' Llewellyn, USA 1994.
Martin Doutre, 'Ancient Celtic New Zealand', De Danaan, NZ, 1999.

The Kaimanawa Wall

Purported to be another pre-Maori Earth mystery, the 'Kaimanawa Wall' lies deep in the forests of New Zealand's north island. I visited this geological curiosity in March 2002.

Jungle mystery

Journeying with Billy Arnold, we wended our way through the thick rainforest, down a narrow dirt track in the Kaimanawa Forest Park, south west of Lake Taupo, as the sun sank low. Would we be able to find the mysterious 'wall' before dark?

The hire car navigated yet another narrow bend as golden rays of sunlight illuminated the tree trunks. There it was! Just a few metres off the track – a line of several neatly joined smoothish, squarish stones lined up along the side of a hill, with trees and a metre thick humus layer growing on top.

Upon inspection of the rock strata Billy and I both felt that it was a natural formation of volcanic stone, said to be ignimbrite, with none other like it about that is closer than some 12km away. Ignimbrite is defined as 'rock composed of volcanic fragments welded together, of 66% silica and generally acidic' A sample analysed in Auckland pronounced The Wall to be closely related rhyolite – 'a fine grained or glassy light coloured volcanic rock containing mineral potash feldspar with over 66% silica, also acidic'.

Energies of Place

Dowsing the energies revealed nothing startling. Then I checked out a gap between two of the boulders and discovered a flow of Earth energy shooting out of it. Looking into the gap I watched as a shaft of sunlight shone down another joint on the side of the wall, illuminating through to the back of the gap, and lighting up the smooth surface of adjacent stones in the rows behind. Certainly some amazing symmetry here.

Tuning in to that spot in meditation I sensed that below the surface there was a great deal of devic activity occurring and this was also Billy's impression. When he tuned in near the energy gap Billy clairvoyantly saw a kind of doorway there and also a 'big mob of spirits beyond it inside the hill'. So the Wall appeared to be acting as a portal to other dimensions, as a natural landscape temple.

The whole spot felt quite special, sacred perhaps. But to who? Perhaps simply a nature spirit temple, as Marko Pogacnik refers to such hot spots of devic activity. Often such spots are characterised by special markings or features, says Pogacnik. So this one could be a classic.

I also got the idea, as I meditated around the site, that the sort of attention that this feature has been eliciting may well be attracting the sorts of devas and landscape energies which make a site especially sacred. That is, by wanting a site to be a site, it becomes one.

And so if enough people go there and meditate and attune to the energies of the place, then it might become quite a power centre ....

What Others Say

In an article on Martin Doutre's website I found a range of differing opinions presented, with even the sceptics getting their two-bob's worth in. Doutre himself has dowsed the stones of the Kaimanawa Wall and finds 'none to be magnetically charged with Earth energies'.

In a major article from The Listener (May 4th 1996) Barry Brailsford, a maverick archeologist who believes The Wall to be made by a pre-Maori culture, describes the uncannily smooth faces, without trace of saw or adze marks; and how many of the interstices where the blocks join are knife blade thin.

However Peter Woods, the Department of Conservation geologist sent in to study The Wall, stated that 'natural fractures with near vertical and horizontal joints are common in welded ignimbrites of this type'. He believes that the molten stone was laid down some 300,00 years ago, when Lake Taupo blew out.

The advocates of the temple or pyramid scenario say the wall is oriented to true north. But it turns out to be 5 degrees off true ... Nature also orientates rocks. For instance – all the quartz veins in the old goldfields region where I live are said to run north-south.

A half round stone lying in front of The Wall is described by Brailsford as a 'touchstone' – that is: a greeting stone placed before an ancient stone structure. Rex Gilroy, Australian archeological anomalist, goes further – believing that this stone is from the top of an ancient pyramid structure and that it was covered with ancient writings which he has translated as describing the site as a temple to the sun. I could see no evidence of this myself! And my dowsing revealed nothing special about this 'touchstone'.

An archeological study has yet to be made of The Wall. The Maori appear to know nothing of it and, indeed, talk of pre-Maori cultures existing in this country is most unsettling for them. But local elders slapped a 'wahi tapu' on the site when media broke the story, although previously they had shown no interest in it.

Until a proper study is made, The Wall will continue, no doubt, to arouse wild speculation and controversy. But an archeological study might prove more destructive than useful and I don't think the devas there would approve. Luckily the 'wahi tapu' label will keep that from happening.

And if you go down to the Wall today, in silence and with respect, your meditational attunement might bring more treasures of insight than the scientist's shovels will ever uncover.

References:
Patricia Riddolls, 'New Zealand Geology', NZ Geological Survey, 1987.
Gary Cook, 'The Secret Land', Stoneprint Press, NZ, 2002.
www.pyramids.co.nz (Martin Doutre's website)

Castle Hill

Castle Hill/Kura Tawhiti Conservation Area is about an hour and a half's drive inland from Christchurch in New Zealands South island.

In 'The Secret Land', Gary Cook tells us that Castle Hill, known as the Birthplace of the Gods, was a storehouse for greenstone. In legend the site marks the creation and battle of the gods.

Some 3000 people once lived here – people of the Waitaha nation, the biggest confederation in New Zealand's history, with over 200 tribes, who say they first arrived here in 250AD.

To feed this big population kumara was grown in shallow pits which were covered over with bulrush mats if the weather was inclement. Here the people managed to grow a tropical crop some 1000km south of its most southerly occurrence in Chile.

Behind the old marae (meeting place) is the sacred ridge Te Tai o Rehua, The Place of the Wisdom Keepers, where there were once schools of learning. Of the prominent 'standing stones' up there, one huge one is known as Marotini, the Kumara Lady. The Kiore stone looks somewhat rat-like (the kiore being a domestic animal in Polynesia) and it is said to be a guardian of the pathway to the sacred ridge above.

According to Waitaha lore there were three marae here, that of the water seekers of Rapuwai, the marae of the Waitaha gardeners and the marae of Tu Mata Kokiri, the old ones who came before.

Gary Cook describes this site as one of *'a vast network that has been "powered down"' and closed. The reasons for this are buried within the mists of time, but in most cases they were shut down for the purpose of protection and security. The history of this land is marked by the passage of many who sought to take control of the people and the energies ... In recent times a number of these places have been "reactivated" to ensure that natural balance is regained. Such places are not only of importance to this country but indeed to the whole planet.'*

My introduction to Castle Hill

I visited Castle Hill in March 2003, after attending the Earth Wisdom Summit in nearby Christchurch the day before. In company with Peter Archerand Glenys, our imagination had been fired by English dowser Hamish Miller speaking of the powerful energies he had recently found there.

As we arrived at the entrance, marvelling at the weird arrangements of the curiously shaped limestone karsts, we were lucky that a guide briefly appeared. The touchstone was pointed out to us by a woman who was leaving who had recognised us from the previous day's Summit.

So we paid our respects to the site at the stone that stood just to the right of the entrance gate (the second one, in from the road) and then spent the rest of the day happily roaming around up and down stones and ridges. Feeling no tiredness, as Hamish had noted too, until a setting sun hastened our departure.

The Touchstone at Castle Hill

Dowsing at Castle Hill

Dowsing the site there I found two big ley lines crossing in roughly the centre above the amphitheatre area, at the point where Hamish had dowsed one of his 'star patterns' of energy. (This is where, in winter, excess water pools in a low point.) So we both established that it was a strong energy point, but we found different energetic configurations, because we were looking for patterns familiar to us. Hurray for diversity in dowsing!

I tried a few times to dowse Hamish's star pattern, but could not detect it until I imagined that I was 'in his boots,' while dowsing. Then I was able to pick up the pattern, which he had conveniently marked out in the white sand a few days previously.

I returned to Castle Hill in December 2003 on my own and sat quietly revisiting sites and attuning to their energy. From the energy ley crossing above Hamish's star point I found a column or pillar of energy coming down. In it a fire spirit was dancing and an Earth spirit hovered below, my dowsing revealed. I felt happy feelings, a sense of ancient people dancing and singing and laughing in that amphitheatre, which would have made a great entertainment area no doubt, to the once large community that lived here.

The fire spirit may well have been attracted to the spot because of fire, as a circle of stones near the base of the energy column attested to a fire being made there in recent times. It felt like a 'nature temple', where the devas congregate. Dowsing also told me that there were two major nature spirits in the vicinity.

Distant dowsing the ridge behind the main site I could detect the dragon /Earth energy line found on my first visit, a powerful one some five paces wide. This began up high on the ridge, where a cluster of 'standing stones' – limestone karsts – looked majestic. It curved down, flowed along to the little valley below me and ended at the back of the main site.

Musing on the nature of this dragon line as I stood beside it I heard in my 'mind's ear' the emphatic words 'Lady Dragon!!' which I gave me quite a surprise. Er, sorry, madam.

Indeed, distant dowsing up the ridge again, where the dragon emerged from deep in the Earth, at the point of a mighty limestone karst 'standing stone', I could detect an important landscape deva, of female orientation, of course. Marotini perhaps?

Following the path of the dragon line at the back of Castle Hill I detected that it would be exiting back into the Earth just up ahead, at a downward vortex. As I approached close to this vortex the energy felt very powerful, although not very big. The pendulum was jolting around in a star pattern rotation cum highland fling as I got closer into the vortex. It was quite electrifying!

I knew that the centre of the vortex is usually the home of an Earth elemental who likes to play the role of guardian to the portal (which the ancients might have described as an entrance to the underworld). But this was something special.

I attuned to the intelligence of the site and asked permission to be there. It was starting to feel familiar and I quickly deduced that this was a Pan site...

I merged with the consciousness of this powerful Earth elemental and went into a reverie, my body twitching with our energy exchange. There was a sense that one might better refer to him as Rongo – the Maori god of agriculture.

Rongo was perhaps the most important god of the Waitaha nation. He rules agriculture and also is the god of peace. Rongo was the son of chief gods Ranginui, the sky father and Papatuanuka, the Earth Mother. In the 'Song of the Waitaha', the first book about the spiritual traditions of the Waitaha nation, Barry Brailsford tells us that Rongo took Te Pani as his first wife. Their child was Te Kumara, the Peace Child, the sacred sweet potato.

(Likewise, the central mystery of the Sioux Nation in America's Hako rite was the Holy Marriage of Heaven and Earth and the birth of the Sacred Child – corn, their staple food.)

It felt to me that Rongo and Te Pani/Marotini are still present at Castle Hill, powerful forces happy for a little recognition by human visitors. And any sincere seeker may find them there.

References:

Gary Cook, 'The Secret Land– Journeys into the Mystery', Stoneprint Press, NZ, 2002.
Gary Cook, 'The Sacred Land' 'In Touch' magazine no 61, Oct/Nov, 2000.
'Song of Waitaha', Barry Brailsford, 2003 edition, Wharariki Publishing, c/o McBrearty Associates, PO Box 35-036 Shirley, Christchurch, New Zealand.

Once there were Rivers

In the times of the pioneering Polynesian explorer Tamatea, a sacred fire, sent by the great high priest Uenuku, was brought to the south island of New Zealand from a volcano in the homelands. It came on the Arai-te-Urel waka /canoe, together with 200 men and women and all kinds of food plants.

After its epic voyage across the Pacific Ocean the Arai-te-Urel nearly capsized at Hawkes Bay and it finally overturned at Matakaea Point, near Oamaru. Here it still lies, says Maori legend, for the great double waka was turned into stone.

The entire crew of the Araiteuru dispersed and were likewise transformed into hills, mountains and pillars of stone. Her cargo was swept ashore at Moeraki, south of the Waitaki river mouth, where eel pots, gourds and kumara were turned into the curious spherical and ovoid boulders seen on the beach there today.

But the sacred fire was saved and a contingent of chiefs brought it up the Waitaki River and placed it in the Earth somewhere up-river. Here a seam of lignite burned 'until about 45 years ago' says James Cowan in 1923.

Wherever that mythological site might be could well be destroyed if Meridian Energy's proposal goes through. This New Zealand government owned business wants to create a 60 km long stretch of canal parallel to the river on the south side of the valley. This would be siphoning off 77% of the river's water for hydro-electricity generation at six power stations along its length.

What would be lost if the project succeeds?
The Waitaki is a partly wild untamed river on the east coast of the South Island between Dunedin and Christchurch. One of the last wild rivers, it is New Zealands largest 'braided river', which are rare in the world. It's many strands fan out into a wide gravelly delta, swelling when snows melt each spring and shrinking in the heat of late summer. It drains a significant part of the Southern Alps including the Mount Cook region.

Although the upper Waitaki has been modified by hydro-electricity schemes, the lower Waitaki flows in extensive braids for 70 kilometres to the coast. It provides important habitat for endangered bird, fish and plant species and offers outstanding recreational fishing.

'On the east coast of the South Island most if not all of the rivers have been seriously abstracted in the last few years due to changing land use. This has lead to conflict in many communities between competing water users and the flow on effect of that water use. In North Otago we have been spared that problem because of the volume of water available in the Waitaki River' says the Waitaki River Users Liaison Group Inc. website.

'Project Aqua will substantially alter that situation and has the potential to create long term conflict in our community.' The New Zealand Green Party says that Meridian will divert 280 cubic metres per second, which is approximately 73% of average mean flow of water in the Waitaki River. This they believe is way too high, being based on high flow periods seen only in the last 2 decades.

'Meridian proposes spending $1000 million on this scheme. For that money you could put solar water heating in every home in NZ and you would have met all our electricity needs for the next 10 years without stuffing up any rivers and reducing everyone's power bill.'

What of the geomancy of place?

'To most of us a river is something to use, but we don't revere it as Maori do. To them it represents their ancestors and has its own wairua or spirit', said Sir Douglas Graham of Ngai Tahu(the local Maori tribe) cultural heritage.

The Waitaki is a Ngai Tahu taonga /treasure, a river of deep significance to the tribe, in 'historical, spiritual, cultural, and historical terms' – as acknowledged in the Ngai Tahu Treaty Settlement Act, just as Mount Cook is a sacred mountain to them, writes journalist Dave Witherow (Otago Daily Times, 21/12/2003).

'For Maori, the land and the sea is more than a property: it is an identity', according to Ngai Tahu's Mark Solomon. Pouakai, the giant native eagle of the Southern Alps, is said to be the guardian of the river.

'Numerous other places are said to be precious, in the hills, by the lakes, by the sea, and in consequence Ngai Tahu have been given many of these, including the Greenstone and Caples valleys, as theirs to exclusively cherish,' says Witherow.

'Ngai Tahu, so far, have had almost nothing to say on the fate of the Waitaki, their special river. Do they oppose its destruction? Why are they not at the head of the queue, leading the charge, determined, more than anyone else, that the "tears of Aoraki" will not be wiped forever from the landscape?'

In his article Witherow talks about the very non-traditional attitude that local Maori leader Sir Tipene O'Regan has exhibited on this issue.

'Sir Tipene is scornful of those who petition his tribe to share the defence of the lower Waitaki. The river is a mess, in Sir Tipene's view. But, as a board member of Meridian Energy, he is perfectly placed to do something useful about it.

'Project Aqua is the answer, Sir Tipene thinks, and will be thoroughly beneficial. The river – once most of it has been safely locked away in a concrete canal – will be "environmentally-improved", and "a whole lot of the values that Ngai Tahu puts on the Lower Waitaki will be enhanced". Just leave it to Meridian Energy.'

'It is long past time that Ngai Tahu were judged by their actions – rather than their windy propaganda. They are opportunists, not conservationists, and their record speaks for itself – on the Clutha, in the Greenstone, and now in the Waitaki Valley,' says Witherow.

'Mercenary considerations have always been paramount, and all the fine talk of spiritual things, of identity and sense of place and the overweening cultural role of the living land is just hot air in the face of a fistful of money.

'And Sir Tipene, comfortable in his Meridian chair, might contemplate the same question: what form of wairua will survive beside a concrete canal, six power stations, and the polluted remains of a river?'

Seeing the river

There is no doubt that the damming of a wild river will wreck havoc on the ecology, the spirits of place and many important sacred, mythological and special energy sites in the process.

My opinion as a professional geomancer was sought whilst visiting the area in December 2003. So, for whatever it was worth, I decided to reschedule my itinerary to pass by the Waitaki, when driving north from Invercargill, via Queenstown.

Wild rivers are not easy to get to. The roads on the north and south sides of its valley are far from the riverbanks. I had limited opportunities and time to gain geomantic insights …

High up in the mountains, after turning off highway 8 onto route 83, I was able to pass through the river's high country and glimpse her three big lakes. Lake Benmore, Aviemore and Waitaki have long ago been dammed and there are eight power stations there already.

Energetically these lakes and power stations were pretty awful. At Lake Benmore I discovered, by distant dowsing assessment, a very angry taniwha (pronounced tanifa, an important water spirit) behind the dam wall. I had already been told of the bad energy felt around there. So here it was confirmed that energetically at least – not all was well with the river.

A few kilometres downstream I got to Kurow and the turn-off to the road that runs up the north side of the Waitaki valley. The bridge over the Waitaki seemed to go on forever … At one point I was able to pull over onto an island and do an energetic assessment of the river water.

A couple of weeks later I drove over the Waitaki mouth on the coast, a bit north of Oamaru, to do likewise and collect a water sample.

The spirit of the river

The first time I got close to the river was on the island up river. Energetically inspecting the river's clear, shallow waters – it felt sadly dull and lifeless. I was expecting a wounded taniwha or something hopefully more dramatic to report on, but no …

All that I can say (and this was confirmed by others later who checked out a water sample) is that the very spirit of the water has been hammered in those power stations.

The Austrian 'water wizard' Victor Schauberger spoke of this kind of energetic degradation of water when it is subjected to heat and pressure. And I pondered on what sort of effect this virtually lifeless, spirit-less water has on the lands it might irrigate.

Nevertheless, I don't think this river deserves to be raped and bled dry along most of its length. It is still a sacred being, with sites of significance for a whole range of beings along it. It should not be written off as a consumable chunk of landscape resource!

Somebody once said that the Vietnam War became a 'war against topograghy', with the extreme ecological damage it wrought. For a supposedly peace loving nation, would New Zealand be doing much different if this project goes ahead?

Long live the Waitaki!

Update 1: On the 2 March 2004, Waitaha are to do their own separate deputation to Parliament in Wellington regarding their feelings for the Waitaki River, in the form of song, dance and legend.

Update 2: Due to the wave of widespread opposition across the nation in early 2004 – Project Aqua was finally abandoned.

References:

J. Cowan, 'Maori Folk Tales of the Port Hills', Witcombe & Tombs, NZ, 1923.
The Waitaki River Users Liaison Group, PO Box 32, Oamaru, New Zealand. Website: www.waitaki-river.org.nz. Email waitaki.users@xtra.co.nz
also www.waitakifirst.co.nz
and www.greens.org.nz/campaigns/conservation/project_aqua.htm
Dave Witherow, 'Ngai Tahu taonga, for what it's worth', Otago Daily Times 12/12/ 2003.
Korero Story – Waitaki River ceremony a Waitangi Day drawcard, 5/2/2004, Fairfax New Zealand Limited, 2004.

Maori Words Glossary:

Ahu – mound shrines

Atua – gods

Hapu – sub-tribe

Iwi – tribe

Karakia – sacred prayer or incantation

Kaitiaki – family guardian spirit

Mauri – resting place of the life principle of something, eg mauri of a kumara crop may reside in a special stone. Special talisman stones for fisheries were called mauri-kohatu. Also refers to fertility, potency.

Mana – spiritual power, essence

Pounamu – greenstone

Rongo – god of cultivated plants and peace

Tane – god of the forests

Taniwha – water 'monster', water spirit

Tapu – sacred or forbidden; a person, place, object or a condition

Te Pani – Earth goddess, kumara mother

Tipua – enchanted object

Tohunga – shaman priest

Toko – godsticks

Tuahu – sacred shrines

Wahi tapu – sacred site

Waka – primarily a canoe, but also a piece of land or an island

Hot mud pool, Rotorua, New Zealand

PART THREE
Geobiology and Electro-biology

Are You Under Geopathic Stress?

That the Earth is capable of producing radiations detrimental to health has been long recognised in the world. It was on record in China four thousand years ago when the Emperor Yu issued a decree directing investigation into building sites to prevent geopathogenic sickness (that is – disease caused by Earth's emanations).

The Australian Aborigines also recognise that dangerous energies radiate from within the Earth, designating noxious energy sites as secret-sacred, to be left alone – taboo. They warn that disturbance of these sites may release dangerous forces into the world. At the Green Ant's Dreaming, now the Ranger uranium mine, legend had it that the green ants, if disturbed, would emerge to wreak havoc on the world. The environment of Kakadu National Park is now suffering, while her uranium spreads, like cancer, across the globe.

Earth energies are found to flow in currents that usually vitalise the landscape. But, just as with human body energies, such energies may also become blocked, stagnant or disturbed and dis-ease result. Old (and outdated) terms used by dowsers for these energies include 'black streams', 'noxious rays' and 'black leys'.

Ancient Earth wisdom has lately been scientifically investigated, noxious energies measured and their effects verified. Defining geopathic stress as *'a geomagnetic disturbance which is geographically localised and which disrupts the homeostatic mechanisms of the sensitive patient,'* many European and Soviet scientists now recognise the significance of its effects. As pioneering Swiss researcher Dr Jopp puts it – *'the preventative building site investigation for geopathic irritations constitutes an important measure of prophylactic medicine.'*

In Germany some architecture students are now taught Baubiologie (building biology), which stresses the avoidance of environmental radiations, be they from underground water, electrical systems or grid nodes.

Sensitivity to radiations

Bizarre behaviour ('lunacy'), suicides and dangerous accidents are rife when the moon is full or magnetic storms suddenly warp Earth's magnetic field. Yet, despite copious evidence, the fact that our bodies could register electromagnetic radiations (e-m-r) was not scientifically accepted until quite recently. Dowsers around the world have been taking full advantage of inherent e-m-r perception, developing it into a finely tuned art. Dowsers were probably the first to investigate 'noxious Earth rays'.

Professor Yves Rocard is a French scientist who braved the ridicule of peers to study the mechanics of dowsing. His publication of 'New Light on Magnetic Healing and the Action of the Dowsing Pendulum' in the January '84 issue of La Recherche (equivalent to the Scientific American), however, heralded the light of its acceptance in French scientific circles. Rocard, retired chief of the physics lab of the Ecole Normale, Paris, and author of 'The Dowser's Signal' (1964), tells of magnetically sensitive points in the body, and quotes the discovery of tiny magnetite crystals in our brow ridges and in certain articulations of the vertebrae. These, he argues, are crucial receptors in the dowsing response, concluding that 'we can no longer refuse to recognise in man a magnetic sensitivity.'

Magnetite, also known as lodestone, is iron oxide – a very unusual metal for the fact that it not only possesses a strong lattice geometry in its component crystals, but these are also aligned together to give it a very strong polarity. It has the unique ability to be able to align itself within the Earth's magnetic field when suspended on a string or floated in water – hence its use in compass needles.

Scientists have established that bacteria, honeybees, homing pigeons and fish possess tiny magnetite crystals in their heads which aid them in orientation and timing. According to the research of Michael Fuller, of the geosciences department of the University of California, whales and dolphins also use these receptors for survival. Fuller and geobiologist Joseph Kirschvink compared geomagnetic data with computerised records of 212 whale sightings, concluding that over long distances these cetaceans prefer to travel along magnetic troughs that run for vast distances from north to south along the ocean floor. Strandings are most likely to occur at local magnetic low points.

Living within the background of Earth's magnetic field gives us our sense of direction and timing, and without its influence our bodies' equilibrium becomes disturbed. In manned space flight it must be compensated for with low-level magnetic generators.

According to Prof Zarboj Harvalik, scientific advisor to the American Society of Dowsers, magnetite is also found in the adrenal glands which, together with the posterior pituitary gland (the master controller of the endocrine system) constitute the major sensing organs of e-m-r.

Under magnetic stress the adrenals secrete adrenalin for the 'fight-or-flight' response, an ancient survival mechanism. During magnetically disturbing earthquake and seismic activity farm animals trying to escape attest to the adrenal response in animals. Their bizarre behaviour has been recorded by the Chinese for thousands of years.

Perhaps the premonitions we call 'gut feelings' are really adrenal jitters? Adrenal glands are attached to the kidneys which, in both Indian and Chinese medical philosophy are said to be associated with the emotion fear. According to the Chinese the kidneys are of paramount importance to the body, the 'root of life'. They accomodate several classes of subtle body energies: congenital and ancestral energies, any excess from the meridians, plus jing – responsible for energising every organic process, ruling development, aging and reproduction. It comes as no surprise then that radiation exposure causes both fearfulness and birth deformities.

The dangers of EMR overload are seen in the highly disproportionate statistics for disturbed psychological activity, formation of brain tumours, eye cataracts and birth deformities amongst telephone and power linesmen (as highlighted on 'Four Corners' an Australian ABC TV programme in 1985). Nearly 20 years have elapsed since then, yet still, the dangers of EMR are not yet widely recognised, although manufacturers are now producing low radiation appliances and VDU screen filters etc.

Another conclusive study by Bristol University in the late '90's has explained the statistically high danger of lung cancer downwind from big powerlines. The e-m-r interacts with air pollution, the study found, causing more of it to be absorbed by the lungs.

How sensitive are we?

Some people are more e-m-r sensitive than others and may experience disturbing head symptoms prior to volcano or earthquake activity. Hours or days before the event and sometimes at a great distance from its location, hypersensitives begin reacting to the magnetic disturbance with afflictions of annoying or painful symptoms such as buzzing or ringing in the head, migraines, nausea and interrupted menstrual cycles.

Reactions to electromagnetic radiation may be observed in the subtle anatomy of the body, says author David Tansley. By dowsing the energy vortex 'chakras' he has determined a defence mechanism. Major chakras situated along the spine (along with magnetite crystals) receive and process energies from within and without, and control their circulation around the etheric body. They are closely associated with the glandular system and govern specific body zones. Tansley originally observed, in a patient who had just received x-rays, that chakra activity had shut down in order to block out the radiation.

If such defence mechanisms fail to protect us, then our organs are the next to suffer, which over the long term, can have fatal results. Organs attempt to block out radiation by putting up a barrier of greater electrical resistance. The blocking mechanism causes much wear and tear. Eventually it may allow disease to take hold in the weakest of the organs. Cancer is a well known consequence.

Just how sensitive people are to e-m-r is the subject of much contention. Officially dangerous threshold levels in the Soviet Union are a thousand or more times lower than in the United States. To measure degrees of sensitivity, Prof. Harvalik devised an experiment in which dowsers attempted to detect an electric current being passed through the ground. He found that 90% of those tested could distinguish an electrical field equivalent to the variation of 1/100,000th of the Earth's field strength. One German master dowser Wilhelm de Boer, was able to detect amplitudes down to one microampere, one billionth of a gauss! This was far more sensitive than the finest magnetometer. However the American dowsers, like other researchers, would have to demonstrate their findings on geopathic zones using measurements derived from machines rather than mere divining rods in order to capture the attention of the scientific establishment.

Landmark research

As long ago as 1916 Nikolai Kaschkar, a professor of engineering at the Institute of Tomsk published research results arrived at by water divining. He was the first to announce that a change in the ionisation (electrical conductivity) of the air above subterranean water veins most clearly characterised its presence. In the 1930's French researchers began experimenting with electroscopes to count atmospheric ions and were able to verify Kaschkar's findings.

French engineer Pierre Cody was able to demonstrate the link between ionising radiation and cancer. His exhaustive studies were conducted over a seven year period before Word War II with the support of eminent physicist Louis le Prince-Ringuet. Using an Elster and Geitel electrometer he registered ion counts in cellars directly underlying 7000 'cancer beds', and compared them with locations two metres away. Beneath the cancer beds the ion count was found to be ten times higher than at nearby locations. The conclusion he drew was that the radiations rose vertically upwards without diffusion. Cody found it a simple job to ameliorate the situation by shifting the beds out of the narrow geopathic zones.

The most famous study of cancer beds was conducted by Baron Gustav von Pohl in southern Germany in the early 1930's. Under the official observation of the authorities of the tiny town of Vilsiburg he was able to locate, by dowsing, 100% of all homes where people had previously died of cancer. In many cases he was able to pinpoint the seat of the cancer by finding which part of the bed the radiations were affecting.

Controlled experiments involving mice and irritation zones were begun in 1932 at the Institute of Biology and Anatomy of the Technische Hosch-schule in Munich, and also in the Swiss canton of Aarau. It was found that mice inoculated with certain disease-producing bacteria fell ill faster when their cages were located above subterranean water than elsewhere. The irradiated mice also exhibited disturbed behaviour, were constantly agitated, gnawing at each other's tails and their cages, and ate all their offspring, which is very unusual.

In Switzerland Dr Jenny carried out similar experiments for 12 years, using 24,000 mice. Mice placed over irradiation zones were observed to flee the area, whilst those forced to live within them had lower birth rates and higher infant mortality. When tar products were painted on their necks a larger proportion of tumours resulted in the mice kept in geopathic zones than in the control mice kept on neutral ground.

In 1955 the German geophysicist Dr V Fritsch implored the scientific world to recognise the problem of 'Earth rays' and the need for combined research studies by teams of dowsers, medical doctors, geologists and physicists, as espoused in his book 'The Problem of Geopathic Phenomena from the Viewpoint of Geophysics'. In that same year Dr Joseph Wust and others undertook the first study with geiger counters to prove the involvement of gamma rays with the cancer beds of Pleutersbach, Germany.

In 1967 Dr Fritsch's hopes were realised. The Research Group for Geobiology from Heidelberg University's Institute of Hygiene teamed up with a group from the Electrophysical Institute of the Technical University of Munich to conduct a multi-disciplinary study. They focussed on a house in the Neckar Valley where three generations of people sleeping in the same bed had all died of stomach cancer. Using a sophisticated 'electronic dowser', an American scintillometer that analyses the sharp increase in radiations found above water veins, they found the especially noxious intersection of a geological fracture and a subterranean water vein where the bed was located. By placing wooden cages of mice over the 'cancer zone' and on neutral ground they were able to observe the characteristic exposure symptoms.

A supersensitive scintillometer developed by Jacob Stangle in the 1970's confirmed its accuracy with the successful drilling of hundreds of wells. Stangle also retraced von Pohl's footsteps, to duplicate the Baron's forty year old findings. In Switzerland a German hydrologist was able to confirm Kopp's dowsing surveys of Zurzach and Eglisau, which led to the opening of fine thermal and mineral water supplies.

'The principal objection against the existence of pathogenic stimulation zones, namely the ability to objectify them, is no longer valid', Stangle could thus state.

In Moscow, at the Institute of Industrial Hygiene and Occupational Disease of the Medical Academy of the (ex)USSR, geophysical and geomedical studies have confirmed the presence and dangers of microwave emissions above underground streams. Russian researches have found that exposure to microwaves may cause dysfunction of the parasympathetic and vegetative systems, and especially affect the heart and vascular systems. The Russians also claim the discovery of a centimetre wavelength radiation above water veins.

The majority of current research into geopathic stress is still largely undertaken in Germany, Austria and the ex-USSR. One canton in Switzerland is so concerned that it offers a public grant towards the cost of a dowser's site survey prior to undertaking new building work and planning permission may not be granted until this has been done.

Well known German oncologist Dr Hans Nieper finds at least 92% of cancer and 75% of MS patients he examines to have spent long periods in geopathic zones. It has been estimated that 10% of German doctors work with dowsers, calling them in to investigate severe cases.

Austrian teacher Kathe Bachler conducted major research with a grant from the Pedagogical Institute of Salzburg. She spent several years interviewing 11,000 people in 14 different countries and testing 3000 flats and houses. All 500 cases of malignant and benign tumours that she tested turned out to be affected by geopathic stress. Other sure signs of exposure were incidences of arthritis, rheumatism, multiple sclerosis and asthma. She also found the learning ability of children to adversely affected, with 95% of children having learning difficulties either sleeping or seated at school in geopathic zones. Highly commended for her research, her book 'Discoveries of a Dowser' became a bestseller.

In the late 1980's the German government commissioned a 400,000 DM study for a team of scientists at the University of Munich to scientifically prove the existence of Earth rays. The study was directed by two physics professors and two 'biolocational' specialists (dowsers). In the Russian sphere scientists studying the problem have been connected with the Interdepartmental Commission on the Biolocational Effect, at its centres in Moscow, Leningrad, the Ukraine, Ural Mountains and Tomsk.

In the early 1990's the Austrian Working Party for Research into Geopathic Stress Sites, consisting of doctors, chemists, physicists and biologists under the direction of Dr Otto Bergmann, a professor at the University of Vienna, conducted exhaustive research over a two year period. 985 people were placed in a geopathic zone for ten minutes and give thorough medical examinations before and after. In most cases harmful effects were registered.

Geological Faults

Faults, fractures, fissures or cavities in the ground may generate some serious georadiation, gamma rays in particular. Constant exposure to low level gamma radiation can induce or aggravate cancer.

Geological faults often indicate oil deposits, and prospectors armed with ionisation chambers actively seek them out, often from a moving car or aeroplane. In the process they have noted that gamma ray emissions are five times stronger at night than in the day. All the worse if you are sleeping over them.

Peculiar phenomena are also associated with active seismic and geological fault areas. These include anomalous meteorology such as curious meteor falls, fire balls, freakish thunderstorms and glowing lights. The fact that geological strata under stress can produce luminous effects has been substantiated by Dr Brian Brady (US Bureau of Mines, Colorado) who applied great pressure to granite in laboratory experiments to produce this effect.

Sightings of 'Earth lights' and Unidentified Flying Objects are also found to cluster around fault areas. Paul Deveraux has explored the subject in his book 'Earth Lights', suggesting that these phenomena are possibly aerial emissions of Earth spirit ('planetary ectoplasm') interacting with the observer. Carl Jung originally theorised that UFOs were the product of our subconscious. Geoffrey Hodson, writing about his clairvoyant observations of nature spirits, has observed their ability to pluck images from his subconscious and rearrange astral matter to create any desired visual affect. These theories help explain why ancient peoples had visions of 'chariots of fire', while modern sightings are usually of more high-tech forms.

Underground Water

Perhaps the most widely recognised source of geopathic stress, however, comes from streams or veins of subterranean water. This concept of underground streams is anathema to conventional hydrology, which clings to the theory that this water is just seepage trapped in layers called aquifers. However this cannot account for the occurrence of water on mountain tops! Also, it has been reported that in the United States an estimated 92% of all rain water either evaporates immediately or runs off unused to the sea (Newsweek 23/2/1981). So how does water end up underground?

Dowsers have been consistently locating underground water supplies since time immemorial, in places where hydrologists would never dream of looking. One theory the dowsers work with is that of the sea/magma cycle, where water, under tremendous pressure in the ocean depths, is forced through fissures and cracks in the ocean bed until it contacts the heat of magma. Then, as superheated steam, it rises up through the Earth to cool and form water 'domes' and veins.

Another theory is that of 'primary water' being constantly manufactured deep within the Earth. Due to the daily stressing of the Earth's crust by its rotation around the sun, the resulting build up of electrostatic charge could allow the interchange of electrons and protons, with the subsequent bonding of oxygen and hydrogen producing water.

However it gets there, water is found running through the Earth, and where it does the above-ground biology may be disrupted. (Likewise above underground cavities and geological faults, and in relation to Earth energy grid patterns.) Certain life forms benefit from the georadiations, others, like humans, are malaffected. (While short term exposure to water energy at sacred sites may have a stimulating effect on people.)

German hydraulics engineer E. Endros has theorised that georadiations from underground streams are caused by the alteration of nuclear processes that come from deep within the Earth. Neutron radiation rises upward and, upon contact with the electromagnetic field created by the friction of water moving along subterranean veins, is modified and concentrated. Radiation then emerges from the Earth as a lethal mixture of neutron and infrared radiation, and is partly converted into microwaves.

Degrees of noxiousness are related to the type of soil strata through which the water passes. Kidney problems, for instance, may be associated with exposure to the energy of radioactive or contaminated water.

In 1978 an Italian dowser in Piacenza used a forked stick to divine an underground stream running under a dairy that produced defective cheese. His experimentation with cheese making (bacterial) cultures showed greatly enhanced microbe activity in cultures placed above the stream, thus solving the mystery.

The fact that georadiations are favoured by bacteria has a practical application, with dowsers finding sites for enhanced compost making.

Georadiation and health

The effects of geopathic stress on people span a wide range of symptoms and diseases, having developed as a result of the breakdown of the body's functions and immune system. Consequences of exposure include cancer, heart problems, rheumatism, arthritis and inflammations; disorders of stomach, kidney, bladder, liver and gall bladder; AIDS, ME, thrombosis, meningitis, diabetes, leukaemia, sterility, tuberculosis, lumbago, exterior ulcers, goitre, headaches and migraines; eye/ear/teeth/adrenal problems; sinusitis, fibrositis, general stress syndromes, nervous/emotional/mental disturbances; constant tiredness and physical discomfort. These, and other illnesses, also prove resistant to treatment, unless the georadiation is avoided or neutralised.

Children, Kathe Bachler found, are especially sensitive, reacting rapidly with such tell-tale symptoms in bed at night as insomnia, restlessness, lying in odd positions, having nightmares and sweating with fear, sleep walking and bed-wetting. They may wake up feeling tired or depressed, having no appetite, or even vomiting. Waves of cot deaths have also been associated with fluctuations in Earth's magnetic field at geopathic stress points.

It has been found that brain signals controlling body functions are disrupted by georadiations. On a cellular level, bioelectrical processes are warped and polarities altered. Such processes as the assimilation of nutrients from the intestines and cell repair mechanisms depend on the proper polarisation of electrical charges on either side of cell membranes. The immune and lymphatic systems are also weakened by geopathic stress, allowing bacteria, vruses and cancer to take hold. Thus georadiations foster the conditions for disease to take hold.

It may take six weeks to shake off the effects of geopathic stress, although there will often be immediate benefit experienced by victims removed from Earth rays. Deep seated chronic conditions take time to heal and sometimes long term effects may need unlocking with homoeopathic and flower remedy treatments.

Dowsing highway 'black spots'

Another insidious effect involves georadiations with car accidents. Often cars inexplicably veer off seemingly safe straight roads and crash, especially at points where water veins cross beneath roads. It is thought that these motorists have had temporary blackouts when adrenalin flooded their system in response to driving over geopathic stress zones.

Dowsers have been able to prevent further accidents at some notorious locations by installing microwave-generating neutralisation devices on roadsides. In one case the accident rate was cut from 32 over two years to just one accident in one year after installation of a device.

The German motoring organisation ADAC has carried out investigations into this problem and lately the Austrian Highways Department has been employing 'Druids' to perform 'Earth acupuncture' at black spots, since initial trials proved successful. ('Druid focuses Earth's energy on road toll', August 11, 2003 The Telegraph, London.)

Animal and plant effects

Geopathic zones are actively avoided or sought out by certain animals, a fact that was appreciated in ancient times for building site selection. Sheep and oxen have been traditionally herded onto land and their behaviour observed – they always avoid geopathic zones. Traditional wisdom has long maintained that people should never sleep where a dog will not lie down. Other such 'ray avoiders' of the animal kingdom include horses, pigs, mice, fish, goats, chickens, swallows and storks. Latvian studies have confirmed the particular susceptibility of cows. Of 35,000 cows with mastitis studied, 78% had been kept for long periods in stalls affected by Earth rays.

In the plant kingdom geopathic stress can cause unavoidable problems. Susceptible plants may become more lightening prone, get 'cancerous' growths, do not produce fruit, become sick, stunted or die. They may lean awkwardly to avoid the rays or start to branch low to the ground when a straight trunk is the norm. Ray avoiding plants include roses, sunflowers, lilies, begonia, azalea, cacti, privet, currants, cucumber, celery, onion and maize. Trees include apple, pear, cherry, walnut, linden, sycamore, birch, plane, conifer, fir and pine.

On the other hand 'ray seekers' will thrive in a geopathic zone. Such animals include many of the insect family: ants, wasps, bees, beetles, termites. Ant nests are often located over the junction of underground streams, while bees will produce more honey in a hive affected by Earth rays. Bacteria and viruses, cats, owls and snakes all appreciate Earth rays.

Ray seeking plants include asparagus, mushrooms, mistletoe, medicinal herbs, fungus, ferns, nettles and foxgloves. Trees include oak, elm, willow, sequoia, redwood, larch, plum, cherry, nectarine, elderberry, apple and apricot. Plants naturally growing in swampy conditions have adapted to thrive above underground water veins.

Detection methods

Is there a place where you get an uncomfortable 'gut feeling', or feel an inexplicable chill in the air? Does the cat like to curl up and sleep just there, but the dog avoid it like the plague? Chances of a geopathic zone will be high.

Dowsers, using their finely-tuned inherent sensitivity plus some read-out device, provide the easiest detection method. Some are so sensitive that they may detect these zones at a great distance, without ever visiting the site. Distant dowsers often use a pendulum to dowse over a large scale map or a sketch plan, and then might follow up their findings with a field check using divining rods or forked stick.

Technological instruments may also be used for detection, and distorted TV and VHF radio reception can occur in geopathic zone.

Our environment provides many other clues for geopathic stress detection. In buildings these might be cracked walls and crumbling plaster, rising damp and corrosion, damaged and colour-changed varnish, swollen timber, loosening wallpaper and veneer, mould, dust explosions and disturbed fermentation processes.

Biophysical test methods for people are becoming more common. An ohm meter, electro-geo-bioscope or georhythmogram can be used to measure skin and body resistance at acupuncture points and to detect organs at greatest risk. Vega testing and electro-acupuncture is gaining popularity. Simple kinesiology, or muscle testing, is sometimes used as an alternative to dowsing for the effects of geopathic stress.

What to do about it?

Once pinpointed, a geopathic zone can often be avoided by moving furniture or changing room usage. However sometimes geopathic stress is compounded by its inter-action with modern building materials and artificial electromagnetic fields. For instance reinforced concrete floors and steel house frames spread georadiations all over a building, which is then unavoidable. If the zone can't be avoided, neutralisation tech-niques used by dowsers often prove successful. Avoidance is always preferable.

With an estimated 8% of all people affected by geopathic stress, it is high time that this was recognised by the medical establishment as a factor underlying many health problems, as well as the reason why many therapies fail.

Of course, were they to act upon such knowledge there might be a dive in the profits of the powerful multi-national drug manufacturers, who would no doubt prefer to ridicule the subject, stifle research and debate. The so-called health industry feeds on sickness, after all, not wellbeing. We live in a sick society!

References:

J.A. Kopp, 'The Present Status of Scientific Research on Soil Radiations', Transactions 1 of the Swiss Society of Science 1970.

'Body, Land and Spirit', ed. Janice Reid 1982.

A. Scott Morley, 'Geopathic Stress: The Reason Why Therapies Fail?', Journal of Alter-native Medicine (UK) May 1985.

Christopher Bird, 'Divining', Raven Books, USA, 1979.

H. Rex, 'Earth Radiations and Cancer Houses', Health & Healing, Oct. Dec. 1983.

Brain/Mind Bulletin, California 1985.

D. Tansley, 'Radionics and the Subtle Anatomy of Man', 1972.

J.A. Kopp, 'Weather, Ground, Man', 1970.

J.A. Kopp, 'Healthier Living by Elimination of Soil Influences Detrimental to Health'. Das Wohnen – official journal of the Swiss Society for Housing. No 11, 1970.

J.A. Kopp, 'The Present Status of Scientific Research on Soil Radiations' Transactions of the Swiss Society of Science 1970.

J.R. McCreary, 'Water Theory', American Dowser Quarterly; Nov. '81.

J.A. Kopp, 'Soil Radiation Research in Soviet Russia' Weather, Ground, Man, 1970.

J.A. Kopp, 'Children's Illnesses Due to Soil Influences' Prophylaxe. Sept 1970.

ADAC Motorwelt, (German motoring magazine) Sept. 1984. 'Who Solves the Puzzle of the B2 Highway?'

J.A. Kopp, 'On the Physics of Geopathogenic Phenomena' Journal for Practical Medicine. Heidelberg. May 1971.

Dr A Schneider, Baubiologie correspondence course, Institute for Baubiologie and Ecology, Neubeuern, Germany.

R Gordon, 'Are You Sleeping in a Safe Place?', Dulwich Health Society, 1988.

Note: This was originally published as an article in Wellbeing magazine (Australia) in 1987.

Dangers of Electro-Stress

Exposure to electro-magnetic radiation – from power lines, home appliances, phones etc – has been linked with many health and behaviour disorders. E-m-r has been described as a carcinogen – not surprising considering the epidemic nature of cancer, leukemia and brain tumours in modern societies. It has also been associated with nervous system dysfunction, genetic damage, allergies … The list goes on.

There are various mechanisms whereby radiation affects us and it can happen at levels much lower than effects associated with thermal heating. For instance researchers in Bristol UK have found that downwind from big powerlines in polluted areas, there is greatly increased incidence of lung cancer. Particles of air pollution become more easily absorbed by the lungs under the influence of the radiation fields, they found.

It is known that e-m-r can disrupt the flow of calcium through our body's cell walls, affecting many important cellular functions, such as cell division. Also – constant low level, long term exposure to electro-(or geopathic) stress can deplete adrenaline, leading to falling energy levels and immune system dysfunction.

Microwave ovens
Microwave radiation has been linked with tumours and genetic damage. Even a microwave oven in good condition is dangerous because of the strong, low frequency magnetic fields present during operation. People who do a lot of cooking with them are at risk. Such ovens need regular checking for microwave leakage too.

Food cooked in microwave ovens has significantly higher amounts of cancer causing free radicals than conventionally cooked food.

Mobile phones
There's lots of talk these days about the dangers of mobile phones to our health. Mobiles operate with microwave radiation and even when you aren't making a call a mobile will sporadically transmit signals as it keeps in contact with the nearest base station/phone tower. Fifty percent of the radiation emitted from a mobile phone is absorbed into our bodies. If it's kept in a pocket or on a belt that is where the irradiation will occur.

High use of mobiles has been linked with brain tumours, cancers, DNA and cell effects. But the increasing incidences have not yet been 'proven' to be as a result of phone use. And as these problems take time to develop, things may only get worse before anything is done about it on a government level.

Landline phones
Then there's the ordinary landline phone. Ever felt drained, tense or stressed by a long telephone call, even a pleasant one? Well there's a good reason – phones have powerful magnets in the ear piece and microphones. This also happens when listening to music through earpieces; the dose is weaker, but people are usually exposed for longer periods.

And as for cordless phones, in terms of radiation, they are just about as bad as mobile phones.

Fluorescent lights
Fluorescent lights have an irritating flicker and produce magnetic fields and many unhealthy positive ions. Too much exposure and they have an unpleasant, de-energising effect on people and can cause eye strain and headaches. US scientist Dr John Ott is of the firm opinion that this type of lighting is involved with childrens' bad behaviour in classrooms. The new generation of compact fluoros are no better.

Computer hazards
Computers produce high levels of e-m-r at many frequencies and also a wide range of radio frequency and strong electrostatic fields. Fields are strongest at the back and sides of computers. Pregnant women should be particularly careful to limit exposure, as they have a doubled chance of miscarriage if working on them for over 20 hours per week. Older computers create far worse electro-smog, which includes a small proportion of microwaves, soft x-rays and gamma rays as well.

Some solutions
One can buy computer screen filters which reduce electrical field levels, cut down glare, and reduce stress, fatigue and sore eyes. Liquid crystal display screens have lesser radiation levels, without the powerfully spiked fields from the transformers in your average cathode ray tube monitors, but they are still not hazard free.

Magnetic fields, while difficult to screen out, drop off quickly across space. So try and keep all computer equipment at least at arm's length away from your body (apart from the keyboard) wherever possible. Modern computers have reduced radiation fields compared with old models. Exposure to VDU radiation in the workplace is limited by EU legislation to 5 hours daily.

To avoid electro-stress while you sleep – turn off electric blankets before you get into bed and unplug them to reduce any potential for stray current to flow through them. If you must use them! They are certainly not recommended to be used by anyone who has cancer.

Also make sure that sleeping areas are far from electrical meter boxes and that your head is not on the other side of the wall from any computer or appliance in an adjacent room. The radiation goes straight through the wall into your head.

There are protective devices on the market (see the end pages of this book), some for personal use and some that can be simply plugged into the electrical system.

Now that you know the dangers, you might start to think about getting rid of unnecessary electrical gadgets, or at least cluster them into specific areas only, and limit your use of them. To be safe – I think we all need to use the precautionary principle.

Reference
David Cowan & Rodney Girdlestone, 'Safe as Houses? – Ill Health & Electro-stress in the Home' by, Gateway Books, UK.
Lyn McLean, 'Watts the Buzz?' Scribe Publications, Australia, 2002.

Radiation emitting satellites

On September 23 1998 Motorola's fleet of 66 iridium satellites began full-time oper-
ation. Also on Setember 23 a large number of electrically sensitive people across the
world developed severe ES (electro-sensitivity) symptoms – including headaches,
dizziness, nausea, insomnia, nosebleeds, heart palpitations, asthma attacks, ringing
in the ears, etc – that lasted until mid October.

During the same period a 4-5% increase occurred in the US national death rate
and thousands of homing pigeons lost their way.

Source: EMRAA News Dec. '98.

Landmark Anti-EMR Legal Case

An application by Energex to erect a power sub-station in a residential area of
Brisbane was rejected on health risk grounds recently and this was upheld by the
Planning and Environment Court. To the knowledge of EMRAA this is the first time
in Australian legal history that the health risks of such a planning decision were the
main focus.

In council's presentation to the court it argued that, given the body of available
scientific evidence, it could not guarantee that approving the application would not
result in a health risk to the community. The court recognised the statistical associa-
tion between EMR fields and health problems such as childhood leukemia and the
fact that the WHO has classified magnetic fields as 'possible carcinogens'. It recognised
statistical evidence that long term exposure of children to fields above 4 milligaus may
be a hazard.

An agreement was reached whereby Energex agreed to construct underground
feeder lines to and from the substation and that it would undertake to ensure expo-
sures at defined locations would not exceed 4mG and to verify these measurements on
request.

Meanwhile, a company in London has developed a website that provides a quick
reference for international exposure limits at all frequencies. It's found at
www.mcluk.org

Source: EMR News June 2002

New Radio Frequency Radiation Standard for Australia

This standard will apply to mobile phones, phone antennas, industrial RF welders,
induction heaters and furnaces. It mainly protects people from the effects of radiation
due to heating. The new standard, which is based on WHO recommendations, allows
people to be exposed to higher radiation levels of up to 4 times as much as has been
allowable, in some cases.

The EMRAA fear health problems may arise at levels of radiation insufficient to
cause heating. There has been a strong link between mobile phone use and brain
tumours in many international studies.

The standard includes a weak precautionary statement in it, which recommends that minimalisation of RF radiation in the workplace should be achieved only if it is 'readily achieved at a reasonable expense,' while it doesn't support doing this to any degree beyond the levels of the standard.

'Why do we need a new standard when technology is operating perfectly well at the present lower levels?" asks EMR News. It seems that 'Last year the committee that devised the standards was told that the higher radiation levels were needed to accommodate new mobile phone technology. That begs the important question: has the standards-setting process been driven by scientific research or by economic motives?'

A copy of the standard and supporting documents is available from ARPANSA's website at www.arpansa.gov.au/rf_standard.htm

Source: EMR News June 2002.

Watts the Buzz?

by Lyn McLean

Book Review

If you have any interest in the impact of environmental energies I highly recommend this book. It was penned by someone deeply involved in the subject, who has fielded many calls from the public complaining about problems associated with e-m-r.

While there haven't been anything like enough safety studies done, you will learn in the book, the public are being used as guinea pigs and it may be ages before there's adequate legislation to protect us from the evils of e-m-r, it seems. In the meantime we must exercise caution.

Australia has one of one of the highest rates per capita globally of mobile phone usage, Lyn, secretary of the Electro-Magnetic Radiation Association of Australia, tells us. Worldwide use of such phones has doubled between the end of '99 and the end of 2001.

Forests of mobile phone antennas have been springing up. These base station towers, as free standing monopoles, are not always obvious. They have often been visually and insidiously blended into our environment, hidden in Church crosses and trees. So-called 'low impact' towers are allowed to be put anywhere. They may be small and inconspicuous, but they still pollute the atmosphere with radiation.

Fortunately you can find out just where mobile phone tower locations are, by logging onto the government website at www.aca.gov.au/database/radcomm/index.htm.

When exposed to mobile phone base station e-m-r, according to anecdotal evidence, plus European statistics and scientific experiments with animals, there is an increased likelihood of having Alzheimers disease, sleeping problems, nervousness, joint pain, blood changes, leaukemia, slower childhood development, etc. Property values also plummet when a phone tower goes in nearby.

Electricians have double the national suicide rate. Policemen using radar guns have very high rates of testicular cancer. Sweden has an epidemic of people who are allergic to electricity and has had to build a special hospital for them... The list goes on.

Studies show that there can be an increased risk of cancer when people are exposed to magnetic fields of a 'mere' one or two milligaus. Yet the Australian government allows exposures of up to 1000mg as okay!

Reports from the vicinity of radar stations have told of clusters of cancer, decreased tree growth, animal reproductive changes, increased epileptic fits, and deteriorating cow health and lactation (– until the cow is removed from the area).

And what about if you want to have a baby? If you are exposed to e-m-r you have an increased likelihood of reproductive problems and miscarriage, while infants exposed to e-m-r will be more prone to SIDS (because of the low levels of brain hormone melatonin after irradiation).

How to reduce radiation damage?

Apart from avoidance of e-m-r, or shielding measures (such as nickel plated curtains!), you can eat a diet rich in antioxidants says Lyn. Vitamin C and E, selenium, herb chaparral and enzyme superoxide dismutase are ideal, she says.

Lyn McLean, 'Watts the Buzz?' Scribe Publications, Australia, 2002.
Electromagnetic Radiation Association of Australia, email – emraa@acay.com.au

'Technology's Curse'

Book Review

From deteriorating nuclear powered naval fleets, leaking power station reactors, residue from nuclear testing and warfare and low level medical waste etc piling up, radioactive contamination is becoming rife world wide.

'During the last five years since the tragic accident at Chernobyl, there has been mounting evidence of much more severe effects of very small doses of radiation from nuclear fission products in the environment than had been predicted on the basis of the study of the survivors of Hiroshima and Nagasak … As much as 100 miles from Chernobyl there has been a very large increase in thyroid disease, leukemia and infectious diseases far above those expected, in some cases ten-fold. Infant and foetal mortality rates as far away as Germany and the US increased significantly in the immediate period following the arrival of the fallout from Chernobyl, just as they did during the period of atmospheric testing, and so has total mortality at all ages from all causes combined' writes Dr Ernest Sternglass, Department of Radiology, University of Pittsburgh School of Medicine on the observance of the fifth anniversary of the Chernobyl disaster (26/4/86), in the Introduction.

This was one of the first books to address the problem of how to survive in radioactive environments. The author, a nutritionist in New York city, presents years of research into the protective effects of eating certain foods and diet supplements.

First Shannon explains the effects to our bodies of low level radiation and radioactivity. Cancerous conditions become prevalent, free radicals proliferate and infants are particularly susceptible. Repeated exposure weakens our immune defences, while increasing the mutation rate of micro-organisms – thus ushering in epidemics of new diseases which prove fatal.

The good news is that 'the body can reduce absorption of radioactive elements by building up reserves of the essential minerals in which it is low' Shannon writes. For example – 'Inhaled radioactive gas or ingested radio active iodine salts will be rapidly excreted if the thyroid is in no need of iodine' (pg 71).

As well – adquate calcium will inhibit strontium 90 uptake, iron inhibits plutonium 238, 239; potassium inhibits cesium 137; sulfur inhibits sulfur 35; vitamin B12 inhibits cobalt 60 and zinc inhibits zinc 65 absorption. A good wholesome diet not high in refined foods can go a long way in ensuring our survival in this nuclear age.

Foods which have protective qualities include whole grains, beans, fresh vegetables, miso, tofu, tempeh, sea vegetables, seeds, nuts, ginger, horseradish, scallions and garlic.

'Technology's Curse, Diet for the Atomic Age' by Sara Shannon, Instant Improvement Inc, USA, (1987), revised edition 1994.

Are You Sleeping in a Safe Place?

by Bill Jackson

Bill Jackson spent over 20 years surveying homes for dangerous levels of e-m-r in the Newcastle area of central coast New South Wales. His copper Ankhs for neutralising geopathic stress were a bit of a trademark. Bill, a long time member of the NSW Dowsers Society, passed away in December 2002, having suffered a brain tumour. Wanting to share his discoveries, he kindly sent me a leaflet about his work prior to his death.

People must be made aware of e-m-r hazards and how they can affect some people. Every day the demand and use of 240V AC 50cps electrical power is increasing at an alarming rate and, in proportion, the levels of radiation are increasing in the home.

A problem in the electrical system of a neighbours home even two doors away can cause reflected current to flow through the water pipes of your home. The manufacturer of the appliances that create or add to the levels of the home are reluctant to discuss these matters, perhaps for good reason. The electrical authorities shelter under the umbrella of excessive levels they claim are safe. They are not.

When I started to survey homes for e-m-r in 1980 I encountered the problem of heavy radiation from water pipes in most homes. All through the home there were high readings around the floor areas and up to chair and bed level. There were no earth spikes or electrodes on a lot of the buildings.

Lifting the earth wire off the pipe eliminated the e-m-r problems. When an A/C volt meter was used to measure between the earth wire only a small amount of voltage was registered, ie 8-10 volts. The only conclusion I could reach was that the main radiation being transmitted from the water pipe had to be of a radio frequency nature, and by the 'sounds' coming out of the test equipment being used, was mainly in the low frequency area of 50-400Hz, plus harmonics.

The noise went completely in one house and the lady who was in the home at the time asked 'what did you do then, the house feels so different.' I had isolated the water pipes adjacent to the water meter.

I went to the Water Board and the Electrical Supply Authority and discussed the matter with them. They suggested that the insertion of one meter of poly pipe into the supply line from the meter to the house be carried out by a licensed plumber i.e. remove copper and replace with polypipe.

The Electrical Authority suggested that a licensed electrician should check the earthing situation and if necessary replace with 6mm earth wire from the meter box to an earth spike and continue on to a bonding on the closest cold water pipe.

I have adopted this procedure on all surveys since and recommended that all homes be isolated as a prudent measure to reduce or eliminate e-m-r in the home and other buildings.

I have seen some amazing changes in peoples sleep pattern, general health and quality of life when we have been able to advise what steps to take to reduce the e-m-r pollution in the home, especially the bedrooms. 'Prudent avoidance' and 'Prevention is better than cure' should be the phrases we adopt.

There are ways people can take action to overcome the problems, reduce or even eliminate them. We need people trained to be able to advise those who wish to make their living and sleeping spaces as safe as possible before their health is affected. Training of such people would not be difficult. Commonsense, the use of simple test equipment and a dedication to the work is all that is required.

PART FOUR
Meet the Devas

*'In an evolving universe it seems to me that the idea of creative intelligences through-
out the cosmos makes a lot more sense than a collection of abstract mathematical
equations beyond space and time, with creativity itself just a matter of chance.'*

Rupert Sheldrake

Discovering the Devic Dimensions

*Deva is ancient Persian term meaning 'shining ones'. It is used as a catch-all term for all the
spirits of nature, ranging from tiny little elemental beings through to gigantic angels. These
beings are a personification of the consciousness aspect of landscape.*

*The devas have been largely neglected by modern society, but I think this is starting to
change. Once dismissed as childhood fantasy or the domain of the pagan fringe, I think the
elemental world has been successfully re-asserting its presence. The fairies (although they have
never left) are apparently making a comeback!*

Devic dimensions historically

Globally speaking, every human culture has, at some time, identified and revered the
spirits of place in its territory, with what is referred to as an animist or pagan belief
system. While ideas about the fairy folk have been kept alive for millenia in the form of
fairy tales, in many parts a denial of their existence has evolved in the wake of witch
hunts and intolerant religious supremacy.

We have been led to only appreciate the psychological interpretations of the fairy
stories and the ability to see the other-wordly beings in children has been largely
suppressed by our rational education systems. Still, in places like Ireland and Iceland
(colonised by Irish people), a great respect for fairies and the like has been largely maintained to this day.

Knowledge of the fairy kingdoms was widespread in Europe up until medieval
times. Some four hundred years ago Paracelsus attempted to categorise the nature spirit
kingdom, according to the medieval view on such things. Nymphs was the term he used
for water spirits, sylphs were the air elementals, pygmies – the earth and salamanders –
spirits of fire. These beings were also ranked into hierarchical levels. Paracelsus's 'About
Nymphs, Sylphs, Pygmies and Salamanders and Other Spirits', published in 1589, 48
years after his death, was the first western book on the subject.

According to this hierarchical model the spirits on the lowest rungs are small and
only concerned with simple, specific tasks, such as opening flowers or nurturing seed
growth. On the next higher level the devas are larger, more complex and sophisticated.
They may be in charge of watching over the biological processes of an individual tree (a
faun, or dryad) or preside over a corner of the garden or forest or pond. On the highest
level they have god like qualities, with a wide area of influence, as we find with the great
god Pan and Earth goddesses.

Robert Kirk's book 'The Secret Commonwealth of Elves, Fauns and Faeries'
published in 1691, described the means by which 'second sight' could be developed to
see the fairy beings.

European traditions

The British Isles have long been steeped in the mystery of the fairy kingdoms, with many species recognised in ancient folk tradition. From household spirits (known as cobbalds in Germany) to Pan himself. There are brownies, gnomes, elves, fauns, mannikins, leprecauns, pixies, fairies, undines, will o' the wisps, and more!

Household guardian spirits seem to have a very long half-life. In the work of household energy clearing, things may get complicated for geomancers when guardian spirits are encountered. 'Old houses often have a guardian spirit, maybe from an animal that was purposely buried under the door or threshold, such as a dog or cat' dowsers Roy and Ann Proctor told us, at the International Dowsing Congress held in Manchester, UK, in 2003.

As for the fairies, in British tradition their's were all the commons and wild land until it was 'cleft by spade' – i.e. by iron implements. It was a definite no-no for humans to till the sacred fairy places or to remove stone or timber from them. Illness or enchantment or death might result, the legends told.

But the lore also stated that fairies might be appeased with offerings, such as part of an ensuing crop. They were also credited with good influence in agriculture and in Savoy they are said to have taught people how to farm. Beneficial brownies and the like were regarded as guardians in many parts, as in ancient Ireland. In the western isles of Scotland they were considered an important part of crop dynamics.

Across Europe so-called cup and ring marks are found carved into ancient megalithic structures, on standing stones, Irish bulaun stones, and on other flat rocks. Archeologists say that the meaning and purpose of these markings is unknown. However in some quiet corners of the British Isles, at least, local folklore and legend provides an explanation.

Where the cup marks sit on horizontal stones in parts of Scotland, and particularly in Argyll and the Isles, the people once collected rainwater for its healing and fertilising properties. And often these cup marks were also places to leave offerings to the local nature spirits. Milk was once poured into them, for the continued goodwill of the 'wee folk', and especially as an assurance of good milk supply.

An old legend of Stonehenge was that the water that washed off the bluestone sarsens has healing properties.

The Irish today talk of fairy forts and fairy rings in their landscapes. These were once the circular ringed farm sites of the Bronze age people whose spirits, they say, still reside there.

Spirits of nature and people also traditionally act as guardian spirits for the sacred sites of old.

Wells are traditionally associated with dragon legends and apparitions of female spirits all across Europe, both being common manifestations of water spirits. There are many recorded sightings of unexplained (spirit?) lights at holy wells.

In Asia

Veneration of nature spirits is the basis of spiritual traditions all over Asia.

For instance, in Burma many people have a nat shrine, for revering the nature spirits, especially the guardian nat of the home. A friendly house nat keeps away evil spirits and brings good luck, they believe. Nat-sayas are consulted to communicate directly with the nats and 3 day annual nat festivals are held to honour the 37 special nats associated with particular localities all over Burma.

In Japan Shintoism evolved out of ancient animistic indigenous folk wisdom. Shinto traditions include pilgrimage to sacred mountains, with their associated spirits. Some Buddhist traditions borrow heavily from Shintoism, as well as the animist Bon Po religion of Tibet.

To this day mountain pilgrimage is still very popular in Japan, the classic peak to visit being Mt Fuji. Fuji was first revered as the abode of a fire god, later it became the home of a Shinto goddess.

Back to the Twentieth Century

In Europe it was not until the dawn of the twentieth century that serious attention was once more re-focussed onto the elemental kingdoms. This was largely coming from the exponents of Theosophy, notably – by Leadbeater and Hodson, as well as Anthroposophy – through the works of Rudolph Steiner.

Later, in the 1960's, at the beginning of the new-age community at Findhorn, extraordinary plant growth in an inhospitable corner of Scotland was a result of conscious co-operation with the nature spirit beings. And at the end of the twentieth century we have seen a rash of bold new authors of the subject – such as William Bloom and, my favourite, Marko Pogacnik.

Rudolph Steiner

Clairvoyant Steiner also made a systematic study of the devic kingdoms and came up with a similar scenario to Paracelsus. In his ten lectures on the subject, given at Helsingfors in 1912, he described a sevenfold hierarchy, starting with nature spirits at the three lower levels and rising up through the angelic kingdoms.

Pogacnik tends to agree with this model, but suggests we talk of levels of unfoldment as a result of evolutionary progress, rather than a static hierarchy of beings. Thus, for example, a highly evolved landscape deva can evolve into an angel.

Bishop Leadbeater's observations

The Theosophist Bishop Charles Leadbeater was another exceptional clairvoyant in the early part of the 20th century who wrote of his observations of the devic kingdoms. His travels in many parts of the world revealed the great variety of species of nature spirits – from the colourful devas of tropical climates to the more staid coloured denizens of temperate zones.

He wrote of blissed-out water spirits playing in waterfalls, fire spirits dancing in flames, and elves dancing in circles. He observed them 'feeding', by drawing in environmental energies and casting out the used up energy.

He saw great angelic beings, such as at Adams Peak in Sri Lanka, a place deemed sacred by all major religions on the island. A place of ancient pilgrimage, he visited the tutelary genius of the mountain, called locally Saman Deviyo, which he said was one of the great order of angels and one of the 'Great White Brotherhood'.

The sacred Irish hill Slieve-na-mon was seen by Leadbeater to have great green angels at its peak, the giants of local tradition. Tradition has it there that if you spent a night on the summit you will awaken either mad or a poet.

Devas mostly avoid cities and humanity, he noted. When they are disturbed they rarely show malice, he said, but rather play tricks and deceive people. They can project images into our minds as part of this deception, in order to mesmerise. But sometimes they will develop fondness for people, usually children, and befriend them.

Geoffrey Hodson's insights

Another Theosophist, clairvoyant researcher and author was Geoffrey Hodson. Hodson described tiny plant devas as etheric points of light hovering around plants, doing specific jobs and feeling keen affection for their plants. He wrote of how they absorb energy from the atmosphere, then enter into the plant under their care, where they discharge the energy. When a new growth phase was imminent and new devas were called for, Hodson clairaudiently heard the calls which attracted the little devas to come and do their work.

Nature spirits stimulate the life of plants and animals, or they may be 'engaged in the raying out of strong influences over certain spots, magnetic centres, which have been put under their charge', he informed us. Highly evolved devas become the guardians of gardens, forests, regions, or whole nations even, and may act as angel messengers. When recognition is given them there is an amazing response forthcoming from them, he said.

The highly evolved devas he saw as having streams of force radiating out from a pulsing light centre, giving them what appears as 'wings' and a vaguely human appearance. In more evolved forms a head and eyes are distinguishable, while a centre of light blazes out at the 'heart' and 'head' positions.

Hodson observed small water spirits absorbing the magnetic forces at a waterfall, 'working' with the energy there. First absorbing as much energy as they could, then assimilating its force, and finally ecstatically releasing it out in a dazzling flash. At other times these water spirits were observed to rest in deep pools.

Hodson observed little elf spirits playing around the root level of trees, sometimes forming a ring by joining hands around a tree or group of trees and dancing.

Hodson spent many of his later years in New Zealand where he was able to observe many powerful devic beings of fire and water, the 'devarajas' of volcanoes, mountains and ocean. Many were described in his book 'Clairvoyant Investigations'. He particularly liked to holiday around Whangarei in Northland and attune to the great 'deverajas' of the extinct volcanoes around the harbour there. He died in Auckland at the age of 96 in 1983.

The Findhorn Devas and Pan

Early in the 1960's a group of four people pioneered a community near the village of Findhorn in northern Scotland. With little money to go around, the growing of food crops was important, but the soil was just coastal sand dunes devoid of much life and the location cold and windy. Dorothy Maclean started to receive gardening advice from the plant deva kingdom and gardener Peter Caddy was thus able to produce astonishing vegetable crops (like a famous 42 pound cabbage!) and magnificent flowers.

Later Dorothy made a connection with the overlighting deva of the area, which she called a landscape angel. An associate of theirs – Richard Ogilvie Crombie, a retired scientist known as Roc – then introduced them to the highly evolved being known as Pan, which makes an interesting story in itself.

Roc had one day found himself in his local park in Edinburgh going into an altered state of consciousness, of high lucid awareness, wherein a faun (an earth spirit) approached him and began to communicate. It looked like a small boy, but had shaggy legs, cloven hooves and a pair of horns on its head. Kurmos, as he called himself, was involved with caring for the trees in the park.

Next Roc encountered a larger faun like spirit which walked beside him one day down the city streets, radiating a great deal of power. He soon realised that this was Pan, deemed by the ancient Greeks to be the great god of nature and later made out to be the Devil. This Pan quizzed him about his reactions to it and when he declared that he felt no fear, it felt most reassured. It spoke of the demonisation of Pan by the Christian Church and the sadness this caused it.

Later another Pan he met on the holy island of Iona told him that 'I and my subjects are willing to come to the aide of mankind in spite of the way he has treated us and abused nature, if he affirms belief in us and asks for our help.' Roc concluded that 'it became apparent that what was happening was a sort of reconciliation between the Nature Kingdom and man.'

Dragons and Rainbow Serpents

The dragon – as a spirit of Earth or water – is recognised from Europe to China. Christianity symbolically subjugated the dragon with it's dragon killing saint legends, but didn't start this practice. Previously in Greek myth Apollo's move to the Temple of Delphi heralded a new era there, when the mercurial Earth spirit was speared. The Earth acupuncture thus performed, an omphalos stone was erected on the spot. Thus the dragon powers of Earth were placed under Apollo's control.

Similar stories abound – Horus killed Aphophis the waters/a serpent, Krishna killed Anatha and Chaldean Belmarduk overcame Tiamat, the waters. James Churchward, in his book 'The Sacred Symbols of Mu', suggests that these legends might represent a co-mingling of the powers of sun and water, rather than an actual battle.

A southern hemisphere equivalent to the dragon is the Rainbow Serpent. Across the vast continent of Australia many varieties of devic beings were recognised by Aboriginal people. One of the most well known and highly revered is the Rainbow Serpent. This being, along with other Dreaming Heroes, was said to have originally created the landscape features when they rested on mythic journeys across the unformed Australian continent, at the dawn of the Dreamtime, the other-dimensional reality.

A dynamic ever-present force and Giver of the Law, fundamental to their spirituality, the Rainbow Serpent represents a primal source of creative inspiration. It could also be classified as the highest level of water deva, associated with water courses and thunderstorms. These serpent spirits come in many sizes and levels of importance, and may be regarded as either male, female or androgenous. They often occur in male/female pairs.

Across Australia they have a snake like form, although in the Tiwi Islands they are said to have the form of huge lizard beings, with horns and long projecting jaws. In other cultures we find similar beings – Quetzalcoatl, the feathered serpent of Central America, is also a controller of rain; horned serpent beings guard the water holes in the lands of the Kalahari bushmen of Africa; and the Naga snake spirits of India and Asia also have great importance. In the Vodun traditions of West Africa Dan is the rainbow serpent, a god of wealth. Feathered or bearded serpents are found in Pueblo Indian lore in Arizona and New Mexico, as well as Egypt. The taniwha of New Zealand tradition is another important saurian water spirit, which will be examined later in this book.

Protecting the Wahgul

A Commonwealth government decision in 1989 to protect a sacred site, where Perth's old Swan Brewery stands, greatly upset the Western Australian state government, who had planned to turn it into a cultural centre. The Federal decision followed a six month protest sit-in by Aboriginals who demanded protection for the very significant site – said to be the home of the Wahgul (Rainbow Serpent). The State Government challenged the ruling.

Earth Spirit Quarterly, August 1989.

Wandjinas and hybrids

Wandjina spirits of Western Australia's Kimberley region rock art are also associated with water, fertility and the Rainbow Serpent. Other water spirits co-exist with the Rainbow Serpent in it's rock hole, sacred site homes. For example the yawk yawk spirit of western Arnhem Land. This is a female water spirit said to live underwater in its youth. Later in life it flies away to live in trees (where it 'makes the tree rotten'). Thus it seems that some nature spirits are capable of metamorphosis from one element to another.

The yawk yawk is usually depicted with a fish tail and long hair like algae. Sometimes it walks around on dry land and a 'clever men' (shaman) might take one as a wife. Yawk yawks have husbands and kids and some have ritual importance to the Aborigines.

While much Aboriginal interaction with landscape devas is now ceased in Australia, that doesn't mean that the Earth spirits and Dreaming heroes aren't still out there!

And where the local Aboriginal people were wiped out their presence may still remain, for their spirits stay in the land, as is their cultural expectation, dwelling alongside the nature spirits and sometimes with the two blended together.

References:
Rupert Sheldrake and Matthew Fox, 'The Physics of Angels – Exploring the Realm Where Science and Spirit Meet', Harper Collins, UK, 1996.
Marko Pogacnik, 'Nature Spirits and Elemental Beings' Findhorn Press, UK, 1997.
Serena Roney-Dougal, 'The Faery Faith', Green Magic, UK, 2003.
Paul Deveraux, 'The Sacred Place', Cassell & Co., UK, 2000.
C.W. Leadbeater, 'The Hidden Side of Things', Adyar, first published 1913.
Geoffrey Hodson, 'Fairies at Work and Play' Quest, USA, 1982.
Geoffrey Hodson, 'Clairvoyant Investigations' Quest, USA, 1984.
Paul Hawken, 'The Magic of Findhorn' Fontana/Collins USA 1975.
James Churchward, 'The Sacred Symbols of Mu', Washburn, USA, 1933.

Deva Dowsing

Deva is an ancient Persian term meaning 'shining one' and it has come to be used as a catch-all term for the spirits of place, the intelligence aspect of nature. Revered throughout the ages around the world, these 'elemental beings' are often described by clairvoyants as spheres of shining light of varying hues. Disappointed that I could not see them, a couple of years ago I discovered that I could dowse for the presence of the devas.

Although my deva dowsing has been a fairly unusual activity, I am one 'who walks on the ones that go before me'. TC Lethbridge has provided inspiration to me and I use his rates method for my pendulum work, as a tuning-in ritual to find the different energetic layers in the landscape.

My partner, Billy Arnold, is able to tune his inner eye to clairvoyantly see the devas, which is a source of much fascination to him. Billy spent time with Aboriginal people in central Australia in order to help with his understandings of the great spirit beings he is able to perceive in the landscapes there. So the devas became a perceivable reality to me through him.

In developing my understandings I read many books on dowsing with a fervour in the early 1980's, then chose to put them away and wait for my own experiences and responses to happen in their own way and time.

Lethbridge's Legacy

I was pleased to recently re-read some Lethbridge and find that he, like myself, spoke of dowsing the fields of energy that correspond with the legendary devas, as well as ghosts and ghoulish apparitions.

'It can be shown' Lethbridge wrote *'both by dowsing and with scientific instruments, that fields of static electricity exist in just the same kinds of places as those in which we have experienced our ghosts and ghouls. They have been studied by scientists. They consist of what is known as ionised particles ... and these static fields are to be found in connection with such things as waterfalls, springs and streams, or woods and trees, deserts and moorlands and mountains. This is extremely important to anyone who is interested in mythology. For these are just the places which were peopled with nymphs and spirits by peoples of the ancient world and by simple modern ones.'*

To qualify the bland term 'field of force', Lethbridge decided to call the water spirit energies he found – 'naiad-fields', 'dryad-fields' he found around trees, 'nereid-fields' were in the ocean, 'oread-fields' in stones, mountains and deserts, and 'psyche-field' was his term for dowsable human fields.

These various fields had the capacity, he found, to draw images and thoughtforms from out of our minds and to project them so they might be perceived of as real, but static, images of ghostly character.

Water is particularly associated with this, and one only has to think of the static apparitions of the Virgin/Mother Mary, who is often associated with holy wells and springs. (The energy fields of some water samples from holy wells that have been checked by myself and students were dowsed as filling up entire rooms.)

In a similar vein one might compare the Polynesian concept of 'mana', which is the spiritual power base of people that can also be conveyed by water and rocks, the typical elements found at sacred sites the world over.

Emotions flow easily between our psyche-fields and the devic fields, and strong emotional experiences of people can be fixed into the field memory of a place, to be triggered and re-lived by people acting upon its power later, Lethbridge found.

I don't know of anyone else who has investigated these phenomena in the manner of Lethbridge and myself. I choose to call what I am finding the 'devic fields' and I believe these to be probably the same phenomena as Lethbridge's various psyche-fields and Rupert Sheldrake's morphogenetic fields.

Layers of spirits in the land

In my work as a professional geomancer ghosts and ghoulish places are a part of the territory and Australia is home to many a murder and massacre site. It can definitely be unhealthy to hang around these types of places. Often they may be permanently cursed.

The Earth's various energy fields become tainted and ghoulish at such places, Lethbridge said. The idea of humans being the creator of ghouls makes good sense to me, as humans are the greatest perpetrators of evil there is. So for angry spirits of place in legend – we might re-assess this as demonised devic fields, which are probably the result of some human destruction.

But there are also peaceful Aboriginal spirits that reside in our landscapes here, especially around the high energy centres. Just as the Tautha de Danaan people of ancient Ireland are said to live in the sacred places in that land. Many non-Aboriginal people perceive their presence too. Aboriginal people say that their spirits come from out of the land, from waterholes in particular, and must go back into it at death. So self-proclaimed new-age 'Earth healers' need to be aware of cultural paradigms and not assume that they are always encountering lost souls that must be rounded up and sent away.

Communicating with the devas

It seems that the nature spirits/devic fields are composed of much the same type of energetic fabric that we are. In Theosophical terminology, they are of an energetic frequency on the mental and astral planes, and this can explain why thoughts and feelings can be transferred between them and us, as Lethbridge noted. In other words they are conscious fields of energy, or energy fields which carry consciousness and feeling.

Our ability to perceive of and communicate with the devas is merely determined by whether we have a serious intention to do so. For instance a student called Esther told me that although she was occasionally clairvoyant, she had never bothered to look out for nature spirits. When she got home after a deva dowsing workshop with me, she asked to be able to see the deva of Mount Wellington, which overlooks the city of Hobart, Tasmania. At this thought she was instantly able to see it. She then asked to see overlighting garden deva – and she could! ...

Our communications with the devic kingdom are best kept simple and more on a feeling level. If we are to warn a tree about some imminent pruning work, for instance, we might put ourselves into a meditative state then bring up an image of the intended actions into our mind's eye. After that we could send a wave of sympathy and say that we're very sorry that it has to be done. And send it some love before and after the act. I'm sure that the tree will be forgiving ...

With practise, attunement to the devic fields/presences, becomes easier and easier. Nowadays they seem to jump out of the landscape at me, whenever I do energetic landscape assessments. But it may take a big paradigm shift for clients to accept them as real.

What do they look like?

As for the visual perceptions that people have of the devas – there certainly is a great variety of images described, which may cause confusion. Lethbridge said that these energies could extract and use images and thoughtforms from our minds in order to clothe themselves in a recognisable form (as Jung suggested of UFO behaviour, and in common with modern crop circle behaviour). Different people, different imagery.

In Europe devas might look like little people in medieval outfits. In Australasia and Asia they may take the traditional forms of rainbow serpents, wanjinas or lizards, while the Chinese might see dragons. The simple spherical balls of light of varying colours that many people I've spoken to can see seem to be their typically undifferentiated, or 'naked' form. My Billy might describe them as a sphere with a big eye, or organ of perception, that looks at him looking at it (usually with some surprise on it's part).

Blanche Merz speaks of similar forms: 'The general impression was of a large eye observing me, questioning me', as does Marko Pogacnik, author of the best books on devas that I know of. At a famous German pilgrimage shrine of the Black Virgin he found himself within the 'universal eye of the Virgin'. It was an 'enormous eye full of grace … its gaze composed of purest water and filled with a noble kind of compassion,' out of which a crystal clear tear drop formed, as a blessing to him.

Finding fairies by deva dowsing, Clondalkin Round Tower, Dublin, Ireland. A Theosophical Society field trip, September 2003.

I suppose my main feeling about all this is that we need to re-recognise the existence of these beings and their need for undisturbed territory to inhabit, if we are all to live harmoniously. To be nice to the devas we can designate a 'temenos' (a sacred, wild precinct in Greek tradition), where we do not meddle with wild nature, in our back-yards. Even if we don't have a backyard, we can find a space for them in our hearts.

Nowadays when I do a house and property dowse and tune in my pendulum to look for any significant energies, important landscape devas might come up. Just about insisting on making contact, it appears to me that they want to be recognised, to be part of the whole equation.

I perceive them as an energy field which can move around its territory, change size at will and tends to be focussed on particular high energy spots, where it 'feeds' from, or works with the energy. And I'm beginning to catch visual glimpses now too.

Devas have their own sacred sites. Pogacnik speaks of 'nature temples' where clusters of devas are found, their influence reaching to a wide area.

Deva types & gender

When I find a deva I might ask, by dowsing, if it is predominantly of either the earth, fire, water or air element, and whether it has a predominantly yin or yang energy. In other words, certain qualities can be distinguished in the different 'species' of nature spirits and they can be personified as either male or female.

And, like us, they are often found in pairs. In England Hamish Miller discovered that the 'dragon line' known as the 'Michael line' was matched by the 'Mary line'. Australian Aboriginals would have known to look for it, for their culture has long spoken of the legendary activities of paired male and female rainbow serpents.

Before I met with male water spirits I had read in John Michell's writings that the element of water symbolised the female principle (represented by the number 1080, which in Australia is the name of a nasty environmental poison!). This new-age gender stereotyping is probably just another limiting concept for the poor abused female half of our species. Give me a fiery hot springs goddess any day!

Deva Mischief

Can devas cause problems for people? If the Irish fairy stories are anything to go by – yes, a whole lot of trouble can be the consequence of wrecking their homes, and all kinds of mischief perpetrated. That's right – the fairies are not just cute little sprites eager to grant wishes, they can get ferocious!

As a consequence of recognising them, we ought not to be building our homes over the top of them (where Earth energies are strongest anyway). Having to move them on or neutralise energies is possible, but best avoided I feel. With so many humans already, so we are no doubt seriously depleting the devic population and creating many a ghoul in the process of 'civilization'.

I have had one experience myself that could be regarded as a bit of deva mischief. I had arranged for Geoffrey Campbell, a talented clairvoyant in Melbourne, to take a group of us on a walk around the Botanical Gardens, where he would be sharing insights about the devic realms he perceived there. First I had to get a group together, but not matter how many times I tried and fiddled around with my printer I could not get the flyer about the walk to print out properly. Every single time the title 'Deva Walk' would not print out. Very strange …

The day before the walk I got a frantic call from Geoff to say that he was dreadfully sorry but he was stuck in Hobart and couldn't get back in time to do the walk for us. I should have guessed by then that something like this was on the cards!

Return of the fairies?

In Irish tradition ancient human habitation sites are the homes of the fairy folk. Fortunately this 'superstition' of the Irish has meant that a great many sites have been preserved fairly intact over thousands of years.

In Yorkshire my friend John Billingsley, long-time editor of Northern Earth (the worlds longest running geomancy magazine) tells me that, according to his enquiries, the fairies, like the otters, are returning to the old ex-industrial areas. Old timers in the area have told him that the much disputed Cottingsley fairy photos may have been faked, but yes! – it was a fairy haunt there nevertheless.

So it seems to me that the fairies want to be found again. That the time is ripe, the knowledge is unfolding rapidly and it is all the better for planetary survival and harmony. There is enough awareness out in the world about their significance for this matter to be talked up and for devic sites to enjoy better protection, hopefully, as a consequence.

In Australia, where we still have a few indigenous custodians of the land who recognise the existence of its spirit beings, I think deva dowsing provides a much-needed bridge of understanding between our ancient and modern cultures, and helps, perhaps, bolster the healthy survival of the Dreamtime/other reality continuum.

References:

TC Lethbridge, 'The Essential Lethbridge' (5 books combined, edited by Tom Graves and Janet Hoult), Routledge & Kegan Paul, UK, 1980.
Blanche Merz, 'Points of Cosmic Energy', Daniel, UK, 1983.
Marko Pogacnik, 'Nature Spirits & Elemental Beings – Working with the Intelligence in Nature', Findhorn Press, UK, 1995.
Marko Pogacnik, 'The Daughter of Gaia – Rebirth of the Divine Feminine', Findhorn Press, 2001.
John Michell, 'City of Revelation', Abacus, UK, 1972.

'Irish Fairy Tales'

by Jeremiah Curtin

Book Review

Fairies are not all sweetness and good wishes

Before my year 2000 research trip to Ireland I attempted to do some homework and discover where I could find interesting, ancient sites to visit. I was amazed to learn of the vast numbers of such sites. For instance, so called ring forts (ancient farm and village enclosures with circular embankments) number in the 30–50,000 mark! There are more ancient sites in Ireland than anywhere in Europe, I found out.

'It's because the Irish are so superstitious', my ex-patriate-Irish dowser friend Sandy Griffin explained. He illustrated his contention with the following story. As a young man working in rural Ireland in the 1940's, he was once walking down a country lane with another young man who was a firewood supplier. They were passing by an old ring fort, covered by an ancient, gnarled hawthorn grove. The trees were mostly dead, with very thick trunks. 'Would you know of any good firewood around here?' Sandy asked. 'Ah, no. Nothing around here' was the reply. 'But what about all that?' he asked, pointing to the ring fort. 'Oh, that ! You can't cut those down, they're the homes of the fairies. They dance around them at night!' he said, intoning that wasn't that obvious? Sandy thought it quite amusing at the time.

When I arrived in Dublin last April and discussed this with Sandy's cousin's family they were much more to the point. 'It is the fairies which protect the sites!' Not just the belief in them, I noted. Fairies, it turns out, in the Irish view of things, are not always the happy little sprites we have been led to believe. They can also be fierce guardians of their homes. Demolish a Bronze Age barrow mound or ancient tree grove and beware the consequences!

Ireland's ancient belief system, which has survived to this day in many ways, is greatly exemplified in those stories which we have inherited as 'fairy tales'. In fact reading the book of 'Irish Fairy Stories', which were collected about one hundred years ago, one is given fascinating insights into a land where the veils between the spirit world and the physical are often quite thin, particularly on certain days and in certain places. There is a real concern that the fairies will be offended by some environmentally unsound action and steal away your spirit, for enslavement in the fairy kingdoms, or some such punishment.

The last story concerns someone who built an extension to his house on the wrong side, where it interfered with a 'fairy pathway', known to geomancers as a dragon line. Despite being warned not to by someone who was friendly with the fairies, the man went ahead, and consequently suffered dire consequences.

These stories can only serve to reinforce the need to maintain the geomantic pathways in the landscape. And they have been very successful, much like Australian Aboriginal scary bunyip type stories have long kept inquisitive people away from dangerous, sacred or taboo places.

The sad thing is that Ireland is currently hurtling into the future at a terrifying rate, being at its most affluent ever, thanks to a burgeoning information technology and tourism industry. Shiny new cars clog the tiny, stone-walled roads everywhere. In 2004 a new motorway is proposed be built past the sacred precinct of Tara. Nothing is sacred anymore.

Old homes are crumbling and new mansions are springing up everywhere. The nation is frantically trying to forget the centuries of poverty and oppression, by sweeping away the past and killing it with neglect. The modern miracle that Ireland is now is just not sustainable. The newfound sophistication comes at too high a price: the rivers are dying, farmland is disappearing under motorways, and the fairy realms are shrinking. If you want to see the old Ireland – be quick!

In the meantime, find a book such as this one and indulge in tales of other worlds. It conveys some part of the white Australian mindset, given that, around the 1850's one third of our population came from the Emerald Isle. Unfortunately the Irish at the time were largely victims of English repression, so their history and rich cultural traditions have been mostly ignored or maligned in the dominating paradigm of Australia's Anglo-centric bias.

Jeremiah Curtin, 'Irish Fairy Tales', Barnes and Noble Books, New York, 1993 edition.

'Nature Spirits and Elemental Beings'

by Marko Pogacnik

Book Review

Slovenian artist Marko Pogacnik has an international reputation in conceptual and land art. Through his work he has developed the skill of geomancy as a tool for unlocking hidden wisdom of the Earth. He leads workshops throughout the world in Earth Healing and advises communities and businesses in landscape planning.

Coming from Slovenia, Pogacnik lives in a culture immersed in traditions of goblins and fairy queens. In his research he makes contact with these fairy tale entities and taps into their wisdom.

Pogacnik explains why people report see nature spirits in differing forms. *'In my opinion'* he writes, *'it is not right to force the world of dwarfs, nixies (water elementals) and fairies into visible forms related to our physical reality. Human beings have developed a very definite, refined outer physique, but we display to only a tiny extent how our inner thoughts and feelings operate. In contrast, the elementals are free of any predetermined form. They can change their appearance to show what is happening inside themselves, which is very different from our human ways.'*

'Whatever form we perceive them in, it is either a mirror which reflects our stored archetypal memory of how we imagine them to be, or it derives from the language of pictures used by the elementals themselves to draw our attention to a certain message they want to deliver. They are without any definite form unless we project our archetypal or imagined forms on them.'

'One of these imposed makeshift images is the little gnome with his red pointed cap, his long white beard and leather trousers. Lovers of nature superimpose this picture onto the being of earth spirits. In turn, this picture influences clairvoyants, who then claim it as the definite, indubitable truth.'

Pogacnik encourages us to 'find a quiet spot to meditate and converse with these beings so that we may re-establish the ancient connection between humanity and these real and powerful realms of Earth.'

OK! – I'm off to talk to the trees!

'Nature Spirits and Elemental Beings' by Marko Pogacnik, Findhorn Press, UK, 1997

The Green Man

In the last few decades many people have been rediscovering the eco-spirituality of our pagan heritage. They recognise a Mother Earth Goddess and even scientists, such as James Lovelock, talk about Gaia. But the masculine spirit of nature has lain silent and invisible to us until only recently.

Enter the Green Man. Most people would never have heard of him. But some may have noticed curious foliage covered faces looking down at them from house fronts or the ceilings of medieval or neo-gothic churches. Could these faces be harking back to a time when Pan was perceived as the potent, Earthy god of nature?

Who or What is a Green Man?

These foliate faces have become a symbol for our connection to nature, in their celebration of the masculine spirit of nature and our own wildness.

The earliest types of green men were faces made up of leaves, often oak leaves with the odd acorn. Later styles have foliage sprouting from the eyes, ears nose and particularly mouth of the faces. Later still mens' and womens' faces came to be depicted emerging from foliage, flowers and fruit. In churches the faces are traditionally painted gold.

The Green Man in the UK

Images of the Green Man are first seen in the UK in 1340 at Manchester Cathedral. There are many from the medieval period, but no mention of them is made in literature.

But the Green Man is no isolated figure of mere decorative character. It is surely related to the once widespread folk customs of the British Isles (and Europe). Leafy figures representing 'Jack in the Green' the 'wild man', Robin Goodfellow aka Robin Hood and the May King (and Queen) once danced upon village greens everywhere, in celebration of spring and the cycles of fertility and plenty. The old folk heroes cum gods certainly are referred to in old writings, they are the stuff of ripping yarns and classic, archetypal myths and legends.

During the Middle Ages many an outcast of society was forced to hide out in the wild forests and they came to be portrayed as 'wild men' (and women), that were also known as woodwoses.

Around this time 'wild men' and 'wild women' were also depicted in architecture, usually as naked figures covered in long hair. These archetypal beings largely exuded benelovence to humanity. They were defenders of the wilderness, where the wild game was hunted.

Robin Hood/Robin Good Fellow/Robin of the Greenwood, is also the defender of the wild woods, and is a highly virile character. He lived in legend with maid Marian – the God with the Goddess – and his 'coven' of 12 'merry men'.

And that great god of nature – Pan, is another important, related being. As the Celtic deity Cernunnos, he sports antlers and leaves sprout from his head, in a famous depiction on the 1st century BCE Gundestrup Cauldron. Sitting erect and cross legged, Cernunnos holds a serpent in one hand, has animals around him and, in other depictions, a stream of coins flow from his lap. His benevolence extends to agriculture, hunting and sexual activities.

The similarity to the Indian god Shiva is striking. Shiva is also shown cross legged, horned, highly sexual and Lord of Animals. The multinational horned god stirs our wild, creative energies to benefit all life.

Grugach was the ancient British Wild Herdsman, a guardian of nature, naked, capricious but largely benelovent a being, whose assistance was once invoked in pastures and farmland. His equivalents Fachan in Scotland and Bachlach in Ireland had similar duties and were considered also as gigantic guardians of the entrance to the underworld (which was usually deemed to be in an ancient tumulus/ mound). They were precursors to the Green Knight of Arthurian legend.

Looking back at earlier epochs, another possible connection is to the Celtic tradition of stone heads, apparently based on the idea that the severed heads of your ancestors or enemies are a source of great mana (as was also thought in Polynesian cultures).

Celtic head cult

The legendary figure associated with this tradition was Bran the Blessed, a demi-god /king of Powys, north Wales, who possessed a cauldron of rebirth. After death, his severed head possessed oracular powers. King Arthur went to consult the head of Bran, it is written.

Bran's head was eventually buried at the White Hill, where later the Tower of London was built, as magical protection for the nation.

Bran's name means 'raven' and the continued residence there of many ravens is said to augur well for the nation. When World War Two was raging, Churchill frantically stocked up on Tower ravens, to ensure the survival of Britain's sovreignty.

Vigilant Celtic heads are found acting as gate guardians, set into barns and walls, and adorning sacred wells. However they do not have the foliate features which distinguish the Green Men of later times.

Bran's legend hints at universal folk tradition, whereby the adornment of buildings with human, animal and mythic figures conveys symbolic protection for the inhabitants. This function may well have been implied in the purpose of the Green Man figures.

Global green man

So foliate faces hark back to ancient times and to other places too. Green Men in the medieval churches of Europe were probably inspired by the foliate heads of classical Roman architecture, from around 2000 years ago.

Some of the earliest examples are seen in mosaics from North Africa, and similar figures have been found in India from 2,300 years ago.

They have also been depicted all around Europe and in ancient China and Mexico. To this day, in San Pablito, Puebla, Mexico (and probably other parts) bark cutouts of people sprouting foliage are paraded during crop fertility rituals.

The first European Green Man in a Christian setting comes from the fourth century and can be seen on the tomb of St Abre, in the church of St Hillaire in Poitiers, France. This was the first of the new type, where the foliage sprouts from the nose.

After the rise in popularity in the Middle Ages the Green Man saw a resurgence in early Renaissance architecture, and then in the classical buildings of the eighteenth and nineteen centuries, such as Queen Anne's Gate in London.

Countless Victorian Gothic and classical renaissance style buildings in the USA, Australia and New Zealand and no doubt many other parts of the world, are also adorned with the Green Man.

The king must die!

Also found globally is the ancient archetypal myth, in various forms, of a great mother goddess, whose son must die at the end of the year, to be reborn in the next cycle. (Christianity is a later version of this story.)

Examples include the Egyptian god Osiris, who, like the grain which he is portrayed with, dies and is reborn each year. Tammuz, the Mesopotamian god of vegetation and fertility is also reborn each year (through a pine tree) in springtime. After fertilizing the Earth goddess he returns to the Earth in autumn.

This classic theme of regeneration (which Sir James George Frazer explores in his classic book 'The Golden Bough' of 1890) can still be seen in a few remaining British May Day customs, most of which were killed off by the Puritans, although a few have been revived in the last century, often as sanitised versions for the kids.

The Hastings (Sussex) Jack in the Green festival (held on May Day) died out during World War One, but it had been carefully recorded and has lately been revived. The

Hastings 'Jack' moves about in a towering frame covered in leaves (mainly laurel) and is accompanied by 'Black Sal' (Black Sal is a vestige, perhaps, of the dark crone goddess, who became the black virgin in Christian times. In over 200 famous Western European shrines of the Virgin, her image is black). Jack has a gang of Green Men to support him, but he is killed off in the end 'to release the spirit of summer'.

A similar custom was held in Castleton, Derbyshire, each May 29th. Castleton Garland Day used to be referred to as Castleton's 'baby night' as the ancient tradition of fertility rites lived on with this ancient custom. May Day celebrations, originally known as Beltane, were once known for their love-making and the consummation of year long 'greenwood marriages'.

London has several Jack in the Green festivals, including a parade to Leadenhall Market, May 1st (Deptford and city) and one at Brentham, Ealing on the 2nd or 3rd Saturday in May.

The return of the Green Man

It was Green Man researcher Lady Raglan in the UK in the 1930's, who gave them their generic name, which she took from the many 'Green Man Inns'.

But it is only in the last decade or two that there has been a real rise of interest in the Green Man. Nowadays there are several books and websites on the subject, as well as wall charts, cards, sculptures, brooches, prints and pendants to be had. The Green Man has also become a symbol for the men's movement in the USA.

Society has been starting to take eco-responsibility and here we are provided with a symbol to remind us of our connection with nature, an archetype of our own wild and free spirits. A fun character, who exudes the boundless joy of nature.

References:

Clive Hicks, 'Green Man – A Field Guide', Compass Books, UK, 2000.
(www.clivehicks.co.uk/greenman)
Peter Redgrove, 'The Black Goddess and the Sixth Sense', Paladin, UK, 1987.
Nicholas R. Mann, 'Reclaiming the Gods – Magic, Sex, Death and Football', Green Magic, 2002, UK.
Patricia Monaghan, 'O Mother Sun! – A New View of the Cosmic Feminine', The Crossing Press, USA, 1994.
John and Caitlin Matthews, 'The Encyclopaedia of Celtic Wisdom', Rider, UK, 2001.

Two more green men.
Tom Grave is on the right.
Tom is the author of highly acclaimed books on dowsing and geomancy , including the classic 'Needles of Stone'.

'Needles of Stone' is no longer in print but can be freely downloaded from the internet.
Check out www.tomgraves.com.au

Meetings with Pan

Who is Pan?

The great god Pan was the Greek personification of the masculine spirit of nature. He was not one of the twelve gods of Mt Olympus, perhaps because his ancient origins go back well before their time.

In the Greek tradition Pan guards the flocks and the forests, as well as the hunters in the forest, preferring to haunt the high hills. Depicted with the hair, horns, legs and ears of a goat, he was the goat god of Arcadia.

The roguish Pan can be jumpy and excitable. His sudden appearance can cause terror and the herds to stampede, and thus the word *panic* is derived from his name.

As a god of fertility, he encourages animals to reproduce. He also possesses the art of prophecy and is an adept with the Pan Pipes. His influence can be felt everywhere and anywhere.

In the ancient Italian countryside Faunus was an early deity whose attributes in later times matched the Greek god Pan. Originally worshiped as a bestower of fruitfulness on fields and flocks, he later became solely identified as a woodland deity.

A goaty figure like Pan, Faunus was also associated with merriment, and his twice-yearly festivals were times for revelry and abandon. At the Lupercalia, a celebration of fertility held partly in his honour each February in Rome well into the Christian era, youths clothed as goats ran through the streets wielding strips of goatskin.

But Pan in later Christian times did not enjoy good press. His image was used to create 'The Devil', his perceived association with evil and debauchery part of the attempts to denigrate all things pagan. But Pan, of late, has been reclaimed from the much maligned mire of medieval public opinion.

Fresh light on an old god

In modern times the spectre of Pan being alive and well in the landscape was finally reasserted when books about the famous Findhorn community, in the north of Scotland, started to become popular in the 1970's. Telling wondrous stories of giant cabbages growing in sand dunes as a result of devic co-operation in the garden, Findhorn became legendary. (Later in the 1980's a gardener/author in the USA, Machaelle Smal-Wright carried on the process, which Findhorn has not.)

R. Ogivlie Crombie (aka Roc), a Findhorn colleague, had been having encounters and conversations with a faun and later no less than Pan in the parks and streets of Edinburgh.

Pan had expressed great surprise that Roc was not afraid of him, considering the bad press that sticks to him. It spoke of the demonisation of Pan by the Christian Church and the sadness this caused it.

Later Roc met another Pan on the holy island of Iona. It told him that 'I and my subjects are willing to come to the aide of mankind in spite of the way he has treated us and abused nature, if he affirms belief in us and asks for our help.' Roc concluded that 'it became apparent that what was happening was a sort of reconciliation between the Nature Kingdom and man.'

As a result of his encounters Roc was able to quickly tune in to the Pan associated with the Findhorn community gardens and was told to preserve a wild corner just for him. In 1993 Pogacnik visited Findhorn and wrote of observing this mighty being on a low hillock in 'Pan's Corner'. This was in spite of his reluctance to believe that Pan actually existed!

'I recognised him from a description by Roc,' he wrote. 'Pan's upper body was human-like. He sat in a squatting position and his furry-haired goats legs were folded.' Pan was able to communicate to him that he 'embodied the highest representation of the earth elemental beings, but he is not responsible for the whole of nature, only for the sum total of natural life within a certain area.'

According to Pogacnik, this highly evolved deva/deity – Pan is *'a focus of the consciousness of nature, holding within his sphere the complete knowledge of any living being of nature that resides in the area entrusted to his attention. His role is to hold the family of living beings united in the common purpose … His quiet, conscious presence in the life processes within his area gives nature its fulfilling sense of being.*

'Each place or landscape has its own Pan focus, which is a fractal of the Earth's Pan … (he) has an all-connecting role within the consciousness of nature.'

Other cultures recognise a powerful masculine spirit of nature. In Siberia, for instance, gazarin ezen beneficially presides over his regions. When he is made angry – drought and pestilence can follow. Mountains are the focal points associated with these major 'land masters'.

Pan as the Celtic god Cernunnos.

My First encounters

I met Pan for the first time in Dublin, Ireland, while staying at an old ex-convent in August 2003. I had dowsed a strong devic energy field located in a corner of the park-like grounds from a distance. It felt powerful and special and I started to feel unusually excited when tuning into whatever it was.

The devic field was stationed in a commanding position in the back corner of the grounds, from where it could look out and see all over them.

But what was the identity of this decidedly regal feeling presence? When I asked who it was, I heard the words 'I am everywhere'. It must be Pan! I thought elatedly.

We exchanged energy and the experience was quite electrifying. I had never met such a powerful deva before and it put me into a state of reverie.

Then I happened to look down at an old solitary fern frond that had survived a recent mowing, in the fading light of the summer's evening. There, in the shape of the fern, I immediately saw the very obvious face of a Green Man. I felt even more awestruck and humbled …

The next day I introduced a couple of women residents to Pan. By dowsing we could all feel and map out his energy field. It was wider at the bottom and seemed to taper off up into space somewhere. Thus he seemed to be in his classic cross legged posture, and gave us a sense that we stood before a sublime sitting Buddha type being that was steeped in wisdom.

The others got the impression, as I had, that Pan didn't like us to walk all over him, although he did seem to enjoy our company. So we were careful to keep ourselves at least one step back from the edge of his energy field. He demanded respect and had asked Julie to take her shoes off in his presence, she told us.

Each day of my short stay I sat near Pan and tried to communicate with him. I felt he was a bit worried by the massive amount of land development that was going on all around his domain. But he was safe living there, I told him, sending waves of love over to him. (And I made recommendations to the residents that his location never be disturbed.) His energy field got larger and stronger each day …

Then one day I was sitting on a Dublin bus and pondering on what would be my next line of research. I looked up and focussed out of the bus window. There I saw a sign on a gate post, proclaiming: PAN RESEARCH.

Seeing the Green Man

And so it wasn't long before I came across a book about the Green Man while I was visiting London about a week later. Since my first Pan encounters I had become fascinated by the archetypal figure of the Green Man. And as the book listed locations I soon had blisters on my feet, from walking the streets for hours and days on end, filming foliate faces wherever I could find them.

Before I flew back to Australia I had lunch with Gill Hale, the editor of the UK Feng Shui Society's magazine. Like some new infectious disease, she caught my enthusiasm for the Green Man and commissioned an article from me. ('I keep seeing them everywhere!' she told me afterwards.) I knew that I would have to do a bit more homework on the subject, but I relished the opportunity which prompted me to do more research.

Pan in New Zealand

Just when I needed some photos for my Green Man article during a visit to New Zealand, my stay in Dunedin couldn't have been in a better spot. Green men and women gazed down at me from many an old classical styled Victorian era city building. Nowhere else on the south island did I see so many. There were even green women, which are much more unusual, and some of the green men and women were sporting little golden horns!

But other work followed and as I travelled later to the fabulous Castle Hill, the Green Man was far from my mind …

There I had been dowsing at a powerful vortex and the pendulum was spinning wildly around in a star pattern rotation cum highland fling as I got closer towards the centre. It was quite electrifying and made my body twitch.

I knew that the centre of the vortex is usually the home of an Earth elemental who acts as guardian to the portal (which the ancients might have described as an entrance to the underworld). But this was something special.

I attuned to the intelligence of the site and asked permission to be there. It was a familiar feeling and I quickly deduced that the vortex must be a Pan focus.

This Pan was even more electrifying and exhilarating than the Dublin Pan. His location appeared to be in the middle of what could well have been an old garden area, next to a dolmen like structure of limestone.

The Polynesian peoples who first came here were right into garden magic. The climate here gets pretty cold and their tropical crops needed extra care and attention, and any other help that could be mustered.

As I merged with his consciousness I went into a reverie, my body twitching with our energy exchange. I had an image of him as the fat little Polynesian diety depicted in stone in gardens of old. There was the realisation that this Pan should more properly be referred to as Rongo, the god of agriculture, and perhaps this is how he grew to be so powerful, from centuries of honouring by the people. I went into a dreamy state and buzzed with his energy

Later I read that the Waitaha people say that Rongo would mate with the Kumara Mother spirit in the Earth there, to spread their vitalising forces around. (I asked 'Rongo' about this and he had confirmed it to be true.)

Rongo Marae Roa, I read, was the son of chief gods Ranginui, the sky father and Papatuanuka, the Earth Mother. Rongo took Te Pani as his first wife. Their child was Te Kumara, the Peace Child, the sacred sweet potato from South America. Te Pani is always honoured in the garden ('mara') and she is said to be sitting there, watching over the crops. (Similarly, in South America, home of the sweet potato, the Inca farmers would some-times place large stones in their fields to honour Pachamama, the Earth Goddess.)

I think Pan/Rongo enjoyed my visit as when I said my thankyou and goodbye and headed off it felt as if he had grabbed hold of me and was hanging onto me with his energy, bewailing my leaving. It felt a bit like moon walking …

Returning to Dunedin a couple of weeks later I looked forwards to running my last 'Deva Dowsing' workshop before I flew home. I had already undertaken an initial dowsing survey to map out the location of important nature spirits in Dunedin's beau-tiful old Botanic Gardens.

On a beautiful mild summer's evening we began our tour, first admiring the Green Men and Women of downtown Dunedin, which participants had barely noticed before. (Typically – it takes a stranger to point out what is in front of you!)

Then we were off to the Botanic Gardens where we arrived just before closing around 9.30pm. A beautiful sunset unfolded and we had the place to ourselves as we dowsed for the energy fields of the Earth and water spirits we met. Most of all I wanted to connect with the Pan of the Park, who resided in a regal position, up a hillside at a stone walled sitting area. ('I like to see' he told me, in my 'mind's ear', when I asked why he liked it there.)

A Pan focal point in Dunedin Botanic Gardens, New Zealand.

Each going into meditation in the vicinity, we attuned to Pan's presence, which, for me, was again an electrifying experience! When I immersed myself in this Dunedin Gardens Pan – I instantly heard laughter. Joyous, bubbling, unabandoned and infectious laughter from that great being.

And we all felt pretty happy for our encounter with him.

Pan in Australia

The next time I met up with a Pan was back home in Australia.

I was map dowsing over a property plan just before a workshop and looking for any important energy centres. A large energy field came up, just in front of the house. An excited pendulum and a few body twitches gave me the clue. It was another Pan.

I looked over from the deck to the section of newly landscaped garden, with its lovely basalt boulders and commanding view over a valley and a peaceful pond. Yes, a nice Pan type of position, I thought. Distant dowsing confirmed the map dowse, so I projected my thoughts over his way and asked him if he wouldn't mind if the group might introduce themselves and tune into him later on …

Later, after lunch, I showed participants how to do 'deva dowsing', which is a way of tuning into the energy fields of the devas, using the pendulum and deviceless dowsing with the hands. I took them to the edge of Pan's energy field, told them to best stay at a respectful distance whilst attuning to his consciousness and to be open to receiving communication, either telepathically, or by asking questions with the pendulum.

We all stood around him and did our own thing, then drifted off to lunch. Later, when we reconvened, we sat in a circle and one by one related our experiences.

Now not all of the 12 people with me did see or sense anything but just about all could feel or dowse his energy field. Others had clairvoyant and clairaudient insights which fascinated me, as they all seemed to mesh together and mostly confirmed my initial impression.

I started with a description of this, my first sighting – in my mind's eye – of a Pan. As soon as I had closed my eyes I had had a strong visual impression, I told them. He looked like he might have just emerged from the earth, a chunky big troll like figure with little horns, pointy ears and rough earthy skin all blotched in red and green. Sitting there looking out over his domain, he was flexing his shoulders a bit and feeling surprise at the sudden rush of attention given him.

Three others in the group also saw the horns and one described the earthy red colour I had seen. As for 'gender' – the majority had sensed his masculine/yang nature.

One woman asked him by dowsing if he was a nature spirit and there was a very strong no! in response and she was told emphatically that he was, in fact, a deity!

A few sensed that they were not welcomed to tread on him, but one woman was invited to walk into his space, and another commented that he had wondered why we'd taken so long in coming out to meet him. 'About time!' he had said to her. Another described the very calm feeling she got from him there.

One of the men had been shown a triangular arrangement of energy that Pan was positioned in, and I wondered if it might be not unlike the geometric energetic structures that angels are known to make for themselves.

Geoffrey Hodson has also noted this phenomenon. When clairvoyantly observing a gang of mannikins (Earth elementals spirits), he had watched the playful dancing beings make a circle with a Latin cross within it. Hodson mused that 'in forming these symbols they are giving expression to some force which flows through them and produces an added sense of happiness and life.' Perhaps it is the Mannikins who make the crop circles? ...

References:
Nicholas Mann, 'Reclaiming the Gods', Green Magic, 2002, UK.
Encyclopaedia Britannica 1994–2001.
Marko Pogacnik, 'Nature Spirits & Elemental Beings' Findhorn Press, 1995, UK.
Marko Pogacnik, 'Daughter of Gaia' Findhorn Press, 2001, UK.
Paul Deveraux, 'The Sacred Place', Cassell & Co, UK, 2000.
Barry Brailsford, 'Song of Waitaha', Wharariki Publishing, c/o McBrearty Associates, PO Box 35-036 Shirley, Christchurch, NZ, 2003 edition.
Brian Leigh Molyneux & Piers Vitetsky, 'Sacred Earth, Sacred Stones', Duncan & Baird, UK, 2000.
Geoffrey Hodson, 'Fairies at Work and Play', Quest, USA,1982.

Angels in Canberra

by Steven Guth

Ecognosis

I saw a definition of Feng Shu a few days ago. 'Feng Shu is a Chinese form of geomancy'. I thought that was pretty good. Well, I have another new word. Ecognosis. The study of wisdom about the earth. I guess it's the next step out from geomancy.

Ecognosis is about the Devas, elementals, the areas of consciousness that exist inside or around geomantic Earth energies.

An example may help here. Frank Moody's interest in Earth energies came out of his background in radio electronics. He constructed radio induction coils to clear areas. I've seen him change an Italian delicatessen from bankruptcy to profit within a week with a length of copper electrical cable placed on top of a pile of boxes. How did it work? I think a gnome came up from the dowsing line that ran under the shop, sat on the coil of wire and spent a couple of enjoyable months playing his mind into the thought patterns of the customers who visited the shop. After that he got bored and reverted back to his mischievous ways – the business collapsed shortly afterwards.

Frank, in those days, had no time for gnomes or elementals. For him everything could be explained by radionics – radio like waves created by coils or radionic machines that directly affected the environment.

Similarly, I suspect that most of the adjustments Feng Shu people do somehow or other satisfy, change or titillate the elementals that live within the energies of structures. Change bad Feng Shu to good and you change the sort of consciousnesses that can live in an environment.

Well, that's what Ecognosis is looking at. Ways to understandings and work with the consciousnesses that reside in place energies. These have traditional names – devas, gnomes, elementals, fairies, landscape angels and gods. They have been seen and described by many people in many cultures.

Findhorn made a breakthrough impact on people because it showed that two-way communication between devas and people is possible. Now 25 years later, many of us have come to realise that human deva cooperation is more than just possible – it's desirable and necessary.

Ecognosis is about trying to create a framework, a way in which the processes of human – devic interaction can be assessed, understood and controlled. It's almost a scientific endeavour. Mysticism is the tool and traditional esoteric writings help to provide a framework. Exchange – communications – helps to separate confusion from fact. Wisdom, can perhaps (thanks to the net) be built up from the sharing of experiences.

About Canberra

Canberra is the main laboratory for Ecognosis at the moment. Findhorn was the laboratory, the showcase, for plant deva and human interaction. Canberra is rich in high energy geomantic locations – hills, lakes, city circles, ley lines. It has ceremonial buildings like the War Memorial (with its shrine of remembrance) and Parliament

House (an underground building topped by a huge metal flagpole). All of this makes for a dense congregation of new and old devas.

But first – how does one describe the world of fairies, devas, elementals, national folk souls and planetary gods? There are so many systems with a confusing looseness of definition – with classifications that hinder rather than help descriptive understandings.

Although the Theosophical literature has many problems it at least has the virtue of a well known terminology – thanks to the writing skills of C. W. Leadbeater. The Theosophical literature also suffers from a confusing overlay of concepts and definitions but it is large and seems about the best available. I find that the Theosophical way of presenting images of devas helps me reach into their kingdoms.

The Canberra geomancy laboratory is not stable. New things are happening all the time. New structures are going up in central Canberra – the newly built National Museum is soon-to-be geomantically balanced by the National Churches Centre. Commonwealth/Federation place with its appendix – Aboriginal Reconciliation Place is being built. New memorial sculptures keeping appearing along Canberra's central ley line, Anzac Parade.

Many groups and people have worked on Canberra's esoteric development. I have knowledge of dozens of them and there must be many more. The activity that has most fascinated me has been the development by a group of a 'crystal' home for angels above the ceremonial centre of Canberra. But first I will back-track alittle.

Canberra Dreaming

In the mid 1980's a group of people, involved with Australian Earth energy work and loosely connected with 'The Renewal of the Dreaming' movement became aware of the need to do work in Canberra to help release old energies.

Mt Ainslie and the War Memorial were the focus of the early work of meditating at sites. In those days the War Memorial was strongly ley linked to the old Parliament House and the Spirit of Anzac still dominated Australian social and political thinking. The mid 80's work done by many groups and people helped to release the pain, frustration, fear and stupidity bound into the War Memorial. As the work was done the new Parliament House rose on Capital Hill.

Without this conscious healing and releasing work the concept of multi-cultural and multi-racial Australia would have taken a different form and taken longer to develop, I feel.

By 1987, as people worked on the energies of Canberra the concept of the triangles became important. There were two of them, the one designed by the Griffins and inscribed on the map as Capital Hill, City Hill and the Defence department hills. The other was embossed on the landscape by the three Canberra mountains: Black, Red and Ainslie.

At first there was a tendency to arrange these two triangles, in visualisation, into what I will call a sort of pentagram shape. I now suspect that this form was placed into etheric Canberra by people interested in power and working through magical rituals.

As this was happening the people I was working with developed a fascination with the tetrahedron as a way of representing personal development. Then a dowseable three sided pyramid appeared in the space above central Canberra between the city, Capital and Defence Department hills. After awhile it began to work its way underground and so become a double pyramid, a tetrahedron – a place for the manifestation of angels.

From 1989 there was a continual play between the pentagram formulation and the double tetrahedron formulations in the etheric space over Canberra. It was not until the March 1996 'Conclave of Esoteric Sciences' in old Parliament House that the battle for the double tetrahedron was finally and completely won. That conference also marked the approximate beginning of the larger interlocking second double tetrahedron that links Ainslie, Red and Black mountains.

Within this developing crystal cluster new shapes are forming – and trying to form. The battle with the power seekers is far from over and a rearguard action is in progress. So all attempts to add new facets to the crystal meet obstruction, confusion and anger. Obstruction comes from individuals, government departments and even from within the personality of the people doing the work.

Deva of Ceremonial

On Anzac Parade I sense balls of radiating consciousness that reach up high into the sky. Around about weave energy streams and clouds of coloured mist. It is a deva of ceremonial, a consciousness that arrives as a purple glow at every ritual, every ceremony, that takes place in Canberra and seeks to facilitate their intentions. Perhaps this is why so many religiously orientated new age groups are setting up in Canberra.

The deva on Anzac Parade is large and reaches high into the sky. It lives in an 'angel house' it has constructed for itself that appears to have square corners set into a round sort of shape, similar to the War Memorial's Shrine of Remembrance. It seems to be linked to similar beings within a geographic area extending from Bali to New Zealand, Perth to Tasmania.

Angel houses

Angel houses can be constructed by ritual, geomantic actions and/or meditation. Perhaps devas construct them for themselves over points of geomantic energy – just like snails make their own shells.

CW Leadbeater has described an 'angel house' created during a Masonic ritual.

> *'The entire figure was thus a nest of four prisms, the floor on which the Angels stood representing the central plane. Having built for themselves a temple of this strange form, the angels proceeded to perform a most interesting ceremony inside it. They moved in a wonderful choric dance, arranging themselves in various figures a seven pointed star, a swastika, a cross and many other figures a sort of hymn voices like the chiming of mighty bells. The multiprismatoidal temple was transparent like crystal, and yet somehow permeated with fire.'*

> *'... Lines of dazzling light shot out into the empyrean, bearing messages and greetings to worlds far away in space. And unmistakably there came a response to this wonderous call – even many responses. Strange to us beyond all words in magnetism and feeling were these replies from other worlds: but that they WERE replies is beyond question. Some, surely came from worlds of which at present know nothing.'*

Surely, fascinating stuff. Gives you something to think about, doesn't it? The material was probably written in about 1920. It predates the New Age and the energy weavers like Melchizedek.

Reference:
C.W. Leadbeater's, 'The Hidden life in Freemasonry.' Theosophical Publishing House. 1949. Page 343.

The Ecognosis site www.kheper.auz.com/ecognosis is run by Alan Kazlev as part of his www.kheper.auz.com site. Contact me on guthltd@mpx.com.au.

Spirit Dimensions of the Pacific Islands

Greater and Lesser Gods of Nature

The Polynesians personified the forces of nature as powerful gods and goddesses. In the mythic beginning Ranganui, the sky god, paired up with Papatuanaka, the earth mother, to become the parents of all the many gods of nature. (The concept of one great chief god – Io – only began around 1880, probably as a concession to Christianity.)

As well as the major pantheon, Polynesians acknowledged numerous lesser gods, as well as deities of place, family guardian gods and deified ancestral spirits, as well as the many usual spirits of nature one might expect. Certain trees and rocks are considered the home of particular spirits of place, local atua, too.

Individual landscape features often assumed the ranks of deities. Important mountains and volcanoes, particularly, were highly revered. In Hawaii the much celebrated goddess Pele and her family live deep within the volcano Kilauea, and when she is angry the earth will shake! Fortunately this is not very often – she is generally docile, occasionally spewing out a stream of lava. Her last violent explosion was back in 1924.

Pele can be as creative as she can be destructive, and offerings of fruit, flowers and vegetables are made to her on a daily basis. In earlier times Pele was honoured as an ancestress, a family ancestor spirit. She is said to have come over to Hawaii from Tahiti by canoe. Usually Pele is depicted as a beautiful or old woman, or as a flame or a white dog. If she manifests herself as a woman in white it is considered a warning of ill health. If seen in red, an eruption might ensue.

Forest Lore

The thick forests of New Zealand are the home of the 'wee folk' known as Tini o Te Hakuturi, the 'Multitude of Hakuturi', being the host of fairies, wood elves etc who are guardians of the forest, avenging any desecration of its sacredness/tapu. Tane is the god of the forests and the 'Children of Tane' are his trees and their associated spirits.

The felling of forest trees was a solemn occasion which a tohunga/priest presided over, a greenstone axe was used and fifteen seedlings were planted as a replacement.

In Maori legend, Rata went into the forest to cut down a big tree for a canoe. When he was finished felling it he went to sleep. During the night birds, insects and fairy people of the forest helped to put the tree upright again. The next day he cut it down again, but again it stood up.

So Rata hid and watched and then asked the Children of Tane why they were doing this. 'You disobeyed the laws of the forest. First you must have a good reason then you must ask permission to cut down a child of Tane' he was told. Rata was ashamed and begged forgiveness. And so the children of Tane helped Rata build his canoe.

Polynesians speak of the menehune or manahune, another forest folk. In New Zealand the maero or maeroero were the wild men and giants of mountain and wilderness, being fierce hairy giants with big claws. Hawaiian legends speak of little people with big eyes, who fear the daylight and perform Herculean labours, such as stonework, in the night, and always ceasing at dawn.

The Underworld

The abode of human spirits, according to Maori tradition, is the region beneath the Earth referred to as Te Reinga, an underworld also known as the 'hidden home of the god Tane'. (A celestial spirit world is also known.)

Tradition has it that the spirits of the newly deceased make their way to Cape Reinga, at the northern tip of the north island. Here they rest awhile on top of the hill Taumata-I-Haumu, where they look back, farewell this world, then go on to the extremity of the cape to an old Pohutakawa tree, where they slide down one of its long roots and down a cliff face, and into a chasm below. There is a similar tradition in Rarotonga.

Interestingly, there is a magnetic anomaly point just out to sea from this spot at Cape Reinga.

The Patu-pai-arehe

Then there are the Maori 'fairy' tales of the Turehu or Patu-pai-arehe, being the fair skinned 'fairy' people of the forest. Rather than referring to nature spirits, a study of history would suggest that these were, in fact, real flesh and blood people, an earlier race of Polynesian people wiped out by invading tribes.

In the 1800's Sir George Grey, New Zealand's governor, wrote that the Patu-pai-arehe were very numerous at the time. A modern sign on top of Mt Eden in Auckland declares that the Turehu or Patu-pai-arehe are considered the nation's original inhabitants. The spirits of these 'fairy people' remain in the land after they were massacred.

Similarly, in the British Isles the word pixy derives from the Picts, an old tribe who were driven into the hills and caves by conquering tribes, to become ensconced, in legend at least, as spirits of the land. And likewise the Tuatha de-Danann people of Ireland became the leprecauns and fairies of today in their ancient mounds and 'fairy forts'.

Cowan was told that the earliest inhabitants of the South Island were the Hawea tribe, who came by canoe from the north or north west. They either looked like Maori of today or their skin was more reddish or copper coloured, as was their hair. Their eyes were black or even blue. They were of normal stature and wore woven flax garments.

Waitaha people also state that there were already people in New Zealand when they arrived, perhaps some fourteen hundred years ago. Stories of fair haired tribes – 'Urukehu' – are numerous. These early tribes may well have been the ancestors of the Patu-pai-arehe.

Credited with having supernatural powers, they spoke the same language as the Maori and played the flute beautifully. Generally it was only the Maori tohunga who had the ability to see them, as they were adepts at invisibility, or else they were only there in spirit.

The Patu-pai-arehe were considered guardians of the sacred places and they 'visited their displeasure on those who neglected the rites of propitiation of the forest dieties'. They had powers of transformation and invisibility, and were said to be repulsed by the steam of Maori hangi ovens and the red ochre of Maori body and building decorations. Peace loving, they didn't play the malelovent tricks attributed to the Maero.

The Patu-pai-arehe were said to prefer wilderness areas and were predominantly found in the wilder south island, where they frequented the highest peaks. Shy of sunlight, they only ventured out at night or on cloudy or foggy days. When the mists hung low, then the 'fairies' might venture abroad and it was not considered wise to hunt up there, the legends went.

People spoke of hearing fairy songs up high in the mountains on still calm days when fog covered the upper reaches. When entering a sacred forest these 'fairies' could detect one's presence and play tricks, such as manifest voices.

These early hunter-gatherers were not wise to the ways of war and were easily wiped out, their memory and spirits fuelling the many tales of the little people out in the woods, hiding for their lives.

Fairy mountains

A famous 'fairy' haunt, Cowan tells us, was densely forested Mount Pirongia in the Waikato district, some 1000m high, with deep ravines. Other 'fairy' haunts include Hihikiwi, a high peak of Pirongia, Moehau (Cape Colville), Maungaroa in the lower Waikato, Waitakere, Te Aroha and the forested hills of Northland. In the Waikato-Waipo regions the ranges of Rangitoto, Whare-puhunga, Maunga-tautari and Taupiri were well known 'fairy' haunts.

The partly wooded 'fairy' mountain Ngongotaha rises above the south west shore of Lake Rotorua. An informant told Cowan that some 1000 or more Patu-pai-arehe once lived there, that they were an 'iwi atua' – a god-like tribe with supernatural powers. Their important chiefs were remembered by name. One was Te Ririo, a chief or atua of great powers, his home being Tongariro and the Kaimanawa Ranges near Lake Taupo.

On the Banks Peninsula, east of Christchurch, hidden in the majestic volcanic heights of Whanga-raupo (Lyttleton Harbour) and the craggy peaks of Akaroa were the old pas and sacred places of not only the Patu-pai-arehe but also the fearsome maero or maeroero, the wild men and giants of the mountains.

Important fairy peaks on the peninsula, pointed out to James Cowan by a local kaumata, was the rock of Te Pohue, the monument between Purau and Port Levy; Hukuika Peak, between Pigeon Bay and Little River, the mountain tor of Te U-Kura, and the high peaks overlooking Akaroa Harbour. Two places of 'particular enchantment' are a peak called Brazenose and a level topped hill above French Farm. The Maori name for Brazenose is Otoki, 'place of the axe', where, above the village of Onuku, on the beach side, lies an ancient burial ground.

There are tales that on dark nights one could see the light of torches moving around the bays across Lyttleton Harbour, where no mortal folk lived. The Maori put these down to the Maeroero, the wild men of the mountains. Or perhaps these were 'Earth lights', a global Earth energy phenomena?

References:
Scott Cunningham, 'Hawaiin Religion and Magic', Llewellyn, USA 1994.
Elsdon Best, 'The Maori', Vol 1, Whitcombe and Tombs, NZ, 1924
James Cowan, 'The Fairy Folk' Journal Polynesian Society, volume XXX, 1921.
James Cowan, 'Fairy Folk Tales of the Maori', Whitcombe and Tombs, NZ, 1939.
A W Reed, 'Myths and Legends of Maoriland', Reed, NZ, 1946.

Barry Brailsford, 'Song of Waitaha', Wharariki Publishing, C/o McBrearty Associates, PO Box 35-036, Shirley, Christchurch, NZ.
James Cowan, 'The Maoris Yesterday & Today', Whitcombe and Tombs, NZ, 1930
James Cowan, 'Maori Folk Tales of the Port Hills', Whitcombe & Tombs, NZ, 1923.
Paul Deveraux, 'Earth Lights Revelation' Blandford, UK, 1989.

Tales of the Taniwha

New Zealand is a rugged land of fire and water, and, not surprisingly, the spirits of mountains, rivers, volcanoes and hot springs are recognised as powerful forces prominent in the Maori mythos.

The mightiest denizens of water are the powerful beings known as taniwha – pronounced 'tunifa', and sometimes called ngarara. Found in oceans, lakes, and water courses everywhere, a Maori writer likens the taniwha to the white mans' dragons of legend.

The Australian equivalent is the rainbow serpent and the bunyip. 'Bunyips live in deep holes in watercourses and punished, usually with drowning, all who trespassed on their domain,' wrote anthropologist Charles Mountford in 1976.

Like the rainbow serpents who mythically created the watercourses and landforms in Australia, some taniwhas were said to have created New Zealand's harbours, by opening channels to the sea. Their temperaments were often said to be ferocious and dangerous, but they could also be ferocious guardians of the people. There are many stories of heroic battles of early Maori with taniwhas, both on land and in the water. Always the people win!

Taniwhas are usually associated with particular areas, but in one Maori story a taniwha roamed about until it settled in the Wellington district and ultimately died, in death forming a small island.

Historical references

In 1983, the Rev. J. Irwin wrote of his burgeoning interest in the Taniwha, after he was told of two taniwha in Ngati Ipu tribal territory in 1942. He also notes that historical references are well established already, with the first written mention of them by Captain Cook in 1777, Nicholas in 1815 and Polack in the 1830's. In each case the taniwha is referred to as a water dwelling monster. Usually they are said to dwell in caves, in the bends of rivers, deep river pools, places with strong currents or dangerous breakers. And they are not always associated with water.

Captain Cook spoke of the enormous lizards at Queen Charlotte Sound – 'eight feet long man eaters'. Nicholas in 1815 described the alligator like taniwha; and Dieffen-abach, about to climb Mt Taranaki for the first time, was warned of man eating crocodiles up there. Wakefield, en route to Wanganui from Lake Taupo, was told of an inland area inhabited by huge ngarara. In 1852 M Martin recorded sightings from the Waikato area and believed the taniwha to be some sort of tradition of alligator, which are still to be found in the rivers in some of the northern Pacific islands.

Some taniwha are traditionally said to be hostile, Irwin tells us, killing the unwary who venture too close to their lairs, while others are guardians of a particular hapu (sub tribe) and are only hostile to strangers. Still other types are only rarely seen at certain pivotal times and are considered to be harbingers of disaster. For example around Lake Taupo the local Maori say that taniwha appear just before a tragedy such as a flood, which they usually connect with the violation of a serious tapu (sacred law).

A Hawaiian scholar S. Kamakau wrote in the 1860s of monstrous reptiles believed to inhabit inland fishponds, as pond guardians. These ponds were built after the fourteenth century. A traditional story from Tonga tells of three man eating giant spirits – one of a dog, one a fowl and the third – a lizard.

Elsdon Best has recounted a number of accounts of taniwha that are not associated with water, some being more like dragons, one being an underground dweller called a tuoro and others are crocodile-like saurian beings. Ruamoko, the volcano god of New Zealand, is a saurian being.

On Easter Island, and in many other parts of the Pacific, lizards represented either life, or illness or death. Wooden figures of lizards had protective functions and were used at dance feasts and placed besides the doors of homes. A reptilian head could also refer to a tribal group – hanau mokomoko, meaning a lizard family. To some Polynesians, lizards were considered to have great magical powers. The belief that lizards can cause death is widespread in Asia and Africa too.

The crocodile is not and never has been a member of the New Zealand fauna, nor of the rest of Polynesia. But it is widespread in Indonesia and South east Asia, from where Polynesian culture is largely derived. The last time the ancestors of the Polynesians co-existed with crocodiles in the Solomon Islands is estimated to be some 3000 years ago, so they are still obviously a potent folk memory. Crocs are capable of long sea voyages, up to 2000km, and they may have wandered in occasionally, as is evidenced by isolated cases throughout history.

Ancestral taniwhas

While lesser native taniwhas are found in all the Pacific's waters, many legendary taniwhas are said to have accompanied the ancestral wakas from the homeland, and then stayed in the new land of New Zealand. These friendly sea spirits, a feature of Cook and Society Islands traditions too, frequently attended great chiefs as guardians, hovering around their canoes and even supporting the canoe on their backs when there was a danger of sinking.

Tuhirangi was a taniwha guardian who guided and protected pioneering ancestor Kupe's ship that came from 'Hawaaikii'(which just means 'homeland'). After arrival it was placed by Kupe in Raukawa (Cook Strait), where dangerous waters in a narrow passage separate Rangitoto (D'Urville Island) from the mainland South Island. There it continues to welcome and protect waka crews. It is said to live in a cave known as Kaika-iawaro (or Taitawaro).

In the late nineteenth century Tuhirangi was associated with a famous dolphin. From 1880 for 20 years this white dolphin regularly met and accompanied passing ships, leaping and riding in the bow wave. The government of the day gave him legal protection. White people called him Pelorus Jack, but to Maori he was always known as Tuhirangi.

Legend says that Takitimu, the great waka of pioneering ancestor Tamatea, was escorted for part of his journey safely around the coast by a great mother of a taniwha called Arai-te-uru (also the name of the companion waka). This taniwha had eleven sons who each helped to create the many branches of Hokianga Harbour. Some still live there with their mother and one of these, Onapa, is a cranky one. Arai-te-uru resides in a cave on the south head of Hokianga harbour, acting as a guardian of the region. Her companion Niua lives by the north head of the harbour.

Te Waenga, a leading tohunga of the Hokianga people in the 1830's was said to have the power to command Arai-te-uru to bring heavy seas or to calm them. Bones of people put in a cave hear her home were thought to be protected by her.

Sometimes taniwhas were held responsible for drownings and the dead person was said to have insulted the taniwha or broken a tapu somehow. Conversely – some people were said to have been saved from drowning by a taniwha.

Forms they take

Elsdon, in 1924, wrote that they are mostly water dwelling creatures of saurian form, mostly man slayers or man eaters, but some are harmless. The Maori say that the taniwha can be noisy, making bellowing or even roaring sounds.

On the ocean a taniwha may appear as a whale or shark. Even in rivers and lakes it might appear as big as a whale, but take the form of a gecko or tuatara. Some were known to assume a range of different forms.

At Lake Taupo a fierce taniwha, called Horo-Matangi, lived on the west side of Motutaiko Island in an underwater cave. It was said to manifest as a reptile, a black rock, or an old man as red as fire. Some would say he is the custodian of the mana of the lake.

The taniwha is sometimes referred to as the ngarara. These mainly dangerous or evil beings are described as having teeth studded jaws, bat wings, hard scaly skin with rows of spines all down the back, and a long and dangerous tail.

In some Maori cave drawings we see lizard like taniwha. One in Hamilton was executed in 1868; others are found in Tangawhai Gorge, South Canturbury. In other Maori art the taniwha appears in the form of merman figures in meeting houses, which represent taniwha sea dwellers from the ocean depths.

Taniwhas, especially the floating log variety, might be referred to as atua, tipua – supernatural presences, beings with extraordinary powers; and maybe as the mauri of the associated human community.

Tribes sometimes referred to their great chiefs as taniwhas themselves. A man closely associated with a taniwha might be considered to become one after death. In China the emperors, in a similar move, likened themselves to the Dragon forces of nature and referred to themselves as Dragon Emperors.

Some people were even said to marry a taniwha and have baby taniwhas together. (The idea of a human-deva hybrid is not unknown in other parts of the world.)

Sometimes when a tribe wanted to subjugate another they believed that they could only do this by first killing its guardian taniwha. One taniwha, Matamata, was placed at a narrow part of a coastal track at Kaikoura at the mouth of the Lyell Creek. It was a vicious one that killed enemy warriors. But an enemy finally snared and 'killed' it.

The sighting of a taniwha that crossed the path of a war party generally indicated a bad omen.

Friendly taniwhas

When treated with respect, taniwhas were usually well behaved towards people. One normally steered clear of their dens, but if passing or fishing nearby one, it was customary to make a propitiary offering. Often this was in the form of a green twig or branch, and approriate karakia would be recited too.

There is a tree located between Rotorua and Whakatane on Hongis Track which was once used as an offering place for such things. Beside it a notice invites visitors to make an offering. Only certain types of taniwha can be appeased with offerings however.

Tohunga would make special offerings to certain taniwha – the first kumara or taro of the harvest, or the first bird or fish caught in the season.

A custom in Manukau Harbour if there was any impending trouble such as illness or war, was for a small raft to be anchored overnight with a mini house on it in which mullet flesh or some other delicacy would be placed for the taniwha. If the food was gone in the morning – the taniwhas help was assured.

Mostly regarded with fear, some families had taniwhas as kaitiaki/family guardian spirits, for some taniwhas took a liking to certain individuals, families or hapu/sub tribes.

When all went well the taniwhas were the peoples' guardians, warning of the approach of enemies, via the interpretations of the tohunga. A ngarara 'dragon' could be the pet of a chief, but only if offerings of food were regularly offered to keep it happy.

At Hamurana Springs, on the northern edge of Lake Rotorua, there are some 15 springs, the largest of which, despite being only spa-pool sized, emits nearly five million litres of water per hour. This main outlet was the home of a female taniwha known as Hinerua. She was gentle, unlike other Rotorua taniwha, and the pet of a local chieftainess. Hinerua would visit her mistress regularly and after her death she was never seen again. The springs have great spiritual importance.

Six kilometres away at Taniwha Springs Pekehaua was known as a man-eating taniwha. The legend tells of a plan made to capture and kill this taniwha. Thus it was enticed into a trap, with the help of the karakia of a powerful tohunga, and then beaten to death.

Taniwhas of the south island

To the Waitaha people of the South Island their great 'waka' Aotea Roa, was looked after by three great regional taniwhas. A female taniwha Huriawa rules the north, while (male) Tu Te Raki Hau Noa rules the snow fed rivers of the east, as well as being able to soar high in the warm north-west wind; and (male) Tu Tekapo is the blind taniwha of the south.

These great taniwhas were entreated by the Waitaha to help the rivers flow freely. They did not enlist the help of a taniwha for the wild, rugged west coast, as they felt it would be too big an ask to keep those rivers clear. With its thickly rainforested mountains and up to some seven metres of rain per year – the task was too difficult.

Northern taniwha

The great northern taniwha Huriawa was considered brave and wise. In formative times lakes were her footprints as she roamed her territory. Sometimes she traversed deep inside the Earth to tend the underground waters, for deep beneath the Aorere Mountains she had created long tunnels and huge caverns to flow through.

She now has many children who take responsibility for individual rivers and lakes.

Huriawa gives warnings to the people should the volcano god Ruaumoko decide to send earthquakes – her underground waters and hot springs suddenly surging up.

When her work is done she returns to her home – the fabulous Waikoropupu Springs, near Takaka. These springs are amongst the clearest and purest in the world. They were recognised by the Waitaha as healing waters, and were once a place of great ceremonies at times of birth and death, as well as the leaving and returning of travellers.

Scientists have determined that in the basin of the main spring there is an astonishing 62 metres of horizontal visibility, making it perhaps the clearest fresh water in the world.

Of the various sources there, the 12 or so springs at the Fish Creek area have been recorded as discharging at a rate of 8m³ of water per second. At other times they can completely dry up.

Stationed above each of the two main upwelling points at the Pupu Springs I have dowsed the presence of a 'lady taniwha' 'dancing' blissfully in the water's upwelling forces.

Eastern taniwha

The powerful taniwha Tu Te Raki Hau Noa is said to live in the Orakaia River and be the guardian of the eastern rivers. The son of the god of winds, he is also the taniwha of the west wind, flying high at times, and at other times following rivers that go underground to the lowlands and freshwater lake Waihora Nui.

In one legend of the ancestral trail making chief of the Rapuwai people, when Rau Kai Hau Tu encountered the fast waters of the Orakaia River his raft overturned and he crashed to the shore. In his shock he struck out at the taniwha Tu Te Raki Hau Noa and inflicted a deep wound in him and much distress. Sky god Ranginui heard his pain and sent a powerful spell to split the rock and create a vast chasm through the hills – Orakia Gorge, releasing trapped waters to the sea.

The injured taniwha disappeared deep into the underground passages to later emerge into the gentle waters of Lake Waihora Nui. Here he met Matakiuru, the beautiful, peaceful guardian taniwha of the lake, and she healed him of his pains.

As a gesture of healing and goodwill to Tu Te Raki Hau Noa, Rau Kai Hau Tu put three large pieces of pounamu into the waters of the gorge. In return the taniwha promised safe travel through his waters. Harmony was restored.

Southern taniwha

Tu Tekapo is the blind taniwha of the south, caring for fiords and deep lakes, and often of an unpredictable, wild and dangerous nature. After he had created all the landscape features this taniwha ending up resting in Lake Wakatipua, which is said to still pulse with the taniwha's heartbeat. Later the gods blinded him for not doing a good enough job, and so he became Te Kapo the blind one, who still lives in the deep tunnels he dug. On calm days he resides at O Mapere.

The prow of an ancient waka found on the southern coast of New Zealand's South Island, depicts the head of a taniwha. Invercargill Museum.

Water quality

Water quality was an important consideration in New Zealand, where water in volcanic areas might be poisonous. Some hot waters ran yellow, green, blue and brownish red. The quality of most waters was considered good – 'waimaori', but it had to always be assessed in case it be bad – 'waimate'. Rain – the 'tears of Ranginui' were always considered to be blessed with goodness and compassion. The favourite water for people and crops was filtered through limestone, the people observed. Information about water quality was recorded in traditional songs.

For a bad water hazard a taniwha would be asked by ancestor Rau Kai Hau Tu to guard the site permanently and warn anyone who came not to drink there.

Log & Lord Taniwhas

Other notable lesser taniwhas were subject to curious stories of them sailing uncannily around lakes attached to old logs. One 'sacred taniwha log' used to drift around Lake Rotoiti. This taniwha, Mataura, had a log that had once been a post for crayfish nets which broke off and went sailing, after which it was said to house the taniwha. It had an Waitaha 'owner' – one Kahu Pukatea, and only he could safely approach it. Mataura was considered an evil omen if anyone else saw it up close.

Another eccentric timber taniwha that cruised Rotoiti was a totara log called Huraki-tai's Head. Considered a magic tree, when it floated to the eastern lake edge people would recite karakia to propitiate the spirit in it and sometimes adorned its branching head with feathers.

Rangiriri was another totara log taniwha, said to bring evil omens, and last seen stranded on the northern Wairoa River. Te Rore Taoho, a chief of the Wairoa River area, told Cowan that there were many taniwhas and demons of both land and water inhabiting the district in days past. From Kaipara Heads right up the Wairoa and the Kaihu, these dragons held sway, he told him.

The high clay and sandy hills at the mouth of the Kaipara were once the homes of powerful sea gods too. At the western head of the Kaipara River, near Shelly Beach and the remains of the once great Okaka Pa/fort, was the haunt of 'a great dragon, Pokopoko', apparently a taniwha-ied hero of olden days, who dwelt in a cave under a half tide rock. Pokopoko was an important 'Lord of the Taniwhas' who could muster an army of sea monsters if he needed to.

The only lesser taniwha who would not bow before him, the legends went, were Niua and Arai-te-uru, who now dwell under the heads of Hokianga Harbour. Legends say that around ten generations ago Pokopoko destroyed the Okaka Pa and all its inhabitants, after a tohunga who had a grudge against the local Ngati-Whatua tribe invoked the assistance of this Lord of the Taniwhas to rise up and destroy the hilltop pa. Wind, waves, lightening and thunder did the job, and the pa crumbled.

References:

Edward Shortland, 'Traditions and Superstitions of New Zealand', Longman Brown; Green, Longmans & Roberts, London, 1856.

Barry Brailsford, 'Song of Waitaha', Wharariki Publishing, C/o McBrearty Associates, PO Box 35-036, Shirley, Christchurch, NZ.

Margaret Orbell, 'The Illustrated Encyclopaedia of Maori Myth and Legend', 1995, Canterbury University Press.

James Cowan, 'Maori Folk Tales of the Port Hills', 1923, Whitcombe and Tombs, NZ.
'Art of the Pacific', Oxford University Press, 1979.
Rev. J. Irwin, 'Maori Leviathon', Historical Review, Bay of Plenty Journal of History, vol. 31 no. 2, Nov. 1983.
 Simon Best, 'Here Be Dragons', Journal of Polynesian Society, Sept 1988.
Kenneth Maddock, 'Taniwha parallels in Australia', Journal of Polynesian Society, Sept. 1988.

New Zealand's unique Tuatara is a mini living dinosaur. In a different family from lizards, these 'living fossils' have been around for over 100 million years. They have a primitive '3rd eye'/sensory apparatus on their forehead, also a third eyelid, as crocodiles do.

Monster stops Roadworks!

The presence of a legendary being, known to the Maori people as the Taniwha, has interrupted road works on a dangerous section of New Zealand's Highway One. The story has bounced around the world since it broke in early November 2002. 'Maori swamp creature delays road' was the splash on the BBC's website.

Meetings were urgently held between the local Maori tribe and Transit New Zealand, who were told that it is believed by Maori that these beings exist all along the rivers, particularly at the bends.

Maori cabinet minister John Tamihere agrees, stating that all Maori children are warned not to swim on river bends because of the threat of the Taniwha, who is considered responsible for drownings.

Karu Tahi is the one-eyed taniwha on this section of the Waikato River, says the Ngati Nho, a hapu of the Tainui iwi. It's lair is a wetland area beside the river about one kilometre south of the Meremere power station, just beside state highway one and smack in the middle of the route of the new Waikato expressway. It also has a second home up river when floods occur, and this is not on the expressway route.

Ngati Naho also recognise two other taniwhas that live north of Karu Tahi. Waiwai, named for a pioneering ancestor, lives on the Waikato banks just over the road from the Meremere power station. Te Iaroa ('The Long Current') lives where the Mangatawhiri River joins the Waikato.

Further north the proposed Northland Prison at Ngawha was also held up around this time, due to the presence of taniwha Takauere. Takauere has been described as a guardian of the waters that manifests as a kauri log or eel. It's presence was raised as part of the Ngapuhi Waitangi Tribunal claim for the Ngawha geothermal resources in 1993.

So what does the Ngati Naho at the Waikato have to say?

'We need recognition that they do exist. We already know that in the Maori sense. They should be identified and be respected for what they are' said tribal spokesman Remi Herbert. '…We are working with TNZ to see how we can accommodate those taniwha there. Maybe the road needs to divert a little bit. It's up to the kaumatua (elders) to make that call … We are not looking for compensation. We're looking to make sure our spiritual needs and our mana are intact. We're confident we'll come to an amicable solution.'

Reactions to the story were very negative. With lots of letters sent to newspapers about such 'mythological claptrap' I sent my own in, which did get published at least.

'… The taniwha is a living and detectable energetic force in the landscape' I declared. 'Just as the Australian Aboriginal "dreamtime", actually an other-dimensional reality, enjoys respect, so the taniwha should have the right to exist, rather than being treated as if it were some kind of collective hallucination.'

The happy outcome of negotiations between all parties on the Waikato was that Karu Tahi's lair was saved, the expressway carefully re-routed around it, and proper drainage installed to keep the wetland viable. The extra works added some $15 – 20, 000 to costs. But it was only done in the name of saving the protected kahikatea trees that grow there. Accepting the real live presence of a taniwha was perhaps just too mind bending for Transit New Zealand.

References:
New Zealand Herald 9/11/02
Transit NZ website press releases, 19/12/02.

Treading on the Taniwha's Tail

I arrived in the afternoon at my destination Te Hue Valley, in the north island of New Zealand, having driven my hire car down winding country lanes in lush farming country south of the Coromandel Peninsula. I was to run a geomancy workshop there the next day and I had to quickly familiarise myself with the energetic character of the property which took up most of the little valley, nestled in amongst forested hills.

My host Udaya was soon taking me around on a four wheel trike farm tour. Without any comments, he took me to important geomantic points that he knew of in the valley and asked me to attune to them in my own way, so we could swop notes.

At the front gate of the property at the entrance to the valley we stopped. Ahead, the road crossed a little stream over a bridge, then curved past a small rocky outcrop of a hill, like a rocky sentinel, on the right.

Dowsing for significant energetic features drew me to the rock outcrop and revealed the presence of some sort of landscape deva in it. Getting up close to the rock and tuning in, it announced itself as a guardian and a somewhat bristling or threatening one at that. Upon sharing my impressions with Udaya he explained why he had brought me there. On two occasions in the past two different clairvoyant people had had interesting encounters down at the creek near the farm entrance.

One woman had seen a bizarre figure approach her, as real and solid looking as anyone. The difference was – it was some 7 feet tall, with a human body, and sporting an alligator head! It spoke telepathically to her and said something like; 'My name is Taia (pronounced a bit like Tyre) and this place is under my protection – or – my domain, and humans can dwell here but they must live within accordance to (environmental) principles or there will be disharmony (trouble) for them.' Udaya told me. Another (terrified!) person had reported this taniwha as trying to attack them in their car.

Udaya thought it just lived around the creek there, but when I popped back to dowse and tune in to the taniwha again later, it was not to be found at the rocky outcrop. I extended my dowsing search further afield and was then able to detect the taniwha's changed location, at another little hill further back, not far from the path of 'it's' creek. The same clairvoyant woman who first described the taniwha to Udaya confirmed to me that she had also observed that it tended to roam around its territory.

Later on, after the end of the next day's workshop I stood looking to admire the Tower of Power we had put up not far from the taniwha's home. I visually sensed a little spirit, monkey-like, with a wicked grin, that was clinging to the top of one side of the tower. Oho! … I felt a bit uneasy …

The next morning I took off at dawn and never got to see what happened to the Power Tower. By then it was lying broken on the ground, blown down by the wind, I found out later. This had never happened to me before, although I knew that the Tower was overly tall. But I was not surprised. I guess we weren't playing by the taniwha's rules.

PART FIVE

Meet the Geomancers

Custodianship at Bibaringa

by Steven Guth

Steven Guth tells us of his developing relationship with the land at his new home, his insights and experiences of sharing that land.

It is now about 8 months since we moved to Bibaringa, a hilly 500 acre horse agistment property ten minutes drive from Canberra's parliamentary triangle.

Our house is situated on the Mt. Stromlo ridge and is open to the four directions. East lies Canberra city, west is the great Australian Snowy Mountain wilderness. To the north is the university Observatory complex – from where cosmic thoughts have been woven since 1904. From the south, along the Murrumbidge corridor, blow the cold high altitude arctic winds, these I call 'Shiva winds' because they enhance spiritual consciousness and so are the precursers of change.

The original owner of our house used the lounge room as a home church for Christian ceremonies and bible readings. I think that these activities hindered the manifestation of the devic forces that pre-owned the house site. The treed farm with its seventy pet horses, hundreds of free roaming kangaroos, and thousands of birds has remained rich in devic life. But the house had its problems – particularly an aggressive female ghost who tried to keep us away. The house problems passed when I accepted custodianship of the property from the Aboriginal spirit man who cared for the ridge, its sites and pathways.

The first to reappear was a gnome. He was easy to visit via a spiral vortex in the ground. He told me about the wisdom he gets from the stars, which he keeps locked in crystals and releases when he senses the time is right – these flow via an underground ley into central Canberra. In time other gnome types have appeared. One even helped me write an article about what is wrong with modern money.

Now an air deva, a sylph, is making her home on our ridge. On windy days she becomes huge and powerful making the household hum with her energy. Its an 'off the ground' sort of feeling. Slowly the sylph has been increasing her contact with Canberra's ceremonial and mountain devas. (But she seems unable to work with the Black Mountain Deva.)

It is through these beings that the future of Australia and the world is being formed.

For better or for worse we are part of all this. We are caught up in the creative forces. One of the things that happened recently was our involvement in the creation of a new deva – a thought form that links Mt Corree (the local old man mountain of the Snowy Mountain wilderness) and gnomes to developing events in Canberra. Here is the story of that event.

'Bubblecode'

'Bubblecode' was the name of the Technomusic event.

Why did we, of all people, do it? It seemed like a good idea at the time. Part of being a custodian is to make 'one's land' available to others.

Who gave us the idea? Friends of son Robert, but in truth I think for a long time there has been the desire by the local landscape angels to interact with people. I now think that there was another reason. A desire by the beings, the gods, the consciousness (struggle for words) that are active in Canberra to establish contacts so that they can weave the desired future. This is a national and international scene.

How? The site was easy to select. A spot much favoured by roos it had its own access gate to the Cotter Rd tourist drive. It also had an open view to Mt Corree, the wise old man of the Brindabella range. Mt Corree enjoys human contact and is easy to travel to in one's imagination.

Ben was the musical director and organiser of the dance party. A week before the event he and three of his friends went to the site and started to set up. The first thing was the four metre high pyramid. This formed the ceremonial entrance to the site. We sat under this, faced Mt Corree and meditated. This appeared to establish a narrow ley line between the Corree and the pyramid, the ley acting as a link to the vast Snowy Mountain wilderness.

In the next five days the site seldom left my mind. I visited, meditated and watched a huge Pan developing. He was international and keen to be at the party to add his touch of magic. On two afternoons I was overcome with an incredible etheric weakness and dropped off to sleep, aware that some part of me was being used to build up the site. Clearly, a ritual of some power was soon to be enacted.

Interestingly, and significantly, no money thoughts were attached to the party. People contributed their time, skill and often meagre financial resources. I suspect that thoughts of unreasonable profit have become a way for terrible beings of greed and anger to enter into human affairs. These beings have a different game plan, they seek to drag humankind on the path of involution into the centre of the earth (what occultists call the 'ninth sphere').

Ben and his tribe organised the generators, lights, speakers and amplifiers. He also did a little publicity for the event. The final amplifiers were analog, digital sound seemingly is less effective, being harder for the human body and nature kingdoms to read. The speakers were designed to push the musical 'dooff' beat through the ground rather than simply place it in the air.

Ben arrived Friday morning in an overloaded kombi and started to set up. Persian rugs, old furniture, bales of hay, a parachute (as a tent for the electronic equipment). Also added were 50 tea candle lights inside paper lanterns, ultraviolet fluoro lights, fluorescent tape, overhead projectors, more pyramids, gas burners, food and heaps of other stuff.

Gradually all this was assembled to make a combined corroboree ground and Feng Shui circle. There were aspects of both design ideas, the fire and tail of the corroboree ground and the nine fold circular division of Chinese Feng Shui. On reflection, I suspect that the lay out and the days of preliminary spiritual work that I was dragged into doing for the site were important.

As the night progressed I sensed that we were inside a huge bubble and outside were the forces of hate, anger, destruction and frustration that couldn't get in. People with alcohol in their breath manifested these beings in their vapour but the huge bon fire quickly gobbled them up. I am told that at dance parties these beings usually are present and wreak havoc.

The events

Ten techno composers each had a minimum set of about an hour. The group – of about 150 at midnight – appreciated the change in style and the slight changes in the basic dooff beat which is seemingly the base of all techno music. Boxes with slides and dials where manipulated to create new sounds. Computers with on screen dials and gadgets were used. Music was being created on the spot for the location, the event, the audience. Strange music, almost instrumental but more primitive.

I let myself sink into the music and allowed it to create images in my mind. The bubble changed, it became a living sponge in which we, as people, pulsated – in and out – the primal pulse of the planet Earth's water borne breathing. Images of trilobytes came to mind – moving on the sandy ocean floor with the flow of the waves ... the Earth's creative evolutionay force.

Pan used the people. As the party progressed friends spoke to friends on their mobiles and by 2 am an uncountable 500 plus people were weaving in and out of the experience. We had planned for about 100, the car park overflowed and hundreds of cars parked along the Cotter road with a police car on patrol. Uninvited the police couldn't enter the property. The party had become a happening.

What happened? Pushed by the music, the planetary pulse of life flowed into all. Relaxed in the triple safety of private property, good Feng Shui and the bubble of spiritual protection, people became neuro transmitters between the devic kingdoms above and below the ground.

Lots of meeting was going on. Mt Corree found its way into the ground. Old Aboriginal beings came, accepting the dooff music as if it were the stamping of a hundred feet. And there was Pan or something giving love and warmth.

There certainly was peace and goodwill, but the traditional Christ? I don't think so, it all had a pre Christian somewhat sexual feel to it ... the land and the human body interacting through the spirits of form and creation. Humans and their nervous system became angels for the night. Or perhaps this is what the Christian experience is all about and we – as partakers in the post Victorian scientific culture – have just forgotten how.

By 5.00 am the crowd had faded. The numbers reduced to a couple of hundred by dawn, about 50 people greeted the day by meditation on a nearby hill. Saturday remained party day. People came and went, some dozed or chatted and all were involved with the music. Little was said in words but we all knew it had been good and the deed had been done.

The final musical set took place just before dusk on Saturday night. I meditated through some of this and noted that Pan had become a huge centaur, with his human body in the air and his horse body reaching deep into the ground. I have no idea what this means.

A friend made the comment, 'You know, the 500 people who attended the event left part of themselves behind. They are now linked to the being, the deva of the site. Spread out through Canberra they are there for the deva to use.'

Now, weeks later, a large noticeable vortex reaches from Earth to sky at the site. A narrow ley line to the Mt Corree wilderness can still be sensed. The nature of the consciousness that occupies the vortex? That's for you to judge.

Maps of the Dreaming

by Billy Arnold

My life's work

My research is about the practice of yoga samadhi. It is especially the practice of the Other Samadhi – a transitional ecstatic (beside one's self) state between the First Samadhi, with an object of focus, and the enstatic (within one's self) Second Samadhi, without an object of focus.

Samadhi, a Sanskrit word, is the final eighth stage of yoga. Samadhi means 'putting it together', i.e. putting together the seven stages preceding samadhi, which are 1. Self Restraints. 2. Fixed Observances. 3.Posture. 4.Breath Control. 5.Withdrawl of the Senses. 6.Concentration, and 7. Meditation.

If the meditation continues and deepens it becomes Absorption in Trance, which is Samadhi (Patanjali Yoga sutra 2.29). Yoga is inhibiting (then stopping) the processes of the thinking principle (Patanjali Yoga Sutra 1.2). Then, 'The Seer abides within' (Sutra 1.3). Yoga is inner vision. Posture, breath, sense withdrawal and so on are stages leading to focused inner vision.

The Other Samadhi is not the goal of yoga but is a stage of consciousness transited as going towards Second Samadhi consciousness. The other is the spiritual reality of Mother Nature. Some spirits are instantly recognisable in nature (water spirits, tree spirits, flower spirits), but some of the bigger spirits in Australia are a mystery to me until I check out sites and their entities with local Aboriginal people.

Samadhi is within everyone's reach, you don't have to be a mystic, an advanced yogi or a Saint to realize the other samadhi. Huang Wei-Chu's commentary on Chinese Sutra 4 ... *'To practice the "Samadhi of the Specific Mode", is to make it a rule to be straight-forward on all occasions in daily life and in meditation, no matter we are walking, standing, sitting, or reclining. Don't let the mind be coloured, while practicing straight-forwardness with the lips only.'* In other words be honest with others and with yourself.

'This Samadhi of the Specific Mode, is not just sitting quietly trying to quieten the mind, nor is it visualising an object or deity, such an idea is a stumbling block to the right Path, as that would mean one does not put in an appearance in the Three Worlds.' These Three Worlds by Chinese definition reiterate the Three Worlds of Australian Aborigines, being the dimensions of the unborn, the living, and the dead.

In his commentary Huang Wei-Chu mentions Virmalakirty saying to Sariputta *As to sitting quietly, it means that one does not put in an appearance within the three Worlds of Desire, Matter and of Non-Matter. It means that while remaining in Nirodha Samapatti (ecstasy with cessation of normal consciousness), one is able to perform the various bodily movements such as walking, standing, sitting or reclining. It means that without deviating from the norm, one is able to discharge various temporal duties. It means one abides neither within nor without. It means that without exterminating Klesas (defilements), one may enter Samadhi.*

This is an extremely important statement because it means you don't need to be a

Buddha to put in an appearance in the three worlds, and to see the spiritual reality of everything in nature.

Discovering the Dreaming

I first went to Alice Springs, in Australia's Northern Territory, with my adult daughter in 1997. I was hoping to meet Aboriginal people who might help me understand some of the things I had been seeing during meditations in nature. I have been compiling material about techniques of sense-withdrawal, combining classical yoga and esoteric astrology, both being about inner vision.

On arrival in Alice Springs we purchased 'Central Australian Religion; Personal

Monototemism in a Polytotemic Community', a book by Professor Ted Strehlow, who shows two of his maps that illustrate some of the songlines running through Central Australia.

One map shows songlines of dancing ancestral women, then a Dreaming of two carpet snakes Kara and Tala – La.lat.utere.le.laka. It also shows the Rain Dreaming of two rain ancestors, which runs through the Ewaninga claypan on the Old South Road, 25km south of Alice. Between Carpet Snake and Rain Dreamings are shown the songlines of Dingo Ancestors, Black Hawk Ancestors and a site of the frost women, all surrounded by Honey Ant Dreaming. Alice Springs lies between the Carpet Snake Dreaming Lalatuterelelaka and the Rain Dreaming.

Lalatuterelelaka is a site associated with the beautiful silver and blue, very frisky, yet profoundly mysterious Carpet Snake spirit called Tala, Strehlow tells us. Tala sleeps in the Hann Range north of Alice with its head east of Arulte Atwatye, its shoulder. He comes up from the Earth through a geological fault line, a split in the Earth's crust caused by ancient tectonics that raised the Range circa 800 million years ago. He flies to sites hundreds of kilometres from here and likes to visit female humans.

The Dreaming of two Carpet Snakes is the story of the two snakemen, brothers, Utnea and Enmalu, being two non-venomous pythons, Tala and Kara. They sang up landscapes, named sites and objects. The two different types of colourful carpet snakes and carpet snakemen still inhabit the same landscapes. They are 'good meat, good corroboree' says Lindsay Bird who sings Utnea as he paints Carpet Snake Dreaming.

Ewaninga Claypan

On reading Strehlow's book and seeing the proximity of Rain and Carpet Snake Dreamings to Alice Springs, I knew I had to return to find other sites on the songlines where I could meditate. A year later I sold up in Sydney and moved to the Alice. I explored like never before, practicing yoga vision everywhere I went. I started to understand the dynamics of discrimination in comprehending inner vision without analysis during yoga vision.

Within a few months I had meditated many times in town – at Corkwood, Caterpillar, Wild dog, Dingo Puppies', and Rainbow Dreaming Sites and at Earth energy sites near the old Telegraph Station, 5km north of town and at the Todd River Gap in the range some three or four km south of the CBD. Out of town I practiced at sites at the other Gaps in the MacDonnell Range, east and west of town. North and south of town I often practised focused inner vision in the dry riverbed of the Todd, also at the Ilparpa Hill and claypan sites, and at Santa Theresa Aboriginal Community, south east of Alice.

I was absolutely amazed at the variety and intensity of landscape energies, the different groups of spirits and different types of energy fields, how they worked and played together in various landscapes. I saw nature spirits living and working creatively together. I saw them combine in an instant to facilitate the manifestation of major local entities, especially at the original Alice Spring, which turns out to be not a spring, but a lens to artesian water.

At Ewaninga, south of town on the Rain Dreaming, I observed a host of local flower spirits that were present around the edge of the claypan. I watched as they combined together into a dense field, out of which manifested a mighty two-eyed water spirit which rose up from the depths of the claypan. This being then gave me a demonstration of its ability in projection of consciousness.

Eventually, I thought, I was ready to practice yoga vision on the Rain and Snake Songlines.

Carpet Snake Dreaming

At the Carpet Snake Dreaming site north of town at Arulte Atwatye (– the shoulder) I first saw the spirit Tala when he woke up, lifted his head and looked down at me. I was awed and impressed.

When I had arrived at the site I talked to the spirits, knocking on rocks with knuckles and with a little stone as I went, saying I was sorry to disturb them. I climbed the range and started to practice outer and inner focus eye exercises. I didn't see the spirit at first. I felt it lift its head up from the range, and then, with eyes closed, I saw the head 40-50 feet above me.

Tala's spirit is huge, a couple of kilometres long, a beautiful blue eyed silver spirit, so peaceful, his eyes momentarily puffy, like an infant suddenly awoken. We looked at each other for a bit then, I continued my meditation. The spirit looked around, stretched up and looked around the compass points some more. Then it went back to sleep!

The spirit appears to be bound to the Hann Range, although it can fly to other sites and waterholes some 300-400km away.

Within a few months I met owners and singers of songs of the Rain and the Carpet Snake Songlines and had seen remarkable things at the sites. The Rain Dreaming song man is from the Simpson Desert south east of Alice and the singer of Carpet Snake is from Anmatyere language country, north of Alice.

Aboriginal songs about sites and the ancient maps seen in their artwork, when used with modern maps can be really helpful in understanding landscapes and the entities inhabiting them. With them I can immediately recognise spirit of place, when attuning in a light trance.

The Geological Map sf5309 and the topographical map of the Hann Range show the geological faults in the Range west of the Stuart Highway (shown running north to south east). The geological map shows the serpentine shape of the western Hann Range.

One man's many Dreamings

The Boss man at Mulga Bore in Utopia, north of Alice, is Lindsay Bird, who is renowned in international art circles for his paintings of Carpet Snake dreaming (– a non venomous python Aspidites ramsayi). I've spent a bit of time with Lindsay in his country and in Alice. He is a born singer and it didn't take me long to hear him singing as he paints.

I have heard four songs so far, and once you understand the songs you begin to understand the landscape of paintings. Without Strehlow's map of songlines, and without Lindsay's songs and paintings of the area I would probably have had quite a shock on first seeing Tala. Lindsay's songs and paintings helped me the most with my understandings.

Lindsay Bird Mpetyane was born in Anmatyere country at Bushy Park Station about 1935. The name of the station owner Mr Jim Bird was the source of Lindsay's European surname. His Aboriginal name is Artola Art Nanaka Yunga Areteca. As a young man he worked as a cattle drover. Lindsay speaks the eastern Anmatyere language and lives at Mulga Bore between the Sandover and the Plenty Highways. Lindsay's country Aremela is spiritually dominated by the oldest rocky outcrops in the area and by the geological faults associated with the Hann Range.

Lindsay has an unusually large wealth of Dreamings – honey ant, two different kinds of snakes, a prickle plant, a white tree, the Perentie lizard, lizard eggs, the Bush Plum tree – including the plum itself and a grub which lives in the Bush Plum Tree. Lindsay paints several Dreamings and sings the songs associated with each painting as he works. He has a snake story which is about two snake men who travelled through Aremela, naming sites in the landscape. They sat down and slept at Arulte Atwatye which means 'back of the shoulder'.

The song has several levels of meaning relating to the men's journey, and the spirit beings inhabiting the sites. Lindsay says some of the stories are good corroboree for men, women and children, and some are secret business. Lindsay says 'It is forbidden in the Law' to sing the songs of some beings, even forbidden to name them. He sings Kala, 'Good corroboree', he says, 'good tucker, good meat', but he won't sing the other one named in Strehlow's map.

Lindsay doesn't own all the songlines in his country, some songs belong to other people. But he is the custodian responsible for the upkeep and the performance of ceremony at open Carpet Snake sites.

Songlines are hundreds, sometimes thousands of kilometres long. Each section of a songline is owned by a different person and only rarely will a group of singers come together to join up the songs. Lindsay's snake story covers a lot of ground starting from Harpers Spring west to Ti Tree, south to Aileron, southeast to Bushy Park, and Aremula. The songline is connected to sites at Wood Green, Woola Downs and Adelaide Bore. Lindsay's part of the snake song ends at Alcoota Creek.

Other peoples' impressions

In September 2001 the Australian Federal Government sponsored a Centenary of Australian Federation celebration at Alice Springs, called the Yeperenye Caterpillar Festival. I invited two ladies to attend the festival – Alanna, a leading dowser and Rhonda, a gifted visionary .

I told Alanna and Rhonda how I had tried to return to the sites east and west of the highway and how I planned to practice yoga vision in female company on Hann Range and had been thwarted by tragic events involving English tourists near Barrow Creek, which closed the Stuart Highway for days. When Alanna and Rhonda arrived in town we set off for the Carpet Snake Dreaming sites. We boiled a billy for tea and admired abundant flora, fauna and geology, before ascending the Range.

Then off we went to sense, in our own ways, the Dreaming of the Carpet Snake Tala. As we ascended the range we stopped to tune in and instantly I saw the huge silver form and blue eye of the serpent spirit right beside me. It looked into my eye and winked 'ok', so off I went up the south face of the range till I sensed a hesitation from the girls and on turning I saw them both frozen in a attitude of extreme alert awareness. I called 'come on' to them; but they were both asking permission to be there. I said, 'It's ok, the spirit said it's ok, he is here beside me and he says, "take them up!".'

The girls seemed inwardly busy. Alanna was doing her thing meditatively scanning, dowsing with pendulum and her hands. Rhonda said 'I know the spirit is here, I saw it'right next to you.' She had felt hot energy burning into her feet, jolts of energy up through each foot. I wondered what Alanna's pendulum had been doing. They both smiled, knowing our presence was acceptable to the spirit, so off we went to the top of the low range.

We admired the wild flowers – Holly Grevillia, and several purple flowered, highly perfumed shrubs amongst thriving native cypress pines, white eremophlia, grasses and lichen on the glazed metamorphic rock associated with the fault.

We descended the Range intoxicated by the perfumes of the blue and lilac flowers, then headed off to explore the fringe of the Eastern Hann Range, a little bit south of Amela, where lie the oldest rocks in the area. This was the area that scared me when I went there alone, yet with female company we were blessed and explored happily in rapt awe of the beautiful landscapes.

The next day an excited Rhonda told us that Tala had come to Alice Springs to pay her an early morning visit in her hotel room. Tala was up close and all she could see was a big eye looking at her, as has been described by other people who have had similar meetings with Tala.

References:
David Brooks, Carol Ruff, Jon Rhodes, 'Site Seeing' 1st published in the 'The Arrente Landscape of Alice Springs' Institute for Aboriginal Development, 1991.
Prof. Ted Strehlow, 'Central Australian Religion; Personal Monototemism in a Polytotemic Community', Flinders Press, Flinders University of South Australia. Strehlow's rare and mostly out of print books can be seen in Alice Springs Library and at the Institute for Aboriginal Development in Alice Springs.

Free downloads of geological, magnetic and gravity maps of Australia are available at www.geoscience.gov.au

Topographical maps are also available for sale from the above web address, and on CD Rom from www.auslig.gov.au

Rhonda, left, and Alanna near Alice Springs, Sept. 2001. Photo – Billy Arnold

Charles Curtayne – Energy Worker in Victoria

I visited Charles Curtayne in his Melbourne factory at Mentone and asked him about his work with Earth healing and space clearing. Charles has an engineering back ground, but is more interested in sacred technologies these days. In his one man business 'Tiamat Global', Charles is happily manufacturing various of his innovative, self-designed inventions.

For a few years in the 90's Charles teamed up with an Aboriginal fellow, a didgeri-doo player, to do space clearing work. When the digeridoo is played in certain ways, Charles told me, energies can be harmonised, hands-on-healing work can be amplified and entity removal is also facilitated. Traditionally Aboriginal people would play it to soothe fractitious infants and the like.

To begin a space clearing his partner would first play the digeridoo, generating a heart beat like drone. The rhythmic tapping of clap sticks might also be used. The intentions of the people involved were a very important aspect of the process.

If an entity needed removing Charles would locate the spot where it was hanging around, by extra-sensory means. He would then talk out loud to it, mentally linking up and asking it gently to move on towards the light and loved ones.

After spirits were released in this way there would be a completely different feel and energy level in the house and Charles would find himself broadly smiling a lot. He never encountered problems performing this work, as he felt that all those lost souls were really wanting guidance and help, and, as long as he was coming from the heart, it was always a successful operation.

For the Earthbound spirits of Aboriginal people a different strategy was used, as the Aboriginal entities seemed to respond better to fire and smoke, with the energy vortex of the fire taking them up and away, in Charles's experience. So the method was to light a small fire and to ask them to come to the fire and jump into it. Often when the entities reached this point other Aboriginal spirits from all around would appear out of nowhere and join in.

One case that he dealt with, at a haunted house in Beveridge, was a good example. In the garden there had once been a stone circle and Charles asked the four resident teenagers to help by replacing the missing stones. He then made a small fire in the middle. Having discovered a female entity lurking in the mother's bedroom, a didgeridoo drone was started up and Charles began to talk to the woman, coaxing her outside and helping her to overcome her reluctance.

Eventually she made it to the fire and as she was about to step into it some one dozen other lost souls appeared and also dived in, and thus all went upwards and were gone. The teenagers were present and most intrigued, so it was a good educational experience for them.

The Renewing of the Dreaming

Philip Simpfendorfer interviewed by Steven Guth, winter 2002.

Earlier this month Philip and I spent time together here in Canberra. We meditated, visited a few of the sites and spent hours chatting about his book, 'Journey to Earth's Dawning,' written in 1983. A time that began 'The Renewal of the Dreaming' process in Australia.

First, a bit about the Renewal of the Dreaming. In 1980 the Aboriginal Dreaming had gone underground and was fast disappearing from the Australian scene. In the 200 short years of white intrusion Aboriginal Australians had moved from being killed, to being assimilated, to being integrated. All processes that would rob any national group of its self-identity and meaningful deeper relationships with its national heritage.

What is 'Dreaming'? Well, it has several layers of meaning. Outermost is the idea of history. Without a written history Aboriginals tell about the creation and formation of the landscape by describing animals and landscape features in mystical terms. Then there is the idea that the 'Dreamtime' is the astral world, the world we visit when we sleep. The world of leftover emotions which people – given the skills and the keys – can tap into.

Then there is 'The Dreaming' attached to sites. Hills and other natural features are alive with CONSCIOUSNESS, not an imagined consciousness, but a REAL 'out there' consciousness. It is a consciousness that can be gigantic, virtually planetary in size. Many dreaming sites are places where this consciousness, finds a home and ends up being described in human terms as the site of a gods or goddesses. Gods and Goddesses are often beings who weave themselves into human affairs – for good and bad – and have done so since the birth of this planet.

Philip's involvement with the Renewal of the Dreaming began in Bali and quickly moved to Kashmir where Philip and his two travel companions, Red and Jann, came face-to-face with a goddess energy that had manifested itself through a Kashmir mystic Gopi Nath Ji. This devic energy undoubtedly accompanied Philip and his companions on their return to Australia, not long before war broke out in Kashmir.

Philip and I discussed how the first and the second Gopi Nath Ji birthday celebrations, held in Blue Mountains bush land, rapidly developed into a surprising number of Renewal of the Dreaming camps held at special sites throughout eastern Australia. Often Aboriginal people came, participated and carried away with them the energy that Philip and his companions brought from Kashmir. The first Renewal of the Dreaming camp, which Philip describes in his book, was at Mt Dromedary above Wallaga Lake on the South Coast of NSW. For the first time white Australians were being actively welcomed by Aboriginal Australians who were happy to share knowledge of their Dreamings.

Philip Simpfendorfer

Obituary by Steven Guth, July 2003

Philip's final request to his friends was not to hold him as a memory, not to consider his earthly part but to regard him as a light body moving into the future. So here I am trying to sum up his life, his notable achievements ...

His greatest gift to us? The critical role he played in the Renewal of the Dreaming – a rebirth of Australian Aboriginal site dreaming. Others were there too; Red, Jan, Guboo Ted Thomas (who passed away also in 2003), Joy, Robyn, myself and many more. But Philip is the one who from the very beginning carried the impulse from Kashmir and put the daily, continuing work into making it happen.

His priceless legacy? Custodianship of Belltrees/Glastonbell – the magic 200 hectares of land in Blue Mountains escarpment bushland, near Sydney. The property, on the Aboriginal walkway linking the West to Sydney is incredibly rich in Aboriginal site dreaming. Philip struggled with all aspects of keeping the sacred location alive and well ... too many visitors, too few visitors, too little money, too many ideas, too little water, too much water, too little firewood, too much fire ...

The site became Philip's life and his path of initiation. He has captured much of the magic of the place in his book, 'A Dreaming' in which photographs and his musings interlink to give the reader meditative insights into Philip's path. It's a jumbled path with confusing insights – perhaps because it's real. It reminds one of the 'Celestine Prophecy' and 'Mutant Message Down Under'.

Philip's book 'Journey to Earth's Dawning' is all about the Renewal of the Dreaming movement, with associated material. A free electronic copy can be downloaded from http://www.kheper.net/ecognosis/Journey/index.html

Glastonbell is still there. It is now run by a group. You can visit it electronically on http://www.hermes.net.au/glastonbell/

Or you can visit it on foot. There is a monthly gathering for meditation there.

Frank Moody:
The 'Feng Shui Man of North Qld'

Frank Moody is known internationally for his dowsing and radionic work and research, and he has been sharing his insights at dowsers' society meetings around the world for many a year. He lives with his family at Holloways Beach, near Cairns, in far north Queensland.

On 22nd April, 2003, Frank celebrated 100 years of a very full life. Hailing from Rockhampton, Frank moved to Cairns in 1926 where he worked for Francis Ireland as an accountant, before becoming a pioneer of the wireless industry in the Cairns and Far North Region (which developed out of his hobby activities). Frank helped with the establishment of the Cairns Aerial Ambulance in the 1930's and often flew to outback and coastal areas to fix or install radio facilities. His business supported him for over 30 years.

Frank was married to Ida for 49 years. She passed away in 1979, after which he travelled extensively to the UK, Europe and New Zealand, doing his dowsing, geomantic and healing work. His well known geomantic/agricultural coils have been described in the book 'Stone Age Farming'.

I caught up with Frank in 2002 in Cairns. He had recently returned from New Zealand, where he had been doing dowsing research with some biological scientists there, which had exhausted him, he told me.

'I have been dowsing since I was 12 years old,' Frank said. Eighty seven years later he's still going strong and was pleased to report his recent success in clearing possums radionically. The nuisance feral possums were removed from an orchard near Kataia, in the north island of New Zealand, using his method of adding Anchor brand coloured cottons to the broadcasting tube of a copper agricultural coil.

'To be fair' he told me 'you need to nominate where the possums can go'. Anchor cottons are getting hard to come by and so Frank is working on a radionic number for possum control. 'It's all in the mind' – is how he explains his work.

His own researches into health have resulted in some amazing healings. As for the health of the Earth, Frank urged that 'The Earth urgently needs carbon, broadcast radionically'.

Inviting cosmic energies

'In all negative areas I can usually find a spot up to 3cms diameter that accepts cosmic energy. Using my walking stick I get the direction and distance, then change to pendulum. One has to be 100% accurate,' Frank wrote in his most recent article in Geomantica (Dec 2002).

'A nursery man asked for help. I found the whole area under topsoil clay. No materials for a Moody coil. Resorted to another way to make the area receive cosmic energy.

'Having seen a 2m steel fence post, I laid it down to neutralise polarity, then drove it in 45cms vertically. Using the Y rod I demonstrated the rod charging 360 degrees and discharging 360 degrees, until the whole area was covered.

'Of particular concern were two side by side 100m long rows of plants that weren't well. Six 2m stakes were placed vertically, two at each end, and two placed centrally, facing each other. On all stake top sides facing the plants I painted in bold type – Iodine 6C (a dowsed remedy).The difference in one week was very pleasing.

'The word "Iodine 6C" was then scraped off and substituted with "Magnesium 30C", resulting in flowers that commanded a top price. This is the first time that I have broadcast homoeopathic remedies on sticks with words.

'Another method I use to introduce cosmic energy to small negative areas is to search for a stone that attracts me. I dig a hole on the dowsed spot, place the stone in it, with dowsed top facing up and dowsed orientation, then fill the hole in. It radiates 360 degrees.'

East west coils

'Experimenters may like to check on coils of one and a half turns exact, using the west-east energy common to both hemispheres. Use insulated wire, negative end to west and positive to east. Ends are 15cms long. Turns go anti-clockwise from negative/west. The coil will radiate energy out over 360 degrees.'

References:
'The Holloways Habit', April 2003.
Frank Moody, 'Just Another Day' Geomantica no. 18, Dec 2002.

Permaculture teacher Robena MacCurdy and one of Frank's geomantic coils, made for the Tui Community, New Zealand, in the 1980's.

Tim Strachan
– Geomancing the City

Perched on a sandstone ridge, its rocks carved in characteristic cragginess over the aeons since the Jurassic age, is the home of Sydney geomancer Tim Strachan and his partner Ester. The Bucketty area is largely unspoilt Sydney bushland, north of Peats Ridge and Tim and Ester's property is bordered by the wilderness of Yengo National Park. A world away from the sprawling city of Sydney that is just an hour and a half's drive away.

Across the steep valley before us – Mt Yengo loomed in the distance. Tim related to me the Aboriginal Dreamtime legend, that the creator ancestor stepped off the mountain and ascended to heaven from that point. In another direction viewed from the porch, Tim and Ester have occasionally seen mysterious lights in lines and triangular formations, fading and glowing inexplicably in the night sky over the rugged terrain. Perhaps there really is some kind of portal in that region.

'When we first moved here from the city when I tuned into this place I could often hear the faint drone of etheric didgeridoo music, like a constant background noise. Perhaps it was some connection to the spirit of place. Now I've got used to it and have to consciously tune in to hear it,' Tim told me.

In front of the house rocks have been laid to delineate two energy vortices, marking a pair of yin and yang Earth dragon spirals there. 'The downward yin spiral is a great place for earthing meditation, while the upward yang spiral helps you to lighten up,' he explained. Out the back a strong node point in the Earth's energy grid has been chosen, by dowsing, as their own sacred site. A circle of sandstone boulders rings the site and this is where the couple come to meditate and tune in to other favourite sacred sites in Australia (such as Glastonbell in the Blue Mountains) and around the world.

Being a Geomancer

Tim has no family tradition of geomancy and he came to practice it as an extension of his work as a natural therapist. Tim has a degree in Mathematics and Statistics, and also studied medicine for a while, before turning to natural therapies. He came to the energy model/perspective from a desire to link mainstream science to energetics.

Tim studied acupuncture at Russell Jewel's college in Paddington in 1972/3, but is not so keen on using needles, preferring to apply acupressure instead, along with a number of other energy disciplines. Over the years he found that there was always a proportion of patients who would not improve, despite their therapy.

He came to understand that their healing processes were thwarted by the stressed environments they lived in. 'Geopathic stress is an important health issue,' he found 'and cities are increasingly becoming more and more toxic, both energetically and physically'.

He took up dowsing to help resolve the issue and also studied the Building Biology course by correspondence from the New Zealand Institute. 'I tell some people who are unfamiliar with geomancy that I practise a kind of western Feng Shui, because so many people have heard of feng shui these days' he explained.

'However I feel that the gross aspects of the energy environment need to be addressed urgently for health purposes – electromagnetics, electrics, chemicals, indoor pollution, etc. Only then does it make sense to use such things as Feng Shui. I think that geomancy is much more fundamental to wellbeing and Feng Shui is merely fine tuning or window dressing for a place. Feng Shui was a very appropriate and high art for the Chinese culture up to a century ago – but 100 years later our western, electromagnetic, polluted culture needs rather stronger measures to deal with it.'

'Dowsing is so useful for finding your way amongst environmental energies. But dowsing competence depends greatly on the clarity of the dowser. Geomancers all seem to operate on their own band of a spectrum and so they may or may not be able to relate to each other.'

'I don't believe there is such a thing as "good" or "bad" energy. It's more a case of whether energy is blocked or flowing, as we relate to it in acupuncture' he said.

Case Studies

'When I visit someone's place for geomancy work I like to see their garden and where they like to sit in it. It usually turns out that they are already intuitively in tune with the energetically best places. I'm often mapping out what they already subconsciously know.'

But in other respects, he explained, some people are quite oblivious about stressful energies and prefer to stay in a state of denial about them. He gave a couple of examples from recent consultancy work.

'Last week I was working with a kinesiologist, who felt her energy draining away seriously at her practice rooms. She was having hip problems too, so the first thing I suggested was to remove the mobile phone that she kept constantly on her hip. No wonder her kidney energy was low! She didn't want to think the problem could be so simple and still carries her phone around in a bag at hip level.'

'Under her practice rooms I found a big stormwater drain was passing and I was able to deal with that source of energy drain. But she was very attached to her phone.'

'In another case, a woman at Bondi had electronic installations on either side of her bed, which was all decked in black, and she kept her electric blanket switched on constantly at night. She thought my suggestions too outlandish and was not even willing to experiment with reducing the amount of electro-stress she was exposed to.'

'Just recently, I was at the house of a woman who is a psychiatrist branching out into energy work, a very interesting woman. Her connection to the land was amazing and completely intuitive – she had no vocabulary to describe what she was doing but she had precisely tuned into a crossing of 2 underground streams and built a stone circle over the crossing where she now holds healing groups. She couldn't have picked a better place. And she had also attracted local birds and devic energies into the garden with water features, lots of flowering Australian flora, and her energy work. She is a natural geomancer.'

'I've also had a few cases recently checking out inner-city flats on main roads. Invariably the readings on the Gaussmeter (magnetic field readings) have been ridiculously high, especially on the side of the flat near the street, and more so when it's a main road. I'm talking about 100 mGauss or more, and when you think that the rather generous Government guidelines recommend no more than 3 mG, you can see these people are being cooked! If you sleep in an area with readings over 1 or 2 you are in serious danger, especially if there is the added problem of geopathic stress due to underground water or Hartmann grid crossings. The best thing is to move out for these people – and the next best thing is to install a combination of my PowerHouse and ElectroGuard.'

The Energy Store
Over the last eight years Tim has been creating and developing a comprehensive range of products to help people to at least live in a healthy 'bubble' within the stress of the city. Through The Energy Store he markets various devices to alleviate electro-stress and geopathic stress in the home and these are easily affordable for all. In several cases his Powerhouse – based on a double Lakhovsky coil, has had the welcome side-effect of ridding a place of a cockroach plague, the cockies seemingly not happy in the energetically changed conditions of reduced turbulence. In combination with the ElectroGuard, he says, most places improve noticeably. A well-known Sydney naturopath couldn't use his session rooms without these devices, but found it fine when they were installed.

Tim sells ceramic beads to reduce 'Electro-smog' from mobile phones and other devices. He also produces water energisers which have the obvious effect on city water of greatly reducing chlorine odours, as well as other more subtle benefits, due to the highly paramagnetic material he uses along with a number of other (secret) ingredients to increase the energising effect.

Well known natural animal therapist Jackie Fitzgerald once recommended his water energiser to a dairy farmer near Lismore, in northern NSW. As a consequence of their drinking energised water the cows became less aggressive and more friendly, and also began to produce more milk.

Dowser's holiday
Twelve years ago (in 1992) Tim and Ester embarked on a three month trip to the UK, Israel and Hawaii, armed with angle rods and Hamish Miller's book – 'The Sun and the Serpent'. They followed the so-called Mary and Michael lines – massive Earth energy lines that some people might refer to as major dragon lines or dreaming tracks. These

yin and yang lines weave their way along the landscape, interacting at sacred sites, in a caduceus pattern. 'It's particularly good to have a male and female pair of dowsers following them' he recommended.

'The trip was like a pilgrimage for me, and great practise for my dowsing. I felt like I was reconnecting to the ancient past, like there was a re-awakening of old traditions buried deep in my psyche or genetic memory. Maybe I was there in a past life, who knows?'

Peter Archer
– New Zealand Flower Power!

New Zealander Peter Archer is the creator of a range of flower and gem essences – the New Millenium Essences of New Zealand – which have proved greatly beneficial for people and animal healing. Peter produces specialist kits of remedies to assist with such things as counselling, recovery from addiction and animal problems. He also makes remedies for feng shui and land healing.

Essences evolving

'I started off with the classical method of Dr Bach who pioneered this modality in the 1930's. He floated blossoms in water in the sunlight – this is now a well proven technology.' Peter said. Unlike Dr Bach, who was contented with just a small range of flower remedies, Peter is constantly discovering new flowers and currently makes up a range of 3-400 different ones to address various conditions, as well as a few animal remedies.

After Peter stumbled across a book by New Zealand flower essence pioneer Mary Garbely ('A New Perception', published in 1990) he was totally intrigued. Fortunately he had the opportunity to study under Mary. After this he then did a major study of the American Perelandra methods between 1994-99.

'I lived, breathed, slept Perelandra' he said. 'I had every book, tape and essence that Machaelle Small-Wright produced and learned the methodical approach she espoused. When you're learning to be a chef you need to follow the rules before you improve on the recipe.'

Peter then launched into original work in discovering new remedies and uses for flowers, including some very deep cleansers. Nowadays he has developed enough short cuts that his style of operation is much different.

He was lucky to have had a colleague – Lisa Bruens – who had the ability to channel the information about the remedies from the flowers. He would telephone her and tell her the name of the flower and she would be able to describe its healing potential. These days he is confident enough to work alone.

With the evolution of his work, processes not possible before are now happening rapidly. For example – a microbial balancing process can now be achieved with just one flower and previously this wasn't believed to be possible. The Perelandra energy balancing technique takes one hour. Peter has discovered ways to expedite this process so that he can achieve the same results in just a few minutes, by connecting to the devas. It can be almost instantaneous. 'The time has come for new ways' Peter enthuses.

Flowers and geomancy

In 1999 Peter was called to check out a house with distinctly bad energy. He was able to do a cleansing on it, but he was called back again. There was a particular spot in one of the rooms that was very creepy and the cat would always avoid walking through it, going right around. Inwardly he asked 'what is it?' and the answer he received was that this was an emotional pattern from pre-European times, where, for over several 100 years there had been a small wooden cage structure where people had been cruelly imprisoned.

Peter asked for help from 'his team' – the deva of energy cleansing. The tainted energy lifted instantly. From that moment on the cat would always walk straight through the area.

Going beyond the Perelandra system, he always checks if there are any energy patterns on a very deep level at a place that needs energy work, such as 'fractures' in the energy matrix. (For example, he once checked out a house with such an energy split, where a woman used to lock herself away from an abusive husband.)

Peter mostly works with people, but is keen to do more Earth healing. For this he generally works without 'props', except for specially selected, energised stones or pebbles. He finds stones in high energy places and wild beaches and keeps them until some are needed. He first charges them up energetically, and either gives them to people to use, or else distributes them around a building.

Peter might place stones in a window to bring in cosmic energies, or put a large stone on an earthing place, to become a focus for earthing, as some houses, he finds 'are kind of just floating.' A stone which he has identified as being a 'heart stone' might be put near a fire place, as it has an affinity with the heart.

Lately he has also developed a range of flower essences to do similar work for land healing and house balancing. Some of his people remedies have also proved useful in this respect.

Peter has created a standard mix of flower essences for Earth healing work in a spray bottle. But that alone may not be enough, he stresses. 'People must be prepared to do inner work on them selves if they want their environment to change' he says.

Peter is mainly marketing his flower essences through his website and he has had many encouraging healing successes with people from around the planet who are using them.

Intuitive method

So just what is the technique that he uses to discover new remedies, I asked?

'Nature reflects to us what we need to know' Peter explained.

When the energies between the Earth and the cosmos are in a suitable alignment Peter intuits to go outdoors and seek a flower of particular usefulness. These flowers, which he finds in parks and gardens, just seem to jump out at him, so he takes their photo and uses that to make remedies with.

The energy signature of a flower is invited to come into a bowl of water from the photo. A popular remedy might have a mother tincture made from it first.

'When I do this work I'm in "auto pilot mode" ' Peter laughs, obviously taking great delight in his work.

'If people want to try this method of healing for themselves they can check out an innovative "on-line healing" system on my website and see the photos of these beautiful flowers and read the story about how it all came about' Peter suggested.

Peters website is at www.nmessences.com

John Billingsley
– Yorkshire Dreaming

John, a geomancer, folklorist and magazine editor, was interviewed by Alanna Moore at his home in West Yorkshire, UK, in April 2000.

JB: 'I originally come from London and in 1975 I came to this valley, the Hebden Bridge area of west Yorkshire. A series of coincidences brought me the information that there was cheap property in the area. It all started on top of Glastonbury Tor one Easter in 1975 when I was sleeping on top of the Tor with 25 other people and made some good friends, and following connections from there I got on a sort of wave that carried me up to this area in August.

This was the first house we looked at, and although we looked at lots more and thought it was in terrible condition – this was the one! Bought it for 1,100 pounds, and prices like that made Hebden Bridge a focus for alternative culture. People in the '70s came here in droves. It was a depopulated area then, but now the demographics are a different thing. So I moved here to a village called Mytholmroyd, which is close to Minchely Moor.

Minchely Moor reveals itself

Quite soon after I found myself attracted to Minchely Moor and one of the things that happened was that I got to know a phenomena called The Watcher. Walking on the moor I'd see a figure watching me and when I'd get to the spot where I'd seen the figure – there would be nothing to be seen. This happened so often I couldn't just dismiss it.

A few other odd experiences happened. The first time I heard a curlew it flew up behind me about 15 yards away and it uttered the most mournful cry that it seemed to me like a message from some other world ... At Minchely Moor there is a standing stone, not an ancient one, but one that is a tremendous focus for folklore. There are bronze age sites and an earth circle, so it is an ancient landscape, but not much is left and I keep finding myself drawn there.

There was one time in 1978 when I had taken a mind altering substance and been driven to walk across Minchely Moor in a hail storm. I felt impelled to climb up there and eventually found myself walking along, head down to keep the hail out, and I found myself following a path that seemed to be going around in a circle. And when I looked up I discovered myself in what turned out to be a bronze age earth circle. So it turned out it be a new archeological site. When I went to Japan in 1980's I found myself going there to ask permission to make that decision, so I'd developed a tremendous relationship with the whole area, particularly with Minchely Moor.

I went to Japan in the '80's and in the '90's I came back and began to visit Minchely Moor again. I eventually discovered several other bronze age structures, including a cairn circle, a cairn field and two possible standing stones. So what we are looking at now at Minchely Moor is a bronze age ritual landscape. It's been there for years, much of it hidden by heather. But for me it seems that Minchely Moor has been saying to me ever since 1975 "I'm going to show you something". And these are the experiences which underpin my spiritual relationship with the area, my very close relationship with the spiritual atmosphere of Minchely Moor and those beings that interact.'

AM: 'So what have you been doing in the folklore area?'

JB: 'My first interest in Earth mysteries was mainly archeological and folklore. But the more I got involved with earth mysteries the more my interests shifted to folklore, and its role in building and maintaining aspects of community. Community, of course, is an important focus for alternative culture, so I grew away from archeology.

I began to realise that to help keep alive community I could tell the stories and help keep the folklore alive and I tend to focus on two areas. One is stories about place, because I think they are very important, they need to be told and retold, preferably at the place, when going on walks and providing some archeological background as well. So keeping the stories alive is important to me and in a sense I'm saying thank you to the land which is feeding me all this information as well. There's a story telling group in Hebden Bridge and anyone can come and hear these stories.

Secondly – I'm gathering and writing up the local legends and putting them in one place because there's not much left of the underlying basic Yorkshire culture, what with all the new people coming here from all over. We can learn from the land and the older people here. I'm not doing so much of this now, more so in the 1970's. I get snippets from the older people, and I'm going to be giving a talk soon where I will be asking the people of Mytholmroyd to help me gather the stories.

But you do have the situation where I am a (relative) outsider coming in and asking them about their traditions and some or most people don't want to tell them to me. So far what I have learnt most are things that are told to me in casual conversations and not as a result of me asking them directly. This is an important point. I suspect I would have to spend a lot more time in pubs for more to be divulged! It takes at least a generation before you are accepted around here, so who knows?'

AM: 'You have had people tell you about fairies, can you elaborate on that?'

JB: 'Well it wasn't so much in this area that this has been expressed, but not far away. And I have the experience myself of seeing, feeling, hearing, being in contact with something that is explicable in terms of traditional fairy lore and that's putting it on the fence as much as I can.'

The Fairies of Cottingley

But about 15 miles from here is the Cottingley village near Bradford, where the famous Cottingley fairy photographs were taken at the beginning of this century. Now these photos were hoaxes, with the exception of one of them. One of the girls said it was a hoax and the other one said it wasn't all a hoax. Generally speaking the whole affair could be put down to a hoax by the girls and there the matter could rest, but one of our Northern Earth readers lives in Cottingley and she's made contact with some of the older people there and some of the old ladies there said to her 'oh yes, there are fairies in that area', they all knew that. 'They aren't the ones in the pictures, but they are there.'

Cottingley these days is rather dirty and polluted however there have been other more recent fairy reports from Cottingley, so it seems that its something of a fairy hot spot. So what does this mean? Are the fairies returning to these old industrial places? Were they frightened away and are they now coming back, just like the otters and kites are? Or have they always been there and are they becoming more familiar to us. But at the moment there seems to be a growing awareness and experience of what you could broadly call the fairy realm. What it is we don't know. There are plenty of theories, theories that you can make anything you like from. But people are coming into contact with some sort of energy, which seems to have a close association with the spirit of place. This suggests that as a culture we are coming a little bit closer to the spiritual dimension.

Of course, we are not supposed to believe in fairies, 'they don't exist' we are told, but the fact remains that over the years many people, and not just in this country, have been seeing fairies. So what do we do with such a weight of evidence? I think we need to re-examine it through the lens of tradition, it's a more positive way than viewing it merely from a, say, new age perspective. We need the weight of past generations to help us to understand this phenomena and to help us to make contact with them.

Today's approach to fairies is to imagine them as little light fay creatures who are only interested in doing good. But if you look at fairy tradition you know that fairies are amoral. They don't want to help us particularly, they're just getting on with their job and sometimes it involves stealing human babies, sometimes it involves creating accidents, if we interfere with their living areas. We know that the fairies aren't that nice. We really need to know that before we go trying to make contact. We should go and ask them to tell us about themselves instead of going in with our assumptions. So this whole fairy thing has several layers of meaning.

But this area of existences of the unseen is very difficult to deal with and open for someone to impose their own beliefs and interpretations and it's very hard to come at it with a completely open mind. This is also where Earth mysteries has its strongest effect in that it tries not to come at something from a reductionist, academic viewpoint, and not from a too wide open and credulous viewpoint, which we find too much in the new age area. It's about trying to find the area inbetween, whereby you can experience something and then see what might be contributing to that and find what the best way of interacting with that. It's the ordinary person's holistic way of dealing with the sacred world around them. Because when it comes down to it – Earth mysteries primarily deals with sacred landscapes and sacred traditions.'

Northern Earth

AM: John – you are the editor of Northern Earth, the longest running earth mysteries magazine in Britain. Can you tell me about that?

JB: The Northern Earth was founded in 1979 with myself and Brian Larkman from Leeds. We got together a bunch of other northern researchers and then linked up with people like Phillip Heselton, John Barnet, the archeologist and Richard Smith, the geographer, and so we created the Northern Earth Mysteries group. It was a fairly active researching group throughout the 1980's, and out of it came a newsletter, which became the magazine, which, in 1982 had its name changed to 'Northern Earth'. We've been going now for 21 years so that makes us pretty venerable, the oldest regional magazine of its kind in Britain and now, since the folding of the Ley Hunter magazine in 1999 we've now become the oldest Earth mysteries magazine in the whole world!

As a small magazine we are not mass circulation at all but have built up a loyal readership committed to a free thinking approach to Earth mysteries which doesn't ally itself with any religious or academic stance but prioritises amateur research and the best of amateur work on alternative approaches to archeology, folklore and the sense of place generally.

There are two Northern Earth websites that we have as well. So we're also trying to keep some contact with rest of the world, but it's not easy to get known out there. There are very few outlets, London's Atlantis bookshop is one. Nowadays there are dwindling numbers of these magazines. Small press economics is a big problem. And the fact of being a small press tends to mean there are some obstacles in getting your name across to interested people, especially in the less populated areas, so we are still not known to all people north of Derbyshire. Small presses have this difficulty of getting the awareness across. But word of mouth has pretty much has kept us going. The website hasn't been too helpful and may have cut sales, because many people will make a magpie search on the internet, rather than subscribe.'

Connecting with the land

AM: 'So is your future aim to continue with your work of connecting with the land?'

JB: 'Yes. In a sense I don't have a choice. When I started finding the archeological sites at Minchely Moor it was just at a time when I was thinking of moving away from the valley and suddenly I had found another five new sites and I had to deal with the fact that I had been shown these and at that point I realised I couldn't move away that easily. I had asked permission to move away and that permission wasn't coming. So for me the interaction with place here has remained and now I've actually bought a new house which is closer to Minchely Moor and is also tied up with a sense of being called to that place, so I can't see myself leaving now until I get called to somewhere else. So for me it's being open to what the land is saying to me.

I'll continue to write about the local landscape and traditions and I'll probably continue to do the walks which integrate the two, telling the stories of the places and running this magazine, unless another editor appears, which hasn't happened yet. But it's too old and venerable to let it die, and with so many similar magazines dropping off, Northern Earth is one of the few left to keep these traditions alive. It's the only organ of holistic free thinking interpretation of place, that steers this middle line between too much empiricism and too much credulity. So it's got to keep going, although I'm getting a bit tired and could do with a break.'

AM: 'You're doing a great job, John! Thanks!'

John and Akiko Billingsley

PART SIX

Working with Earth Energies

Suburban Sacred Site

The enigma of the vortex

Since time immemorial humankind has revered the spiral form. Its image crops up around the globe – etched into rock, in body design, marked out as a labyrinth …

From a geomantic perspective this fascination comes as no surprise. The spiral form is how energy tends to manifest and unfold in great intensity, such as the frond of a fern unfurling. And in terms of Earth energies an Earth vortex can be a powerful in or out breath point, where Earth acupuncture might be needed.

Sacred sites around the planet are often to be found in association with a powerful Earth energy vortex of seven or eight rings. Labyrinths at cathedrals are found to be located at an Earth spiral and, in Australia, I have found that Aboriginal bora grounds (circular areas used for corroborrees and intitiation) are also located over a vortex.

Whether the vortices were there first, or became manifest in response to activities happening at these sites is another thing …

As a geomancer I have had to attempt to either move or shut down vortices when they were found in peoples' homes. The energy is usually too intense to live with. But what may happen when we embrace the potential that is offered?

In the following cases an Earth energy vortex in a suburban home goes through an energy activation process and gains the potential to become a sacred site – a healing site for the local area and beyond, a vibrant node in the Earths energy network, 'like a shining beacon that is connecting with other sacred sites around the world'.

Vortex in the house

My friend Barbara Galloway had lived in her home since 1986, aware of powerful energies there. But she did not recognise the existence of an upward flowing spiral energy vortex in one of the bedrooms. Her daughter, who had been sleeping on the vortex, had had some unusual and unwelcomed psychic experiences.

The vortex was fairly dormant in those days, but it was still capable of affecting consciousness. Barbara and her daughter began their own self-healing journeys and eventually Barbara started to work as a spiritual healer, using the vortex room after her daughter moved out. This was the beginning of the activation of the vortex.

I was invited to stay over when passing through Melbourne and feeling the need to do some energy dowsing of the house, I discovered the presence of the vortex. Having explained to her what a vortex was all about, my assistance was then enlisted to work with the energy there and to be a part of an activation process.

Vortex characteristics

An Earth spiral can act as a spirit portal and my first impression of Barbara's vortex, in April 1999, confirmed this. On entering the room I perceived that it was rather crowded with invisible visitors. However I always slept well there when visiting.

When originally dowsed, it was found that the vortex had two or three energy rings and covered just one corner of the room. By February 2000 eight wide energy bands were found to be spreading across the small house block and Barbara was told by her spirit guides that these would be increasing.

Earth energies vary in strength and character according to the cycles of the sun, moon and planets, and the vortex is strongest at full moon. (However the strength, clarity and purity of peoples intentions is always the greatest factor in this and all transformation work.)

After several sessions of meditation work I was invited to 'interview' spirit energies about the site. These are their words, as channelled by Barbara.

Connecting up

'There are countless opportunities for this work to happen throughout the world. The key is self-knowledge, self healing and awareness. Now universal energy has been connected to the site, spirit set it up as a transmitter and since then new energies have been assisting the work from beyond the Earth. There is an energy grid connecting all the planet's sacred sites and they are like little power houses. As people become aware, divine forces are brought down and Heaven and Earth are connected.'

'The site has the effect of accelerating healing processes, not just for individuals on-site but also there is a 'fall-out' effect for a long distance. The rest of metropolitan Melbourne is acted upon by this energy going out. With more people coming and using the site, more consciousness is brought to this space and the influence will be spread further. Still more anchoring work is required to be done relating to Earth changes.'

'In the network of sacred sites people provide the heart centre, connecting Heaven and Earth. These sites are the chakra points and they are found all over the universe. There is a perception that there are a fixed number of sacred sites. We have facilitated the development of this site to show that these sites can be anywhere and everywhere, just as this vortex covers an ordinary house block in the suburbs, acting as a beacon of light and connecting with the other sites. So healers can connect with this site, which acts as a portal to bring down the highest healing forces. They can connect with it from wherever they may be.'

It was requested of me to spread this information far and wide, to assist both personal and planetary healing, to improve the vibrancy of the planet's energies and to accelerate healing processes.

Another Site in the Making

Some time later, after relocating to a country town north of Melbourne, Barbara found herself going through another energy activation process with another vortex that, co-incidentaly – was found in her new home.

'Heart House' as it had became known, had been empty for some time. I was asked to do an energy dowsing survey and soon found that there was a small four ringed, upward flowing vortex, located in the corners of several rooms. A photo of the Dalai Lama had been put up in the vortex corner of the lounge room.

Standing on one of the bands of the vortex I closed my eyes, sank into a meditative state and attuned to the latent energy there. Almost immediately I became aware, in my mind's eye, of an old Aboriginal elder man in spirit, standing before me. He was friendly and I asked him mentally if it was okay if friends did spiritual work there. Yes it was, he told me, and he would help.

Behind him in the distance I saw a host of Aboriginal spirits connected to him, perhaps an ancient ancestral line, which stretched out upwards ad infinitum. I was quite surprised at my rapid introduction to his world, especially as I usually didn't perceive spirits visually. But such is the nature of the vortex that one's experiences are accentuated and amplified, and this certainly seemed the case.

Dancing the site

As Barbara lay in bed on her first night there, she clairvoyantly saw a group of Aboriginal spirits dancing a corroboree around her in joyful welcoming. Perhaps this place had been a corroboree ground in the pre-colonial past? Or a sacred site of some kind.

One weekend we ran a series of daily group meditations, as a component of World Environment Day events. At the first meditation with the group Barbara perceived a spirit corroboree being held inside the circle of participants. The old spirit man who I had met before joined with us in our healing meditation and Barbara was aware of a great host of other spirit energies around us. The atmosphere was positively buzzing.

After our second group meditation my dowsing showed that the vortex had swollen rapidly in size, gaining an extra two rings, and with all the rings much thicker. In the third meditation that evening, with eight people participating, I sensed a wise old Aboriginal woman elder spirit behind me, a bit shyer than her male counterpart, with short white hair. I felt her putting her hand on my shoulder and resting it there for a short time. I felt greatly honoured by her presence.

Later, when Barbara was relaying her guidance about connecting to Mother Earth I suddenly felt electrified, my spine and nerves seemingly wired up to some great energy current. Barbara had felt similarly 'switched on' earlier that morning. The activation process seemed to be really moving along.

After the final meditation on Sunday my dowsing revealed the vortex to have grown to seven rings – the number which often signifies a sacred site- with its energy reaching to the neighbour's walls. So most of the house was filled with vortex energy. And we were extended our energetic influence to around the town, particularly to the nearby Theatre Royal, where WED events were taking place with much goodwill. Barbara said that our Aboriginal spirit friends were involved too.

That night there was a wonderful closing ceremony at the Theatre Royal to cap off a great weekend. Craig Nelson, a Queensland Aboriginal man, treated us to an amazing didgeridoo performance. He told us to relax, close our eyes and let ourselves be taken away by the sounds. And what a sound feast it was! Like an incredible sound massage, reverberating deeply to the core of our being.

I became aware that my Aboriginal spirit friends were both standing behind me, their eyes blazing, shining with excitement at the thrill of hearing those vibrant sounds.

A couple of months went by.

Expanding vortex

Before it was time for Barbara to travel overseas we decided to do some more group energy work with the vortex. Barbara organised a spiritual workshop, for women to connect with the goddess energies. It was a powerful day of inner work. We all had some revealing, challenging and intense experiences throughout the day, no doubt accelerated by being on the vortex.

By that time there were at least a dozen vortex rings counted by pendulum and it reached half way across the street. After the workshop I dowsed that another exponential leap in vortex size and qualities had occurred. It now reached further down the street, each ring greatly strengthened and widened. I could feel each ring as an energy 'wave' in my whole being as I walked down the street. I could count 16 rings, but later distant dowsing suggested there might be up to 28. Barbara's guidance was that the vortex was covering much of the towns CBD and it's vibrations were now more powerful than ever.

Thus, it seemed, for a second time we had achieved the raising of the latent potential of a vortex, potentising the site and elevating the consciousness of its denizens.

Postscript – After Barbara left 'Heart House' it was necessary to shut down the vortex so that the next resident would be able to live a quiet life!

'Practising the Witch's Craft – real magic under a southern sky'

Book Review

Rather than a practical how-to that this title might suggest, this book allows ordinary people in Australia, who have discovered that life is enchanted and that Witchcraft works for them, to speak about their ideas about and experience of the Craft. What has it got to do with geomancy, you might ask? I'll let Yarrow, author of the chapter on 'Sacred Landscapes', explain:

'The current within Witchcraft and Paganism that concerns me here is often a hidden one and is about having a right relationship with the sacred land. This undoubtedly doesn't fire the public imagination to the same degree as visions of Witches working magic and spells, or of groups of people dancing naked around bonfires. However, within Witchcraft and Paganism, there are also those who have an ongoing intimate relationship with the land on which they live. The public face of this is the environmental and political activism of groups and traditions such as Dragon Environmental Network, Reclaiming, and others of a similar nature, which often concern them selves with civil disobedience and working magic in an effort to prevent inappropriate development of particular locations.

'The more hidden face takes the form of a direct and intimate relationship with the very land itself. Many people might label this as Shamanism or Druidry rather than Witchcraft. I find these sorts of distinctions are often rather arbitrary, as many Witches freely acknowledge the Shamanic roots of their religion and practise.'

Yarrow gives practical tips about relating to the sacred land, such as:

'Treating a landscape as sacred involves practical tasks that Nigel Pennick refers to in "Celtic Sacred Landscapes" as "spiritual gardening" Some of this involves picking up litter, removing noxious weeds, restoring damage, adding only those man-made things that are strictly necessary and in keeping with the environment, and removing those things that aren't. It also means ensuring that biodiversity is retained and helping the right species to grow. These sorts of activities can be easily undertaken on either an individual or a group basis, and many "friends of" groups have been formed to care for particular reserves, rivers and other sites. Using and visiting a sacred site requires some form of repayment, and lugging several huge sackfuls of other peoples' rubbish a kilometre or more up a dirt track often feels like payment enough!'

As for ethics:

'When interacting with the landscape consciously, we need to become aware of what it is actually telling us. In neo-Paganism, people often talk of concepts such as "asking permission" to a tree, for example, when cutting a wand. The underlying assumption seems to be that permission for our activities will inevitably be granted. Sometimes, however, it is not, and we need to become more aware of that possibility Similarly, permission to go into certain locations may not always be granted, even to someone who has been there many times before The natural world is not inherently benevolent to humans, and some landscapes seem not to particularly care to have us around' says Yarrow.

In another chapter Lesley-Caron Veater tells us about the delights of A Witch's Garden and overall the book is a great read for all those who aspire to eco-spirituality.

Douglas Ezzy (and others), 'Practising the Witch's Craft – real magic under a southern sky' Allen and Unwin, 2003.

A Workshop of Earth Attunement

It was a workshop to introduce people to geomancy in a small country town in central Victoria. The afternoon would include visiting a local site which has been special to the white villagers since the gold rush days of the 1850's and to the Aboriginal people before them.

Geomancy defined
Our exercise in connecting to sacred space firstly needed some definition. To start with – just what is geomancy? Geo means the Earth in Greek. The –mancy bit means divination, also from the Greek. (Gaia-mancy sounds even better!)

The Macquarie Concise Dictionary gives two meanings. The second being that it is a type of divination where shapes made at random are interpreted as prophetic. But the more common meaning is that geomancy is 'the achievement of harmony, physical and spiritual, between a person and their environment, with regard to the placement of buildings, monuments, etc. Cf. Feng shui.'

I would hastily add that geomancy is a lot more than just putting the shack in the right spot. Aboriginal geomancers would give much deeper meaning to the term, and speak of the consciousness and life force of the landscape.

What is a sacred site?
And what of sacred sites? Do white fellas really have none? What has the Macquarie got on this?

The Macquarie provides three definitions, which range from the intensely sacred to the highly secular. We are told that a sacred site is:

1. a site of significance or sacredness in Aboriginal tradition.
2. a site or institution with a particular religious, cultural or historical significance; eg Lourdes is a sacred site to many Catholics.
3. (usually ironic) a site or institution of significance to a particular group of people eg the Melbourne Cricket Ground is a sacred site to cricketers.

Well then, it seemed that we were indeed heading for a proper sacred site that day, a site of cultural significance to the local white people at the least. Unfortunately little is known about the Aboriginal significance of the site, although some people have been aware of strong spirit presences there at times.

The legacy of mining
As a sort of warm-up for our 'pilgrimage' the group ambled up the slope of a ridge that comes down off Mt Tarrengower, a mountain behind the village. Here the ravages of intensive gold mining are obvious and ugly. Open shafts only partly filled in and mullock heaps are everywhere. Topsoil is mostly gone and the regrowth of the eucalypts is typically scrawny, the coppiced limbs weak.

Billy Arnold, my co-facilitator, described to the group how he comes here to visit a huge Earth mother spirit – with rayed headdress and powerful presence. He first observed this Wandjina type nature spirit when we were in Western Australia late 2001. In this part of the world are found, in the Kimberleys at least, depictions of the Wandjina at rock art sites, and she is considered to be a supreme Earth mother being by the Aboriginals. When he described the being to Malcolm Borgward in Collie, it was suggested that Billy was actually seeing the great Wandjina.

When Billy first saw Wandjina here at this place she was weeping. Weeping for the degradation of the environment, no doubt. When we visit her we send our respects and good energy to her. It was good to hear that Wandjina was not crying any more.

We sat on the rocks that covered the area – white quartz left from the mining, now encrusted with lichen – and tuned into the spot, going into meditation and opening up to any impressions received. There was the usual good feeling to the area, despite its past history.

A Nature Temple?

Billy reports seeing many nature spirits in the vicinity and we suspect that the area is what author Marko Pogacknic would describe as a nature temple. That is – an area where strong energies and nature spirits abound. Such sites, with added cultural signif-icance, would be known as sacred sites as well.

Nature temples often comprise groups of high energy/spirit centres in a triangular arrangement. Here it is so, with three mountains – Mts Tarrengower/Moorul, Alexan-der and Franklin – at each corner. It's certainly a magical area.

The longest running pagan festival in Australia, the Beltane gathering has been held annually in the crater of Mt Franklin, over the last 30 odd years. Recently (July 2004) a mobile phone tower was prevented from being erected on its summit, due to the heritage value – the sacred iconic reputation of this conical ex-volcano.

At Mt Alexander the Dog Rocks site, with its enormous granite oulders, is used by local Aboriginal people and the Aboriginal reconciliation movement for gatherings. Prof. Callahan has also checked out Dog Rocks energetically, finding it to be very powerful paramagnetically (see it in the back of his book 'Paramagnetism,' published by Acres USA).

At The Rock of Ages

We then headed off to the site known as the Rock of Ages, the summit of Mt Moorul, close to Mt Tarrengower. We wound our way up the charming little dirt track, through the regenerating forest of the Nuggetty Ranges, up to the magnificent pink granite bouldered hilltop site. (The hills were denuded during the gold rush. Now a new threat to the site emerges, as a mining development threatens to send trucks roaring past here, with the rustic track enlargened, cleared and straightened for them. We have been writing letters of protest to the council.)

The Rock of Ages site has a wonderful energy, thanks partly to the presence of the pink granite. I have been told that it is a Rainbow Serpent site of Aboriginal signifi-cance. Billy usually observes a lively pair of Rainbow Serpents frolicking around the site, and I have sensed their presence too.

The site also has significance to the rest of the local community. With its wonderful views of nearby Mt Tarrengower and distant plains punctuated by extinct volcanoes, it has drawn white people to have picnics there since the days of the gold rush, one hundred and fifty years ago. The miners and their families would attend church on Sundays, then walk up the track to the hilltop singing the song 'The Rock of Ages'. That is how it got it's name.

The first thing we did was to ask the spirits of place for permission to visit. We laid our hands on the 'touchstone' at the site's entrance and silently attuned to the place. After a few moments I felt a flood of loving energy going straight to my heart. A good sign of welcoming, I thought.

We then sat in the shade of a tree and played around with pink granite pendulums, using them to help us find interesting spots to attune to. Previously I had dowsed that an energy ley line was coming over here from Mt Tarrengower. Without knowing about it, one of the participants placed herself just where it touched down!

I was guided to a huge boulder that jutted out from the hillside and afforded great views. Oddly I had always previously got the message to avoid this spot and had never before gone there, although I had always wanted to. This time we all went and sat there. We had a ceremony of thanks and chanted harmonically, our hands joined as we sat in a circle on the rock.

Billy observed that the nature spirits were delighted about our activities and positioned themselves above us, directing our energies upwards as we sang. It certainly felt magical.

Pogacnik says that the devas love to be recognised and acknowledged. This is why people have long gone on pilgrimages to sacred sites, where their offerings are reciprocated as they receive the blessings of the spirits of place. I felt that we had also been successful at making a good connection with the devas here.

Postscript – The gold mining company's application to widen the road for truck access near the Rock of Ages has now been withdrawn!

Sacred sites rule – OK?

Gariwerd Gathering

by Junitta Vallak

On a winter's weekend in 2003 about 2000 people gathered from far and wide to attend a gathering of indigenous elders and others at the fabulous Brambuk Aboriginal Centre at Halls Gap, The Grampians/Gariwerd, Victoria. Junitta Vallak reported the events in Geomantica.

'World Peace and Prayer Day' was founded in 1996 by Chief (Dr) Arvol Looking Horse, Spiritual Leader of the Lakota, Dakota and Nakota Nations (collectively known as the Great Sioux Nation).

Along with thousands of concerned citizens of the Americas, Chief Arvol Looking Horse began to promote this Wolakota (Lakota word for Peace) event. This vision was then extended to the global community and he is now pursuing a UN world proclamation declaring June 21st as 'Honouring Sacred Sites Day', where all people join together for the healing of the Earth and all beings to live in sustainable harmony and peace.

The international delegation that attended WPPD at Gariwerd included peace leaders, cultural representatives, multi-faith dignitaries and representatives of social and environmental causes.

This was the 8th WPPD and the theme was 'Coming Home'. It was directed at youth in culture and the arts and was synchronised with other gatherings at local sacred sites around the world.

There was no charge for this event, which featured traditional ceremonies and prayer from indigenous elders, cultural leaders and representatives. After a march from Lake Bellfield on the first day led by Chief Arvol, a sacred fire was lit on the plateau above, flanked on either side by spectacular Ranges. The fire was made in the center of a huge medicine wheel that had been marked out with stones and showed the four directions. Everyone except the elders stayed outside the circle.

At the end of the first round of ceremonies, everyone queued up clockwise outside the circle and entered through the east gate to make an offering and say prayers at the sacred fire. They then exited through the west gate. It was very cold and wet the first day but things proceeded regardless. As elders spoke, flocks of white cockatoos flew overhead, usually at most appropriate moments. As the weather improved, rainbows arched over our heads and the sky became blue with sunny breaks.

By the last day, people were shedding winter clothes as they watched Tony Ghost Hawk dance and listened to Blue Feather and other elders speak. There were many profound moments and much wisdom shared.

There were many cultural performances including music, dance, story telling and songs and there were also many speakers from a variety of cultural backgrounds including Aboriginal people from all over Australia, Maori people and Native Americans.

Chief Arvol Looking Horse is the 19th Generation Keeper of the Sacred White Buffalo Calf Pipe Bundle. He says 'We are now in a time of prophecy, when Animal

Nations would stand upon Mother Earth a different colour than their natural being and be born white. They are speaking to us with the only voice that can be heard. These messages are of a blessing and yet of a great warning. It is a time of great urgency to unite for Peace and Harmony upon Mother Earth in order for our future generations to survive. Mother Earth is not a resource, but rather a source of life itself.'

The next WPPD is being held on June 21st in Japan 2004. The Hoop will join in 2005 when the 10th and final one will be held back in the United States.

For more information – www.wolakota.org
www.worldpeaceandprayerday.org

Exploring an Earth Vortex – Grid Point 44

by Annie O'Grady

'There are many forces and energies at work in nature, which we accept ... (and) equally, I suggest, there are many of which we are simply unaware, that have always existed.'

David Kennett, Geomantica no. 8, June 2000.

Campers in the northern Flinders Ranges in South Australia experienced strange energies on a special safari pilgrimage to replenish their spiritual connections with the Earth. I took two weeklong groups to powerful and beautiful Flinders locations at different times in the 1990's. I hoped that, by living close with the land under sun and moon – and by continually sensitising ourselves via a program of simple personal processes and practices – we would generate healing interactions to benefit both ourselves and the planet.

Would the impact of natural energies help to spontaneously push up transformational forces within each person? It did. In fact, we could not separate the land energies from our own spiritual opening and emotional healing. Participants later said things like, 'The whole Retreat was a new initiation of my spirit', and 'I'll never be the same again.' As for Earth healing, we can only go by the widespread impressions group members received, of our Earth welcoming us, soaking up our admiration, respect, love and care.

Outback gorge

We were aiming to finish the week at Chambers Gorge, known to many as Grid Point 44 on the Becker-Hagens Earth magnetic grid system. Grid point 44 is one of this grid's 4,682 global locations with potential for unusual experiences, including magnetic anomalies. Earth grid technology was highlighted in the 1960's by three Russian scientists who examined the globe for any pattern linking significant places in history. They discovered an energy matrix built into the structure of the Earth in dodecahedron fashion.

Subsequent researchers added more information, and deduced that ancient cultures utilised bio-magnetic grid information to site their sacred structures (often later appropriated by Christians). New science investigators employing ultrasonics, microwave and geiger counters found British standing stones responding to cosmic shifts of energies. Physics shows us that vortex energy experienced by many at the material face of the planet spins off into space. No wonder these locations have ancient histories of 'communication with the gods'! We wanted some of that.

In Australia, the Becker-Hagens planetary grid system shows Chambers Gorge vortex as the focal point of all Australian leylines (British terminology for energy beams that traverse the landscape). As Australian researcher Paul White says of vortex energies,

'These power places are like electrical switch points or energy transducers spread around the planet in the precise geometry of an icosadecahedron.'

Seth, a widely read dimensional intelligence channelled for many years by American writer Jane Roberts, points to vortex energy in his mention of 'the interrelationship that exists between all systems of reality, including certain contact points that include them all. These various points can be mathematically deduced, and will, in some future of yours, serve as contact points, taking the place of space travel in some cases.'

Mysterious rock carvings

Chambers Gorge, as well as – or perhaps because of – being a vortex area, possesses a mysterious gallery of rock art which is Aboriginal heritage. The mystery about its carved glyphs occurs because archaeological reports from the 1930's reputedly make it clear that the local Aboriginal people of the time had no knowledge of these carvings, and insisted they were made long before their people came. Paul White says, 'The Adnamatna elders said the carvings were made in creation times by the mythical "serpent men" who were called Iti (pronounced E.T.) in the Adnamatna language.'

An archaeologist who gazetted this site for National Parks and Wildlife said, according to Paul, that carbon-dating of the interior of the carvings indicates they are 40,000 to 60,000 years old – older than the Cave of the Bulls rock art in Altamira, Spain, previously thought to be the world's oldest.

Similar characteristic symbols are also carved on sites scattered in a crescent shape across Australia, traversing a number of Aboriginal national territories. Paul and others wonder whether these hieroglyphs were carved by early visitors from ancient cultures. While orthodox archaeology pays no attention to this view of the carvings, people have found comparisons with the writings of other ancient peoples, ranging from early Sanskrit to Easter Island and early Chinese. Adnamatna language and customs have been compared to Hebrew. So central to the mysteries we would be exploring was: 'Who did these carvings and why, and what do they mean? Can we intuit answers?'

Because Chambers Gorge is a tourist attraction, to obtain privacy we spent the previous days preparing in another bush area, kilometres away but still in the vortex area.

Human and universal energies

In these remote places we respected the powerful Aboriginal energies that are woven into the landscape. We carefully asked permission of Aboriginal spirit guardians to visit. A number of us felt we had meditational contact with ancient Aboriginal spirits. Some of us felt we saw these, with our eyes either open or closed, heard them, spoke with them, had them touch us. Other people tapped experiences of having been Aboriginals in previous lifetimes.

Yet our intention was wider than human groupings, Aboriginal or Caucasian. We wanted to touch the subtleties and power of energies of the Earth itself, even perhaps energies of the cosmos – because vortex areas are reputed to be sacred gateways to interdimensional contact: to other realities and ways of being.

The people drawn to these interface explorations included public servants, teachers, a miner, a housewife and therapists, who held varying spiritual views but shared a love of Earth and Nature. We all did things we had never done before. Except for the miner, we were addicted to living 'normal' lives in houses, so we left behind a number of barriers that usually blunted our sensitivities to the subtleties of nature: TV, radio, tele-phones, alcohol, intellectual distractions, etc.

For a while we rode camels. We ate unfamiliar camp food, around an evening campfire. We stayed together. We had no toilet block. Our water was rationed. These things alone pushed us out of our comfort zones. Some of them brought up fears that had to be faced and conquered right then.

Added to that, the groups each experienced a full-on Retreat program with three facilitators, to open up our personal and mystical awarenesses – beginning with rebirthing (breathwork) sessions each dawn, under circling eagles and noisy flocks of galahs, with an occasional kangaroo or emu observer.

One of many other processes was learning to dowse. We located a leyline. Recalling a workshop I had attended in a Sydney park with Alanna Moore, I suggested the group meditate silently for half an hour beside the leyline, then recheck its location. To us, the leyline seemed to have curved over to our meditation site: energy moving towards the highest vibration. We were soon tuning into the countryside in new ways, each of us becoming an explorer. We felt our environment continually opening to us, through both our inner and outer experiences.

A woman said, 'In my swag under the sky I went to sleep with tears in my eyes each night, at the beauty of being bathed in starlight while I slept.' Another group member said, 'The amethyst I brought with me was on our rock altar for three days. When it came back to me it was so powerful I couldn't wear it without becoming nauseous, until I adjusted to its new energy level. It looks clearer, too.'

A man reported feeling at one stage that he had become an eagle, first as a large energy imprint in the rocky cliffs, then flying far over the countryside. A European woman in her swag was profoundly moved when she was visited one morning by a willy wagtail, totem of an Aboriginal woman friend who had recently died. (Subsequently, this participant changed her name to signify a new sense of herself, and eventually married her late friend's husband.)

People's meditations embraced universal themes, as some felt they made contact with goddess energy, immortal beings, and varied divine blessings that interacted with the land.

Arrival at Chambers Gorge

Finally, spiritually and emotionally prepared, we travelled by 4WD to spend twenty-four hours (without sleep) at the heart of the vortex, Chambers Gorge. This is visually just another beautiful camping spot in semi-arid bushland, with the low peak of Mt. Chambers, dry creekbeds with rock walls, and sometimes a few waterholes. We set up camp among other scattered campers – but no meals, as this was a day of fasting.

Some of us noticed that cloud formations above the gorge periodically formed spiral and circular shapes. A woman said, 'I was surprised at how open I was to feeling the energy of the place, through my body, especially in my hands.' A man said, 'In medita-tion I became the mountain – and felt a homecoming to myself!'

Our heightened intuitional senses ran riot with the heavily fissured walls of the main gorge – we 'saw' pictures and faces and symbols everywhere. At night all the low bushes around the camp seemed to take on other shapes. In the night sky, we agreed we saw areas of red haze, and small lights travelling about. We heard distant drumming and occasional didgeridoo (was this from other campers?).

Much later at night we formed a silent procession in the dark, filing between rock walls into the ancient dry creekbed that cradles the gallery of carvings, to spend two hours taking part in our own reverent ceremony. We could picture our toning sounds spiralling out into the solar system, carrying our homage.

Individuals' insights

During this and the vigil that followed, as we each found a separate place to sit on the ground through the night in silence, each person had different mystical experiences. Some brought inexplicable joy, or sadness, or amazement ... A woman said, 'Was I "seeing things" – or was I REALLY seeing things?'

Here are some other reports:

'My hands were drawn to "read" the rock walls.'

'I experienced a great energy force moving along the gorge.'

'I was surrounded by a mob of Aboriginal male spirits, talking and laughing with me, urging me to click stones, then to dance, which I did.'

'I saw an angel who gave me a key, I could feel its weight in my hand.'

'During this solitary vigil, a part of me opened to love again, after my heart had been closed for eighteen years.'

'Spots of light seemed to dance on the cliff edge.'

'I saw some people inspired to kiss Mother Earth. My tears flowed.'

'Wind in the gorge sounded like a heavenly didgeridoo.'

'I sensed beings coming down from the stars, and joining with another group of beings at the top of the gorge.'

'On my rock, great streams of energy passed through me, back and forth.'

'I received a yellow river of light bearing symbols, coming too thick and fast to copy them down. It was coming from somewhere very far away.'

'I couldn't believe it – but I saw a craft flying down from the mountain to the gorge. Not like a flying saucer, but a weird cross between a transformer toy and a racing car, with a derrick type of structure on top, and wheels too. I felt it could carry a large number of "beings". Then it disappeared. Into another dimension? Later I was relieved when others said they'd heard it.'

'Some of the meanings of the rock carvings came to me.'

'I felt I was looking down a long tunnel, and the face at the end of it was of another kind of being. We looked at each other! Was 'he' an interdimensional artist, scribbling pictures in the cliffs?'

'With my eyes open I saw three blue beings around me. It felt so natural.'

'I felt I was an Aboriginal boy in this gorge sixty thousand years ago, and I had the knowledge. I was told that in the future I would be back in this same place, to revive the knowledge.'

'I saw a light around each person in turn, that emanated up into the DNA double helix, quite eerie.'

'Magic in time and place! My left and right brain hemispheres will never be the same! I had prayed for this connection.'

'I was being anointed by the energies of the mountain.'

'Three elliptical shapes drifted from the floor of the gorge up past me. Spirits or mist? There was no mist.'

'A rather inconspicuous oval carved in the rock felt like "mine". It hit me with a blast of energy to the third eye.'

'Familiar yet unfamiliar symbols flooded my being, a bit like crop circles. It went on for a week afterwards.'

'I feel a new dimension of knowing.'

And by the way – did any of us solve the riddles of the oldest carvings in the world? Actually, some of us thought we did, and I was one. I feel I found their origin as I sat alone on a rocky ridge towards morning. I didn't need dowsing rods or any gear; only my (by then) heightened sensitivities and a moonless night.

So what is the secret? Well, if you're interested enough, you're free to go camp there and see for yourself. After all, you might discover something different ... But if you're thinking we were all victims of our imaginations – don't knock it till you try it. The fact is, we are all part of a vast universe that is largely unknown to us.

References:
Paul White, 'Ancient Secrets' video film series, Australia.
Nexus magazine, April-May 1993, Australia.

Rebirthing, or breathwork, is a personal growth practice in which breathing with intention in a simple way, for about an hour and a half, deep-cleanses accumulated life stresses from body and mind, and facilitates inspiration.

Annie O'Grady is a self-transformation practitioner, teacher and writer based near Adelaide. She is the author of 'Past Lifetimes – Keys for Change!' She runs training courses in rebirthing breathwork, also in past lifetime resolution, both for people who want these career options and for those who want to accelerate their personal life journey. Annie also trains people in spirit/entity release therapy, teaching compassionate methods developed by international therapists. Expressions of interest are welcome. Telephone 08 8537 0447   Email annie@alt-therapies.com Website www.alt-therapies.com

Chanting at Sacred Sites

Not all sacred sites have uplifting energies. They can be mis-used over time by all sorts of people with all sorts of intentions. But we can help to restore them, I was told at the International Dowsing Congress held in Manchester, UK in September 2003.

'People don't even realise that they are mis-using a sacred site' softly spoken dowser Bart O'Farrell told me. 'We get a sense of sadness and weakness at these places, when originally they were places which gave out energy.'

'Sometimes I get together with a group of friends in order to give back something to the site, to give some healing. We hold hands in a circle and chant a few "aums" … We slowly chant is as aaaaaaa, then au …, then mmm. When we've boosted the site's energy this way, then the site is self charging, as we've helped it back on its feet. Chanting is a balancing process, it helps the immune system of a place to self regulate.'

Bart and his friends encircle standing stones that 'feel sad' and energise them with chanting. A stone circle in Cornwall was also felt to be depleted and Bart's dowsing and a tape measure showed the meagre extent of the energy field associated with it.

The group encircled it, chanted a few 'aums' and the energy 'just went out'. Dowsing and a tape measure showed the growth in the size of the energy field and there was a sense that the site was grateful for their efforts. 'The standing stones are just like us. They have seven chakras – five above ground and two below' Bart explained.

'At East Kennett Long Barrow (near Avebury) last January our group went in there, as it was very sad and depleted. We chanted three "aums" to recharge the energy within the Barrow. We've since been back and the improved energies continue to grow. At full moon time the energy field goes right out to the edge of the nearby field. There's a footpath there and if I step over it into the field and put my hands up into the air I can feel the field there and my body starts to sway with it.'

Gundagai Earth Connection Weekend, May 2001

by Steven Guth

The gathering

We met for the Earth Connection Weekend on the Saturday morning in the Returned Soldiers Club, with about fifty people attending. Vince Bulger, a local Aboriginal custodian gave a greeting. Although given an hour to talk about the local Aboriginal experience Vince was reticent and finished in three minutes.

The atmosphere in the club's function room with its plate glass windows out looking out to the car park was terrible. It smelt of alcohol and beer. In it floated the left overs of war.

My talk

I used the overhead projector to show artist's impressions of huge landscape sized devas. They were drawn in the Theosophical tradition, some from well known books, some created by a friend from what he discovered around Canberra ... I was succeeding in building up a framework of belief.

I reached out for Vince and asked him about the local Aboriginal guardian spirit, who's presence I could feel as a blue haze over layering the room. Reluctantly he named the spirit, 'Munja' who lived on a Cypress Pine ridge upriver towards Tumut.

With Vince's help – which became less reluctant as he realised people were accepting his statements – I explored the importance of Gundagai as a Dreaming place that linked the hills that encircled it to the Murrumbidgee, which flows slowly down hill from the town, eventually reaching Adelaide.

Gundagai was important in British times too. Again it was the river. It was the highest point from which goods – the extractions of Australia – could be sent down river. 'The Road to Gundagai', a popular folk song sets into the record of myth the point at which the land journey home with its horses, drays and terrible roads ended and the soft, cool river journey could begin.

I showed a slide of Shiva in Nataraj form, superimposed on the eastern hemisphere of the Earth and explained how his limbs represent the main energy pathways over the planet. These follow the main mountain ridges, peak in Tibet and flow to world's holy places. I explained how Shiva – the God of destruction and creation – dances, ripping apart the old as he puts the energy in place for the new to happen.

I presented my understandings as to how these Shiva energies which, when they flow, enliven creative and spiritual thought. How this energy is attractive to people and draws the talented to locations to begin new cycles of civilisation.

I suggested that in the last 15 years there had been profound changes in Shiva's dance. The freshest energies on the planet had totally changed direction and now flowed from south to north. South-east Asia and India now received energies, interlaced with Australian thoughts, rather than the other way around. Australia's eastern mountain range was the main line along which the Shiva energies flowed. Canberra had become a key place in this new development, giving Australia the potential role of becoming a spiritually and culturally important place some time in the future.

These winds were also affecting Gundagai. The fact that we were here, as a group was proof of that. I asked the question … 'What next in Australia, what next in Gundagai? How do we move from here to the future?'

People responded, I suggested meditation as a way to work from the spiritual into the physical. But my answer was as hollow as theirs. We didn't know. Surprisingly, the next day was to provide the answer.

Gundagai insights

Three of us independently, and in different ways, were to get the same answer. Ross, from Canberra, awoke at four and received in writing a message about the prime importance of the Gundagai location to the future spiritual awakening. Ilyanha Kennedy had a sleepless night, all too aware of the energies that were trying to make their way from the ground to the sky through her body.

And I, in my morning meditation, visited the Gundagai river flats with its surrounding circle of hills and witnessed the howl of anguish that took place as the dancing elders (who I saw in their huge etheric shapes) shut down the relationship between sky, hills and the river system. Perhaps some time in the 1840's.

That howl still lingers in my ears. It seemed that the weekend was about connecting the Dreaming between the surrounding hills, the river flats, the river and the sky. The energy was to plume into the pathway of the Shiva winds racing north from Antarctica.

I saw that the devas, some of great age and majesty, needed people. Stuck in the landscape they needed humanity to act out their creative impulses.

Linking Earth and sky

It was Ilyanha's job to lecture to the group in the morning. The three of us discussed the situation and decided that she, with Ross's help would do what they could to help the group link between earth and sky. I elected to sit in a corner and meditate, watching over what was happening, helping to protect the group and facilitate the energy flows. I asked that I remain undisturbed and that my name not be used during the talk.

Ilyanha's talk described the situation in intellectual Merkabaha terminology using the concepts of projective geometry and crystalline structure. Slowly, ever so slowly, the energy in the room started to lift from ground level to the solar plexus area. To me it looked as if the room were filling up with a navy blue liquid, which sort of sloshed around the edges.

The energy level raised and fell with the activities taking place. Toning increased the level. American Indian drumming decreased the level. Songs, mostly hymns, had little affect, except for the 'Road to Gundagai' which gave a good boost.

Some Aboriginal (spirit) figures appeared holding spears, I counted five. The group, struggling with its task did a dance – a circle dance in the shape of the figure 8/ infinity sign. This helped and the energy finally raised itself tentatively to the throat chakra level.

Coming out of meditation I was asked to speak. Using the white board I drew 'The Dog on the Tucker Box', a symbol of Gundagai that is world famous. I rubbed out the dog and opened the lid.'That's what we are doing,' I said, 'The tucker box is the

Pandora's box holding the creative energies which have been placed there when the Dreaming stopped. The dog, the guardian has been removed. It is now our work to open the lid.'

As I looked around me at the tired bodies and confused minds I wondered if anyone understood what I had said. Clearly, the RSL function room with its steel and cement floor, low flat roof and stale air was an impossible structure to work in. We needed a cathedral or a least to get out into the open.

Visit to a bora ground

We asked Vince to suggest a suitable area. The best place, he said was ten kilometres upstream where the Tumut and Murrumbidgee rivers met. Too far. So we went to the river flat monument area – it marked the site of the first (and quickly flooded out) township. It also, Vince said, was the location of the local Bora ring.

Parking our cars near the eight metre high pyramidal monument Vince walked a little way and lined up three old man guardian trees. The ring's outline could just be seen as a circular impression in the grass. It could easily be felt. The group assembled, Vince told a man carrying an American Indian drum to leave it outside – please use clap sticks if you want to have a rhythm.

And so, in our different ways – singing, breathing, toning, dancing, mime, movement – we all worked at raising the energies from our throats to our heads and the sky above. (We really do need new understanding and new ways of doing Australian ceremonies in Australian places.)

I meditated and softly did an etheric dance. I felt contented. People wondered in and out of the ring. After about ten minutes a sort of climax was reached. At this point I counted 32 people in the ring. This seemed significant because it was half of 64 – I have no idea why this should be so. The job was done.

We had our picnic lunch near the monument and listened to a farmer telling us about his experiences in improving his health. This light story telling seemed to help ground the work.

How did it all go? Now four days after the event my meditations lead me to the Gundagai river flats with its ring of encircling hills and I sense a plume of energy rising far into the sky. It's still unconnected to the planetary network. Will this need further human involvement? Or perhaps it will all sort itself out on its own?

Cycle of Pilgrimage in Yorkshire

John Billingsley, interviewed by Alanna Moore, continues the story of his developing relationship with nearby Minchely Moor and around his local area, culminating in a cycle of pilgrimage that evolved out of that.

A Terrestial zodiac reveals itself

In 1977 I'd done a lot of walking around my area and discovered that the landscape features in the area fell into a complete zodiac configuration stretching around a circle of recognisable figures, based on a centre in Hebden Bridge.

Now I can't claim that it was an ancient engineering feat, because it feels to me that it's more like some kind of an interaction between higher intelligence, higher imagination and the generations of people who've lived and farmed and settled there. And most of the patterns seem to have taken shape around the 16th to 18th centuries, perhaps by chance. I was the first person to see this zodiac and, without wanting to sound arrogant, I always felt as if it was a product of my own interaction with the landscape, an extension, of a kind, of my own experiences and connection to Minchely Moor.

As I said before, in the '70's a lot of alternative people were setting up and there was a strong alternative feel and pagan movement here, so it felt like there was a good alternative community here. When I came back to Mytholmroyd in the '90's it seemed that something was lost, the centre had been lost. I suppose in keeping with the Thatcher years people had become more materialistic, more self seeking. The old hippies were buying and selling houses and making profits from that and there was just something that had gone. People who had been involved in alternative spirituality had become born-again-Christians. One of them even said to me 'John, the goddess is no longer strong in this valley, it's Jesus that's strong here now.' It didn't seem a positive direction and I was dismayed that the centre wouldn't hold, that the centre was spilling out everywhere and nothing alternative seemed to have kept going.

Walking the zodiac

So one of the things I did soon after moving back was to reawaken interest in the terrestial zodiac and I organised a series of guided walks around each sun sign, walking around the corresponding figure on the terrestial zodiac. There soon gathered a core group of 5 or 6 people and we followed the sun in its movement through the year around the terrestial zodiac. The reasoning behind this was because it was a possible way of creating a magical ring around the landscape, of possibly holding the energy in and allowing it to grow again. I didn't know if it would work or not, but it would be good to do anyway.

Each of the walks that we did was accompanied by odd little coincidences, curious things, like a lamb that just detached itself from a flock of sheep and came over to this group of some 25 people. It's not like it mistook us for its father or anything. It actually came over to be greeted by us, to the great consternation of its mother. And that happened on Aries, the figure of the lamb.

And as we went around the guardian figure of the crow, one of the group found on a little hill that forms the head of the crow – a perfect skull of a crow just there. Just little things like that, trivia, kept happening, that kept reinforcing the sign that we were walking on. It was on Gemini one really awful rainy cold day that we briefly stopped and looked back over the landscape we had walked. And as I looked back where we had walked, the land just seemed to breathe.

It was 30 seconds of an impression, but this kind of thing happened as we were doing this and as we came up to the end, back to the first sign, which was the guardian spirit, the crow, several of us got independently the image forming in our brains of a kind of brooch, or a clasp of a brooch, a circuit if you like, coming together. So it was like making a connection. The final thing we did was to gather around this standing stone on Minchely Moor in a ring and that was the act that seemed to fasten the circle.

Life since then

Hebden Bridge since then, in the last nine years has had a lot of ventures started and they keep going and it's very alternative. The born-again-Christian movement is almost nowhere nowadays and a lot of pagan groups are back as well as complementary health people. So alternative and forward looking ideas are now flourishing in Hebden Bridge.

It would be nice to think that this year of magical walks around the terrestial zodiac has had some part to play. The terrestial zodiac in an area is the result of some kind of unconscious communion between peoples' work and action and imagination and some other wider energy. What that energy is I don't need to know and I don't ask. If it works – let it happen. By us doing it, people put out waves which affect positively the area that we live in.

In a sense I feel that this is what is needed to be done with all terrestial zodiacs. That people should be getting out, putting their boots on and actually walking the zodiac, not waffling on about them, and just talking or writing articles about them, but actually putting themselves in contact with the land. There's nothing to prove on terrestial zodiacs. They were not engineered, they're not totally wishful thinking … some might be wishful thinking, but not the ones with good designs. They exist in this limbo territory between the real and imagination and that's an area where some good positive energy can be created and maintained. People and land working together, creating something which is far more than either could do consciously.

'Healing the Heart of the Earth'

by Marko Pogacnik

Book Review

I highly recommend this book as a must-have for any one who aspires to Earth healing. It's a great follow up to his wonderful book 'Nature Spirits and Elemental Beings.' Once again we have a refreshing, original voice in the wilderness of hype, giving us the essence of geomancy and Earth healing, casting strings of pearls of Earth wisdom before us, that require repeated re-reads!

Pogacnik, a Slovenian artist and Earth healer, puts the subject on a sound and grounded footing. He starts with profound definitions. *'(Earth healing) is not a repair kit for the landscape, nature and the Earth. The urge to heal everything originates from our superficial modern consciousness which expects problems to be fixed medically the moment illness sets in,'* he says.

To be effective Earth healers Pogacnik encourages us to develop understandings of life processes without the hindrance of dualistic thinking, ridding ourselves of the need to classify all things as good or bad; and also to take on board responsibility for humankind's relentless destruction of the Earth, whilst adhering to a strong ethical base.

> *'As a culture and as individuals we are especially called upon to become acquainted with the invisible realms of the Earth, nature and landscape and to their reverberations on the visible plane. Only this way can the largely unconscious repression of the vital-energetic, emotional and spiritual-soul dimensions of the Earth systems be alleviated step by step.'*
>
> *'I do not see any value in Earth healing activity that is done surreptitiously without giving public awareness a chance to participate … I only found the solution to the problem some years later when I discovered the possibility of combining Earth healing with art, thus tying it into social processes of awareness as an activity accessible to the public. This is how the technique of lithopuncture came into being, a method that is still based on the principle of Earth acupuncture but does not bypass the deciding element of consciousness in the process of healing the Earth.*
>
> *'The "acupuncture needles" forged from iron that I had been using I now replaced by standing stones that are very visible in the countryside and cannot be ignored. As needles of stone they directly stimulate or balance the energy currents with which they resonate. At the same time they direct the attention of the onlooker to the process of Earth healing'*

In this book we are given examples of some of the many Earth healing projects that Pogacnik has been involved with in Europe. Sometimes it is the local authorities of towns and cities in Europe who employ him to help improve the energetic atmosphere there.

In part three Pogacnik espouses the view that personal development and clarification must precede any attempts at Earth healing, while it is suggested to constantly monitor ones motivations to be doing this work.

Pogacnik warns us – *'Does the urge to heal the Earth mask a continuing determination to dominate the Earth and her nature realms? Traditionally this dominance has taken place through the power of human intelligence; therefore today this superior attitude towards the Earth could find expression through a misguided "intention to heal" that continues to debase the Earth by regarding it as an object.'*

'Before interfering with the tissue of a place in order to give Earth healing we should ask the consciousness of the place: Do you wish me to intervene? Is it allowed? Is it time to do so?"

In the following four parts the methods of diagnosis and healing that he uses are described. To me, the most important point is his opinion that – *'We can understand that each living space or garden is different in nature and that there is never a case where it is possible to act following fixed guidelines. In my opinion we can in no way do justice to life's infinite variations if we try to implement an inflexible plan when examining a family home.'*

He stresses that we need to exercise our intuition at all times in Earth healing activities, whilst adhering to certain geomantic laws, but never acting in a robotic way, merely mimicking the techniques of others.

He urges people to become familiar with the geomantic features of their area and to visit these regularly. *'This includes points in the vicinity of a house that are visited by its inhabitants on a more or less regular basis during walks, outings or journeys. They may be focal points in close proximity that can be visited on a daily basis or they may be located further afield, including places that are visited only rarely, at weekends or on holidays. Everyone can find places within the range illustrated here which have either the characteristics of places of power or represent focal points for individual elementals or else in some other way embody the sacred quality in the landscape.'*

'... If, in the course of approaching the chosen places in this way, signals emerge that indicate hidden problems from which the place is suffering, you can apply the appropriate Earth healing methods on your own or, better still, with the help of friends. Finally you can regularly create a protective cloak for the places in your care.'

And yes, Earth healing work isn't always sweetness and light, as the section on 'Dealing with Destructive Forces' explains. Pogacnik has encountered destructive forces coming from both the elemental and human realm, including black magic as a result of jealousy of his high profile work. So-called evil is always generated by humankind, he points out.

'Unfortunately the ambition of being an Earth healer all too often opens the door which lets in the opposing forces, and, carried along on waves of false messages, they then occupy the place disguised as "Earth healing forces" ' he warns.

Can you afford not to have this book?

'Healing the Heart of the Earth – Restoring the Subtle Levels of Life', by Marko Pogacnik, Findhorn Press, UK, 1997.

Fountain Groups

Community peace and healing is the aim of informal Fountain Groups which are active in some 20 countries around the world.

In a type of applied geomancy, members of informal Fountain group networks link their healing thoughts at common times in the day, directing them to chosen community focal points to radiate out, fountain-like, into the area via its subtle energy networks.

Sometimes trouble spots in the community are targeted as secondary focal points for specific energy harmonising work. Over 50 institutions were targeted by the Adelaide Fountain group, as a response to requests for help from people working in them. Enthusiastic feedback, relating improved working conditions and more caring managerial decisions, has affirmed the benefits of Fountain work.

UK Origins

The Fountain movement has grown steadily since the founding group began in Brighton (UK) in 1982. Prior to Fountain activities in Brighton there was a high rate of violence and crime, mainly from gangs of rioting skinheads who would gather there for weekend gang fighting. Twelve months after its work began local police reported the crime rate to have been reduced by 50%.

The Brighton group, inspired by talented psychic healer Matthew Manning, chose a local fountain as its focus. Not only was this an appropriate symbol of their activities, but deeper significance lay in the fact that this particular fountain had long ago been built on an ancient pagan site, the remains of a stone circle still apparent beneath it. The site was also an Earth energy centre, at a node of energy lines, dowsers, like Colin Bloy, then discovered.

How does it work?

The principle is that our thoughts are powerful and, as energy follows thought, so they can be directed to help harmonise Earth ch'i, when needed, and thus influence peoples' behaviour.

When meditating, we resonate with Earth spirit and places of regular meditation become centres linked into the geomantic system of a place. Similarly, when psychic healers are at work a cross of dowseable energy lines manifests above them, connecting them to the nearest major energy ley (also known as 'overground'), dowsers have found.

People in telepathic communication are likewise connected via the energy ley network. Healers not only 'plug in' to the ley network, they enjoin into a common etheric field with the receiving person via the energy pathways. The subject takes on the healer's brain rhythm, no matter the distance apart.

Dowsing patterns

When Fountain activity begins local energy lines swell in magnitude. The major ley of Brighton multiplied 2,400 times and a series of dowseable energy squares about 2m wide appeared. These eventually formed a checkerboard, a pattern that also appears around individuals receiving healing energy. It is believed that the checkerboard energy field has the effect of shifting brain rhythms of those who enter it. The flag of the ancient Earth-wise Order of the Knights Templar was a chequerboard pattern.

The more active the chequerboard energy grid, the greater the number of (smaller) squares are in it. The pattern is seen clairvoyantly as cubes of various colours. Other geometric energy patterns may be superimposed over this field, developing at node points where ley energy goes into function mode.

What to focus on

Modern civic focal points are usually selected to be used for a Fountain 'hara'. Even if neutral in an Earth energy sense, they will acquire the necessary energy dynamics.

Energy-leys can result from focussed human thought (both consciously or unconsciously directed), and link centres of group activity to create local energy networks. The energy ley system could thus be considered an aspect of the collective consciousness of humanity.

Fountain International explains, at its website, that 'Communities, like people, can be sick. This can be recognised by finding one or more of the following within the community: war, ill health, crime and violence; re-occuring conflicts and riots; tension, stress and upset; people starving, in famine; life-forms dying, or missing; pollution and excessive noise; lack of caring and awareness, joy, love and enthusiasm.'

The key to this type of simple community healing is to express unconditional love via local focal points.

Fountain in Australia

Australia saw what would become the largest fountain group in the world start up, in Adelaide in October 1983. The group evolved over 15 years until winding down at the end of 1998. The focus of their projected thoughts was the Victoria Square Fountain in the city centre. Roger Brown was a key member of the group, helping to produce over 100 newsletters. He passed away a couple of years ago, as has Colin Bloy, one of the UK founders, in May 2004.

Melbourne had a Fountain Group for a while and small groups come and go, here and there in Australia. Albany in Western Australia has seen a Fountain Group start up around 2002. Their focal point is a statue of an Aboriginal man, in the Alison Hartman Gardens in York Street. Gillian Cotterell is the contact for the group there.

How to run a Fountain Group

To help bring improved harmony to an area anyone can start up a group. Fountain International suggest the following method.

First select a focal point or 'hara' for your community – a clock tower, tree, war memorial, fountain, market cross or church spire, for example.

Then, working in a group of 2 or 3 or more people, meet together to meditate and send a initial pulse of light/prayer or whatever suits your way of thinking, to the focal point in order to activate it.

It is only necessary then for individuals to focus their attention for a few moments each day (wherever they may be), to tune into the focal point together at an agreed time of the day.

References:
John Michell, 'The Earth Spirit', Thames and Hudson, UK, 1975.
Jill Purce, 'The Mystic Spiral', Thames and Hudson, UK, 1974.

www.fountain-international.org

Community geomancy

In January 1988 at Mt. Oak Community near Bredbo (southern NSW) the author
ran a geomantic dowsing workshop aiming to enhance community harmony.

Dowsing by the group in the field detected a noxious telluric current. The dragon line, emanating from a hilltop, passed through a hut that had been the centre of much political intrigue and negativity in the recent past. The energy line went straight across the middle of the bed.

The last unfortunate occupier of the hut, once a strong young man who loved to plant trees in that semi-arid landscape, had died of a liver condition. The medical fraternity had decided that this was caused by his regular consumption of comfrey leaves. As a sad and unnecessary consequence of his death comfrey became a restricted herb. We reckoned it was more likely the dragon that killed him!

Following the energy line along further through the village centre, it passed between the main buildings of the community and right through a large dome meeting hall, where many heated community meetings had occurred. It was difficult to feel comfortable within its field of influence. No doubt its effects were having a detrimental influence on community life.

By questioning with the pendulum, I was able to divine a remedy. With thoughts of healing we ritually hammered an old length of copper pipe into the ground mid-stream in the energy line and just before it entered the village. We then covered the pipe with a pyramid made from small white quartz rocks that lay around us on the ground. This was to cleanse and harmonise the tainted energy. Meditating in a circle around the pyramid we worked at mentally reinforcing the task at hand.

Indeed, on completion of the task we noticed a sense of relief in the air, a lightening of tension. And the next day residents commented on the mellow morning vibes, of increased friendliness amongst people ...

Some time after returning home I heard that the community was beginning to resolve political problems and finally attract more members.

Devas and the Towers of Power

Towers of Power are paramagnetic antennas, inspired by the Irish Round Towers, which act as wave guides for cosmic and Earthly energies. They can act as Earth acupuncture needles – much as our megalithic ancestors might have done with standing stones. But primarily they have been used to create beneficial energy fields in gardens or farms, as they help to accelerate plant growth, increase the quality and quantity of crops, and generally enhance the health and harmony of a place. The author has built over 150 of such Towers all over Australasia over the last ten years (and even some in Ireland!)

When I was researching and writing my book 'Stone Age Farming' in early 2001 I asked around for peoples' ideas on why some Towers of Power were not working. I was offered a message from someone's spirit guide. 'Orion' alluded to the possibility that the spirits of place were not happy with the ineffective Towers , that their consent or co-operation was perhaps not being elicited.

This did ring a bell to me. When a Power Tower has been built and blessed, it is easy to perceive something of a touch of magic coming down, which many people can sense, and I had sometimes wondered how the landscape devas fitted into the picture.

A few months later I was fortunate enough to be able to collaborate with Billy Arnold, who has the ability to clairvoyantly see the spiritual entities of nature. Billy had been visiting Aboriginal dreaming sites around the Alice Springs area and observing the spirits of the Dreaming there for several years. Billy then travelled with me across the country and brought fascinating insights to my Tower building workshops. Now, some 20,000kms later, I can sit back at home at last, and reflect on the quantum leap in understanding that this has brought me.

The power of ceremony

When Billy first saw the joyous reaction of the nature spirits to a Tower of Power going up he was amazed. It was certainly unexpected. Nonetheless they were attracted, as if by a magnet, to what Billy thought of as an ugly plastic pole. But this only happened once a good Tower ceremony got started. Spirits really resonate with human ceremonial activity, it has been noted by many, and the quality of the ceremony can make quite a difference to their response.

Usually the devas had an enthusiastic response and a landscape entity would come over to inhabit the Tower on a permanent basis, often in a pose of prayer. These beings were sometimes huge, with only their hands in prayer pose fitting over the Tower.

Billy saw them doing similar at a one week old Tower and again, at a Tower at a strawberry farm in South Australia, that had been constructed several years before. At the latter he saw a huge being directing cosmic energies with its hands, working with the energy within the general energy field of the Tower, which appeared as a field of silvery blue colour to him.

What powers the Towers?

Tower Power is the synergy of four critical aspects – the antenna form, the paramagnetic and other energetic qualities of the Tower materials, the appropriateness of its siting and the qualities imbued into it via our intentions.

Along the lines of the art of radionics – in the Tower ceremony we send out into the ether our charged thoughts/energies, through the medium of the Tower's energy field, to affect changes. We verbalise simple affirmations and, to reinforce the process, we then chant several 'aums'.

The potential power of our individual focussed thoughts is awesome, and this is not really appreciated by the average person. The collective power of a focussed group's thoughts is much more powerful still.

Some way of explanation given to me for the odd ineffective Tower was that someone present at the 'blessing' ceremony (which concludes my Tower building method) had been polluting the intended thoughtforms of growth and harmony with the force of their negativity. Some participants had felt a bit nauseous after this.

Negative thinking can be so poisonous, a toxic force in our beings. Imagine amplifying that manyfold within the Tower's sphere of influence. No wonder it felt a bit yukky and there was no beneficial Tower action!

Sometimes at Tower ceremonies Billy observed various nature spirits coming over with great curiosity to check us out but then go back into the Earth or the trees, from whence they came, somewhat unimpressed. Once again – these were the odd times when people brought scepticism and negativity to the ceremony.

Harnessing the power of intention

So the biggest lesson I learnt from it all was about the power of intention and this has helped me to fine tune Tower energies all the better. People are required to bring positive enthusiasm to the task to help charge up a Tower energy field and imprint beneficial intentions. Any doubts, scepticism, cynicism or negativity may imprint on the energy field and be a real dampener.

You can always repair the damage later, I suppose, with a really good follow-up ceremony at the next full moon. But it's best to avoid propagating bad vibes, by filtering out inappropriate thoughts and people.

Asking permission of the spirits of place when siting the Tower is also an important start to connecting to the place and might help avoid non-functional Towers. Acknowledging the presence of these devas and tapping into their wisdom may well be appropriate action to take.

Deva Dowsing Workshop

It was an unusually hot weekend for Hobart, where a large group met for my first 'Deva Dowsing' workshop, on 22-23/2/2003, which we held out in a paddock in the shade of the gum trees. Angel Hill Sanctuary was a perfect venue, the home of spiritual healer, Dr Jocelyn Townrow, and set up with many sacred structures that Jocelyn had been lovingly crafting. We were fortunate to have several clairvoyant people there who provided some interesting insights.

Towards the end of the weekend we constructed a 'Tower of Power'. Although merely a PVC pipe filled with basalt rock dust, it had been beautifully painted in advance by a local artist. After its construction one of the participants, Vicki, saw a column of light come down into the Tower, as well as a deva descend into it.

The next day we had two geomancers visit. Darron Phillips said that as he and Phillip Simpfendorfer drove up the valley towards Angel Hill they had been watching a fountain of energy that was pouring up into the air. It was from the Tower, they found out. We all went to see the new Tower and several of us stood around checking it out. Francis said that she could see a teardrop shaped deva 'perched' on top of the Tower which also connected up into space.

Later we did a re-programming ceremony, as Phillip thought the energies of the Tower to be too yang and that it needed some goddess energy for balance. After this Francis said that the deva had now compressed down into a disc shape (a toroidal vortex perhaps?). Amy saw it as being heart shaped. I was able to roughly dowse changes in its shape. We happily watched as a red robin appeared and flew a rapid loop around the Tower, and then three tiny blue wrens hopped daintily all around it. Towers are definitely an animal attractant.

I had noticed red coloured (yang) energy coming off the top side of the Tower before the balancing ceremony. Later Esther saw that it had a yellow aura, and it certainly felt much better balanced and mellower afterwards. I was grateful to Phillip for his insights into the yin/yang harmony of the Tower.

I am also most thankful to Billy and the devas for their assistance in helping me gain an improved understanding of the invisible processes at work in the environment. I feel these understandings have brought a greater richness and effectiveness to the esoteric agricultural technologies that I have been working with. And they've also brought me more joy and wonder at the amazing powers of nature.

Power Tower ceremony in New Zealand, 2002

Stone Age Farming

Was secret knowledge of enhancing plant growth practiced by early medieval Irish monks? Were our ancestors influenced by an advanced culture from the Sirius star system? ...

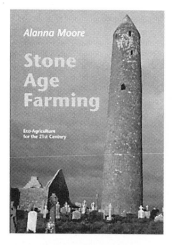

All this and more is explored in Alanna Moore's book – 'Stone Age Farming, Eco-agriculture for the 21st century 2001' – which describes the latest ideas on the benefits of magnetism and paramagnetism to plant growth and how to impart it, in order to bring dead soils back to life.

In this 213-page book are described numerous natural and simple techniques which help to counteract soil sterility and salinity, restore chemically poisoned land and waterways, improve farm profitability, help counteract the effects of radiation and radioactivity, improve plant, animal and human health. Chinese edition is now out too.

Contents of Stone Age Farming: The Eco-Farming Imperative. Rock Dusts can Save our Soils. Natural Resonance. The Art of Dowsing. Radionics & beyond. Plant Energies. Stones in the Garden. Psycho-Spiritual Techniques. Agricultural Coils. Modern Biodynamics. Earth Spirited Permaculture. Homodynamics. Agnihotra. Ireland's Magical Heritage. Irish Round Towers. Dowsing the Round Towers. Towers of Power. Building Towers. Problems with Towers. Amazing Olives. Organic Dairying. Wheat in the Mallee. CERES in the City.

Some feedback:

'I think your book is simply fabulous!' Maurice Finkel/'Health and Healing'.

'Your book pulls a lot of things together for people who are confused by the question of energies.' Tim Strachan, The Energy Store, Sydney.

'Clear, lucid and practical' Tom Graves, Victoria.

'What a tremendous book ... an inspiring read.' Pauline Roberts, NSW Dowsing Society.

'My experience of the book helped to crystalise so much information I had acquired from so many different sources – I was in danger of overloading!' from a reader – Loret.

'Every so often, a book comes along that will change your perception of the world. Stone Age Farming is such a book'. 'Conscious Living', Sept. 2001.

'A much needed, easily understood and concise book on subtle energies and their use in agriculture.' Natural Resonance Study Group.

'Finally an Australian book that stands out in content from an eminent researcher, practitioner and dowser.' Rosemary Stevens.

To buy this book: send $33 for your copy post paid within Australia
or $AUD45 posted overseas, by cheque.
to Geomantica PO Box 929 Castlemaine 3450 Vic. Australia

email – info@geomantica.com

Geomancy Resources and Dowsing Contacts

GEOMANTICA Magazine

Australia's only quarterly Earth mysteries, dowsing and geomancy magazine is freely available at the Geomantica website.

Fascinating articles by/about Australia's top dowsers & geomancers, with Alanna Moore the editor. Check it out at:

www.geomantica.com

Get on an email list for quarterly magazine notices – contact:
info@geomantica.com

Geomantic Site Surveys

Not sleeping well? Not happy in your new residence? Health problems won't improve? (You might be affected by geopathic or electro-stress, or sick building syndrome.) House haunted? Need to find a good spot for a Tower of Power, or a safe site for your dream home? …

Have your home, office, house site, property or whatever checked out energetically by Alanna Moore. Earth, sky and household energies can be checked out remotely by map dowsing. Areas of noxious energy to avoid can be discovered and energy harmonising work can be suggested.

Simply send a house or property plan. A sketch will do. Something that can be written on, with the north point marked in. Send with cheque/money order in the post. Ideally with an email address for further correspondence.

Map dowsing fee: (generally) small job $50 – larger $80.

Enquiries: Alanna Moore – P.O. Box 929 Castlemaine, Vic, 3450

or email – info@geomantica.com

Dowsing Group Contacts –

Dowsers' Club of South Australia – PO Box 2427 Kent Town, SA 5071.
Dowsers' Society of NSW – c/o 7 Maycock St, Denistone East, NSW, 2113.
   Website: www.divstrat.com.au/dowsing.
Dowsing Society of Victoria – PO Box 4278, Ringwood, Vic 3134.
American Society of Dowsers – PO Box 24 Danville, Vermont,
   05828-0024, USA.
British Society of Dowsers – 2 St Ann's Rd, Malvern, Worc WR14 4RG, UK.
   www.britishdowsers.org, email – secretary@britishdowsers.org
New Zealand Society of Dowsers – PO Box 41-095, St Lukes Square,
   Mt Albert, Auckland 3, New Zealand.

Environmental Energy Enhancing Products

Geomantica recommends Energy Store products for being effective, no-frills, guaranteed and based on proven energetic and scientific principles. They are reasonably priced and are produced in Sydney by geomancer/natural therapist Tim Strachan.

The Powerhouse – A general energy neutraliser (comprising two Lakhovsky coils) to neutralise the effects of electro-magnetic pollution and Earth radiation. Has also been known to rid homes of cockroaches, due to the harmonising or neutralising of the energies of place – cockroaches prefer 'turbulent' energies. The Powerhouse plugs into a power point and uses the wiring of a site to trap noxious frequencies. It is considered, in scientific terminology, as a 'wave trap', and has been tested at the University of Newcastle. Price – $198. A car unit is available for the same price.

The Electroguard – reduces effects of electricity on us. It is attached to any current-carrying cord in the house and uses the principle of paramagnetism to reduce electro-stress effects on our bodies. Price – $258.50.

Together or separately these two products are effective indefinitely and many users have reported significant differences in their health and vitality levels, with significant reduction in stress and depleted energy conditions. These products are also effective with animals such as dogs, cats and horses.

Catalyst Bead – ceramic bead for personal energy protection. Price – $49.50.

Phone tab – ceramic bead for neutralising mobile phones. Price – $49.50.

Toroid – for electronic equipment. Price – $49.50.

Energised water systems – These systems use principles of paramagnetism, resonance, scalar energy etc to energise tap or rain water. They are simple, portable, last for years and are extremely effective. They also work as effectively as other much more expensive systems, such as Grander water units. For the 'AquaCharge 2' – a unit for household use – price is $258.50.

Postage fees – include $10 for post and packaging, or use a courier service for the same price. Overseas orders – add 10% to the order (or ask for exact rates).

To order contact – Geomantica, PO Box 929, Castlemaine, 3450, Vic, Australia or email – info@geomantica.com

GEOMANTICA
FILM PRODUCTIONS

'The Art of Dowsing & Geomancy' film

Two hours 20 minutes of workshop training sessions with Alanna Moore.

Learn the geomancer's art at home. Students are introduced to dowsing and other bio-resonance techniques. Earth mysteries are de-mystified! Skills in water divining and neutralising geopathic stress are imparted. Electro-magnetic radiations from underground water, household appliances and mobile phones etc are checked out. Suited to beginners.

Send $AUD55 (overseas – $AUD70 cheque) for a post paid copy
to Geomantica PO Box 929 Castlemaine 3450 Vic.

'Dowsers Down Under' film

One hundred minutes of interviews and dowsing demonstrations by fascinating dowsers around Australia, filmed by Alanna Moore.

Hear about water and gold divining experiences, see the graves of Ned Kelly's gang, found by dowsing; watch an Earth acupuncture job. Check out opal divining in Cooper Pedy; find out how to test soil and what is blink dowsing; see how map dowsing can be handy and watch a profesional health dowser at work.

Send $AUD40 (overseas – $AUD55 cheque) for your copy posted to Geomantica.

'GEOMANCY TODAY'
a film series by Alanna Moore.

If you would like to see some of the people and places written about in this book then these are the films! The first in this series (Glastonbell Dreaming) has been completed, by the end of 2004 more will be available.

Others in the pipeline will look at sacred sites and power centres in Australasia, examples of practical geomancy and geomancer interviews.

Check the website at www.geomantica.com for updates.

'Glastonbell Dreaming' film

an interview with Philip Simpfendorfer by Alanna Moore.   35 minutes

Phillip talks about his life, from his very first stirrings of love for the land, through the growing understandings he gained. He speaks of his many spiritual adventures, journeys to Kashmir, central Australia, Tasmania and Antartica, and his involvement with the 'Renewing of the Dreaming' movement – showing great wisdom and humour in the telling. You'll get to see some of Glastonbell's sites as well.

VHS film – $AUD20 plus $5 postage. DVD – $20 posted in Australia, or

$28 for a PAL or NTSC DVD posted overseas – paid by cheque.

'EARTH CARE, EARTH REPAIR'

A film series made by Alanna Moore

Scientists have been painting gloom and doom scenarios for the environment for too long. While they are busy writing up reports about widespread land degradation there are ordinary people out in the back blocks practising creative, intuitive, innovative and practical solutions to the environmental crises they face.

This film series is a call for all people to consider positive approaches to their environment, and to discover backyard solutions to global problems. Alanna Moore is a great believer in the power of positive focused thought put into action.

Parts 5 – 8 are available now:

Part 5: 'Remineralising the Soil'   24 minutes

Land degradation is rife in Australia, farmland topsoils are vanishing rapidly and our foodstuffs have ever decreasing nutritional values as a result. Mineral imbalance in modern society is abysmal, and is linked to disease on physical, mental and spiritual levels.

Crushed rock of many varieties can help to rejuvenate soils in a short time (given enough organic matter and the presence of moisture and soil microbes) and provide greatly improved nutrition to us, from crops grown with it.

We get to see soil testing by dowsing, then learn about the energetic value of volcanic rock dusts, with Professor Phil Callahan's discoveries outlined, at a training session run by Alanna. The dowsing approach is also demonstrated.

A case study, of an olive farm where phenomenal growth resulted from using biodynamic growing practices combined with rock dust, is then showcased.

Part 6: 'Making Power Towers'   32 minutes

Irish Round Towers act as wave guides for cosmic energies which can have beneficial effects on Earth. We get to see several in Ireland, then find out how small replicas can be used in the garden and farm to enhance plant growth, enliven livestock and a host of other effects. Alanna Moore outlines the theory of modern Power Tower building, then we get to see one being constructed, and dowsing of the resulting energy field.

Eight Tower owners around Australia then talk about their Towers and the effects they have noticed since they went up. From lusher orchards, more wildlife, happier chickens, improved business, greater family harmony and more rainfall, to increased productivity in commercial strawberry, herb and wheat crops.

Part 7: 'Agnihotra'   33 minutes

A revival of ancient Indian tradition, the practise of Agnihotra can help restore harmony to the environment and make plants grow better. Frits and Lee Ringma talk about the benefits of Homa farming at their Hunter Valley, New South Wales, property 'Om Shree Dham' and demonstrate the fire ritual.

Part 8: 'Radionic Farming & Landcare in Australasia'   42 mins

Agricultural radionic methods include soil testing and balancing with remote dowsing. Alanna Moore interviews four radionic practitioners who talk about their methods and experiences in this cutting edge of esoteric agriculture. Find out how they treat health problems of livestock, soil imbalances, rain making, and more. From pioneering work in Tasmania with radionic coils to weed busting on landcare projects with a distant radionic box.

The next films to be made in the 'Earth Care, Earth Repair' series are parts 1–4:
Part 1: 'Dowsing and Re-afforestation' (dowsing and tree planting)
Part 2: 'Soil Saving Solutions' (grassroots solutions to soil salinity control)
Part 3: 'Permaculture Pioneers' (tour the gardens of permaculture pioneers)
Part 4: 'Measuring Success in Eco-Farming' (devices that assess plant and soil health and quality).

To purchase these films:
<u>PAL VHS video films</u>: can either be purchased and posted within Australia,
for $20 for two films (only in pairs e.g. 5–6 or 7–8) (plus $5 for postage),
or four films on VHS for $40 (plus $5 postage);
<u>DVD films</u>: 1 for $20 posted in Australia (pairs) and $36 for 4 films/2 DVDs;
<u>New Zealand:</u> $NZ50 for the 2 DVDs, $NZ55 the 4 on VHS, posted.
<u>Elsewhere overseas</u> – $AUD28 for a 2 film DVD and $AUD45 for 2 DVDs/4 films
in PAL or NTSC.

Email enquiries to: info@geomantica.com

Diploma course by correspondence, since 1989:

Dowsing for Harmony

1) The basics of dowsing.
2) Wholistic diagnosis & treatment.
3) Body systems.
4) Analytic dowsing.
5) Dowsing for remedies.
6) Distant dowsing & harmonising.
7) Earth energies & health.
8) Building biology.
9) Map dowsing, Earth healing.
10) Towers of Power. The Professional Dowser.

Some examples of comments received about the course:

'I am thoroughly enjoying the course ... Thanks a lot, the information has been of real practical help' Mrs R Ogden, Brunei Darussalam, Malaysia.

'I think it's an excellant course.' H. Young, Mosman, NSW.

'Your section on chemicals is quite comprehensive ... I have found the course very informative.' S. Becker, Perth.

'Another enjoyable unit and for me a great unfolding of my dowsing ability occurred. I think this was due to the amount of hands-on work in the lessons. It has built up my confidence ... The last unit of study has brought me to the finish of one and a half years of most enjoyable learning. I have reviewed my progress spiritually, physically and emotionally over this time and feel that personally I have grown in leaps and bounds. I feel that the connection with my true self/nature has been established.' A. Rafferty, Lismore NSW.

The following comments pertain to the original textbook –*'Dowsing and Healing Manual'*:

'... By far the best work on the subject I have come across.'

Dr Jocelyn Townrow, PhD, BSc Hons, Sandfly, Tasmania.

'... The best manual on the modern system of dowsing principles and information I have found ... a splendid book.'

J Rubie, secretary New Zealand Dowsing Society, April 1990.

'A veritable bible ...' Jeni Edgely, Wellbeing magazine no 26, 1988.

Fee: $AUD380 in 10 instalments or $AUD350 in advance
(overseas – $AUD420 or $45/unit, by international bank draft in AUD).

Send a self addressed stamped enveloped for enrolment form to:
GEOMANTICA COLLEGE, PO Box 929 Castlemaine 3450 Vic.